THE THEORY AND INTERPRETATION OF NARRATIVE SERIES

FRAMING
ANNA KARENINA

Tolstoy, the Woman Question,
and the Victorian Novel

Amy Mandelker

Ohio State University Press / Columbus

Library of Congress Cataloging-in-Publication Data
Mandelker, Amy.
    Framing Anna Karenina : Tolstoy, the Woman Question, and the
Victorian Novel / Amy Mandelker.
        p.   cm. — (The Theory and Interpretation of Narrative Series)
    Includes bibliographical references and index.
    ISBN 0–8142–0613–1
    1. Tolstoy, Leo, graf, 1828–1910.   Anna Karenina.   2. Women in
literature.   3. English fiction—19th century—History and
criticism.   4. Tolstoy, Leo, graf, 1828–1910—Aesthetics.
5. Feminism and literature—Russia.   I. Title.   II. Series.
PG3365.A63M63   1993
891.73'3—dc20   93–5570
                                                                     CIP

Text and jacket design by Nighthawk Design.
Type set in Caledonia by Connell-Zeko, Kansas City, MO.
Printed by Thomson-Shore, Inc., Dexter, MI.

9   8   7   6   5   4   3   2   1

For my son, Nicholas

The prison-house is the world of vision.
Plato, *The Republic*

The better a person understands the degree to
which they are externally determined (their
substantiality), the closer they come to understanding
and exercising their real freedom.
Mikhail Bakhtin

"What woman, what slave could be to such an extent a
slave as I am in my position?"
Anna Karenina

CONTENTS

ILLUSTRATIONS

PREFACE

The main sources of inspiration for this book were three seminal studies: Richard Gustafson's *Leo Tolstoy: Resident and Stranger,* Gary Saul Morson's *Hidden in Plain View: Narrative and Creative Potentials in "War and Peace,"* and Mary Ann Caws's *Reading Frames in Modern Fiction.* I had the good fortune to discuss my work with all three and to benefit from their comments, suggestions, and encouragement. Gary Saul Morson read most of the manuscript as it was written and offered extensive constructive criticism. In addition, I had the opportunity to teach a course on the avant-garde with Mary Ann Caws, an experience that transformed my perceptions of painting, frames, the visual, and the interrelationships of art and literature.

I would also like to acknowledge the numerous friends and colleagues who read and commented on portions of this book in manuscript, and whose insights, ideas, and often libraries were always generously made available to me: Elizabeth Allen, Pamela R. Bleisch, Ellen Chances, Caryl Emerson, Lillian Feder, David Goldfarb, Gina Kovarsky, Jerry Leo, Robert Maguire, Deborah Martinsen, Cathy Nepomnyashchy, Seth Schein, and Anatole Vishevsky. Cathy Popkin read and commented on the entire manuscript; her invaluable suggestions and encouragement are deeply appreciated. I am particularly grateful for the close attention my manuscript received from Stephanie Sandler, who read my book for the Ohio State University Press, and from the editors of the Theory and Interpretation of Narrative series, Peter Rabinowitz and Jim Phelan. Naturally, any errors or infelicities of the text are entirely my own responsibility.

My most profound gratitude goes to my teachers and counselors: Shelley Angelides, Emily Dalgarno, Deborah Mandelbaum, Roy Mendelson, Katherine O'Connor, Rosalia Rosenbaum, Victor Terras, and Thomas G. Winner. I must also thank the members of my discussion group on Russian theology and scientific thought, Ellen Chances, Richard Gustafson, and Alex Mihailović. I appreciate the expertise of my research assistants Tanya Serdiuk, Elina Yuffa, and Maria Makowiecka. The graduate students in my seminars "Tolstoy and the European Novel" at Columbia and the CUNY Graduate Center provided a challenging forum for discussion and constantly forced me to rearticulate and clarify my ideas. My colleagues at the CUNY Graduate Center offered the best kind of stimulating and supportive environment for research and writing; I would like to thank in particular Vincent Crapanzano, Fred Nichols, and Burton Pike. A generous grant from the National Endowment for the Humanities provided me with a fellowship year in order to complete this book.

I am grateful to my father, who makes writing books look easy, but who has never allowed me to forget how much hard work is necessary; and to my mother, who was willing to discuss Victorian novels and feminism with me for hours on end. Friends, students, and colleagues too numerous to mention by name have put up with a great deal of obsessive talk about Tolstoy over the years.

Slightly different versions of chapters 5 and 7 were published as articles: "A Painted Lady: The Poetics of *Ekphrasis* in *Anna Karenina*" (*Comparative Literature,* 43 [Winter 1991]: 1–19) and "The Woman with a Shadow: Fables of Demon and Psyche in *Anna Karenina*" (*Novel,* 24 [Fall 1990]: 48–68). A portion of chapter 2 was published as a review article, "Feminist Criticism and *Anna Karenina*," in *Tolstoy Studies Journal* 3 ([1990]: 82–103).

Note on Translation and Transliteration

To accommodate those who do not read Russian, I cite whenever possible from existing translations. It has often been necessary to correct or emend available translations and I have done so, relying on the authoritative texts in the ninety-volume Jubilee Edition of Tolstoy's complete works, *Polnoe sobranie sochinenii*, Iubileinoe izdanie (Moscow: Gosudarstvennoe izdatel'stvo khudozhestvennoi literatury, 1928–58). Direct citations to this edition, indicated as *PSS*, or to any other source in Russian, indicate that the translation is my own.

All citations to *Anna Karenina* are to the translation by Constance Garnett, revised by Leonard J. Kent and Nina Berberova (New York: Modern Library, 1965). References to this translation are indicated by page number alone. References to the Jubilee Edition are to volume and page number.

I have used the Library of Congress system of transliteration from the Russian Cyrillic alphabet, with the exception of common proper or geographical names, which may be given in their more usual, anglicized form (e.g., Kitty instead of Kiti; Moscow instead of Moskva). Exceptions occur when a work is cited that has used a different transliteration system.

INTRODUCTION

Snakes at Yasnaya Polyana

There are no cats at the Tolstoy estate at Yasnaya Polyana. Curled, or rather, coiled in the sunny patches in the Tolstoy house, protecting it from pestilential infestations, instead of the expected feline emblems of domesticity, there are now, and were in Tolstoy's time, snakes: large garter snakes that rub their scales against the ankles of readers in Tolstoy's library and usurp the warm windowsills and sunny spots usually occupied in country houses by somnolent, contented cats. The ancestors of these ophidian house pets were adopted by Tolstoy's ailurophobic wife, Sophia Andreevna, to rid the house of rodents.[1]

Picturing snakes in the center of Yasnaya Polyana home life disrupts our mental image of the Tolstoy family idylls in the years before Tolstoy's conversion to a radical Christianity and seems all too suggestive of what may have transpired after his conversion. To the extent that we allow knowledge of an author's life to color our reading of his works, the presence of snakes in Tolstoy's life radically alters the imaginary scenes with which we may have illustrated our readings of his novels. Those who have seen the carved wooden portico of the Yasnaya Polyana house have easily recognized the setting for the domestic scene in *Anna Karenina* where the Shcherbatsky women make jam on the porch. The attendance of snakes at such a family event seems as disruptive and disjunctive as the insinuation of the original intruder into Eden.

Imagining an unsettling presence among the unremarked details of daily life depicted by art or literature among other things chal-

The portico at Yasnaya Polyana

lenges the very premise of representational realism, and the promise of realism to tell the whole story or show the whole picture. Since we do not expect trivial objects to have more than a relative, transient value, their original meaning or importance is often irrecoverable by viewers from another time and place. Thus, the simple minutiae of daily life may suddenly acquire potent symbolic power when considered from a different perspective. Film adaptations of novels exploit the impact of visualizing trivia by transforming trivial details into symbols; for example, in a sequence from the Soviet film version of *Hamlet*, Ophelia is shown being strapped into a metal corset and dress form. These standard accoutrements of court dress are used by the director to signify Ophelia's feelings of confinement and oppression, which precipitate her madness. They also prefigure the direct cause of her death, when ". . . her garments, heavy with drink, / Pull'd the poor wretch from her melodious lay / To muddy death" (IV, vii, 180–182).

Making an emblem out of a domestic detail and then rereading an author's work to note an idiosyncratic or even fetishistic usage of these same details in the text has often been the work of psychoanalytic criticism. Taking a psychobiographical approach would make the snake in the grass, the viper in the bosom, the serpent on the hearth, into images suggestive of the well-known strife in the Tolstoy household and, in larger terms, of the falling out and mutual recriminations between man and woman and their fall into the sex roles determined for them by the God of the Old Testament. The serpentine presence can easily be construed as the impetus to carnal knowledge; a demonic, sinuous aspect of sexuality, repressed into its animal avatar, yet nonetheless given the run of homes and gardens.

Much has been made of Tolstoy's biography and attitudes toward sexuality in the literary criticism of his greatest works, but this is not the use to which I wish to put the image of snakes at Yasnaya Polyana. Instead, I would like to emphasize their presence as a phatic symbol, to call attention to our own habits of reading, picturing, and imag(in)ing, to welcome the sense of disturbance we may feel when the reality does not fit our preconceived image, and to direct our attention to the ways in which Tolstoy and his art have been stereotyped both in the biographies and in the criticism.

This book participates in the current critical revision of Tolstoy initiated by Richard Gustafson's challenge to the traditional view that bifurcates Tolstoy's oeuvre and aesthetics into two estranged pre- and postconversion periods. Recently, Rimvydas Silbajoris has extended the implications of reading Tolstoy's art and aesthetics as a unified text. Both Gustafson and Gary Saul Morson have noted Tolstoy's deviation from the conventions of European literature and questioned his placement in that canon: Gustafson creates the concept of "emblematic realism" to accommodate the symbolic features of Tolstoy's art, while Morson institutes a theory of prosaics in his studies of Tolstoy's resistance to the strictures of causality and narrative.

The thesis of this book is first that Tolstoy's literary-historical placement at the apex of realism is problematic, and second that *Anna Karenina* reflects Tolstoy's polemic with realist art and his quest for mythopoesis—two key elements of his aesthetic philosophy that are made explicit in his later treatise, *What Is Art?*[2] By reading *Anna Karenina* from this perspective, a different interpretation of the novel emerges. This interpretation argues that just as *War and Peace* was the place where Tolstoy explored the failures and dangers of causal narrative representation (history), so *Anna Karenina* problematizes the theme of visual representation to critique the aesthetic category of the beautiful, the framed, the embodied, and the feminine.

As I pursued this approach to the novel, I often encountered shocked incredulity from the majority of colleagues and students with whom I shared my impressions. My thesis was shipwrecked before I ever set sail, the response went, because Tolstoy was a known sexist in his private life, in his journals, and in his novels, especially *Anna Karenina*. This view is deeply entrenched in the criticism as well. Indeed, with one or two exceptions, the critical consensus is that Anna dies at the point of Tolstoy's punishing pen, and that the novel upholds what is perceived to be Tolstoy's conservative position on the woman question. Thus, in order to be able to explicate my reading of the novel, I was forced to challenge the critical consensus of Tolstoy's novel as misogynist, a move that necessitated a larger evaluation of the charges against Tolstoy as a sexist. My extended survey of Tolstoy's thinking on the political aspects of women's representation reveals the ways in which, in *Anna Karenina,* he makes the theme of the artistic representation of women stand for issues in aesthetic philosophy.

Thus I find that, in *Anna Karenina,* Tolstoy conflates the aesthetic question—what is the beautiful and can it be represented? what is its nature? what can it show us?—with the woman question—what is woman and what is her proper role in life?—to interrogate the literary conventions of realism and the social conventions of romantic love and marriage. *Framing "Anna Karenina"* thus refers first to the literary-historical framing context and the frame of expectations and critical conformation that focuses our reading. The frame is also the "frame-up" of Anna by a critical tradition that condemns her and also frames Tolstoy as a misogynist. Finally and most important, the frame is Tolstoy's act of framing within the text that makes Anna, the heroine, and *Anna,* the novel, a work of art. Her status as objet d'art and the novel's emphasis on the visual as the venue for knowledge make *Anna Karenina* a novel about the boundaries of vision and a tragic narrative of beauty framed.

My approach to the novel will be tropological, intertextual, and feminist. Tropological in the examination of tropes, figures, and imagery in the novel, especially those related to the themes identified above. Intertextual in the exploration of these figures' intertextual resonances, particularly with the Victorian novel that *Anna Karenina* both imitates and resists, and with the folktale, fable, and myth—the genres Tolstoy emulated and valorized in his quest for a universalist art that began at the time of writing *Anna Karenina* (1873–76), when he was engaged in compiling fables and parables for his *Primer* (1875). Feminist in that the themes of the novel—the fallen woman, the question of marriage, and the aesthetic problem of the beautiful versus the sublime—demand a critical practice, a canon of interpretive strategies, and a vocabulary for reading with attention to these issues that make feminist criticism most appropriate. Furthermore, the direction of much recent criticism of Tolstoy and of *Anna Karenina* forces the reconsideration of Tolstoy's own relationship to feminism along with the reevaluation of his novel as a misogynist text.

My methodology will be the close reading of key passages, some of which are notable for considerable critical traversal, others of which have been overlooked or have usually received a more literal interpretation. Each chapter is intended to stand alone as a self-contained essay, and this book may be read in that fashion. My practice here has been rhetorical and associative; my argument does not rely on a linear, chronological progression. Rather I intend to explore each issue thematically in all of the theoretical, textual, and contextual complexity that it demands.

The feminist intention of my close reading is not to argue for the existence of a repressed, subversive text of gendered imagery that "exposes" Tolstoy. When feminist criticism pursues this line of interpretation, it sometimes demonstrates its affinities with psychoanalytic criticism in shifting the focus from the text to the author and his or her unconscious. I do not subscribe to the view that the strands of imagery many critics (not necessarily feminist or psychoanalytic) have noted in the novel can be relegated to the sphere of the authorial unconscious. Rather, I argue that these "labyrinths of linkages" belong to the active powers of the creative imagination. I shall therefore demonstrate that Tolstoy's subtle attention to the visual field in this novel directly engages his theme of beauty framed.

Part I of this book, *"Passe-Partout*: Tolstoy's Image," explores and explodes the mythologizing that has formed Tolstoy's biography and has served as the supportive, interior frame, or *passe-partout,* for critical readings of the novels. Chapter 1, "The Myth of Misogyny: De-Moralizing Tolstoy," questions the traditional view of Tolstoy as a misogynist holding reactionary views on the woman question. Chapter 2, "The Judgment of *Anna Karenina*: Feminist Criticism and the Image of the Heroine," considers the ways in which the image of Tolstoy as misogynist has shaped critical evaluations of the ideology of his novels and his representations of women, particularly in *Anna Karenina*. The concluding chapter of this section rejects the popular view of a sexually repressed, misogynist Tolstoy and instead upholds a perception of the author as a conscious, aware, and caustic critic of social institutions, particularly those based on gender. This view of Tolstoy is supportable when we allow that the feminist views he expressly stated in his postconversion years were forming prior to his conversion and are emergent and discernible in his literary works. In his statements and literary works of the postconversion years, Tolstoy quite explicitly rejects the concept of a sexually consummated Christian marriage and declares chastity to be the ideal Christian state. In *The Kreutzer Sonata* (1889), *What Then Must We Do?* (1886), and *Resurrection* (1899), he repeatedly compares the married women of high society to prostitutes and characterizes marriage as a form of institutionalized prostitution that oppresses and enslaves women.

I am therefore also employing the serpents on Tolstoy's hearth to emblematize the disquieting darkness Tolstoy perceived at the heart of the domestic idyll, the problematic nature of the sexual contract of marriage and the resulting conflicts of domestic life. In his earliest depiction of family life in *Childhood* (1852), Tolstoy draws on Victorian—specifically Dickensian—models and conventions to idealize and romanticize domesticity and family life. Yet even in his first sustained exploration of the contractual marital relationship at the heart of the family in *Family Happiness* (1856), Tolstoy does not hesitate to probe the negative, darker side of sexual politics and the failures of romantic love through its bourgeois institutionalization in marriage. Although his masterpiece, *War and Peace* (1863–69), may seem to conclude on a note of connubial bliss, this mood is undercut by the apparent dissolution of the main characters' potential for heroic action and the limitation of their ultimate interests and passions to the everyday world of mundane events and concerns. In returning to the theme of the family, marriage, and sexuality in *Anna Karenina* (1873–76), Tolstoy again reveals his affinities for his beloved Victorian authors Dickens, Eliot, and Trollope, who, while exalting the Victorian ideal of the family, simultaneously, if not always consciously, expose its pathology. Yet Tolstoy carries the exploration one step beyond the Victorians in addressing the issues of sexuality and the psychological effects of repression in direct and explicit terms, especially by the time of writing *The Kreutzer Sonata*. The Victorian literary influences on Tolstoy are summarized in chapter 3, "Beyond the Motivations of Realism: Tolstoy, the Victorian Novel, and Iconic Aesthetics," where I examine the ways in which the conventions of the Victorian novel are adapted and polemicized, even parodied, in *Anna Karenina*. In its exploration of interiority, *Anna Karenina* turns away from the textual conventions of realism to a different, more mythic mode that allows the unsuppressed exploration of the most disturbing and anarchic forces of the human psyche. And in its use of imagery and tragic narrative structure, the novel itself violates the conventions of realist fiction. Tolstoy's revision of realism in *Anna Karenina* marks the beginning of a development in his thinking that would culminate in his infamous rejection of Western aesthetic theory in *What Is Art?* (1898) and his formulation of an original theory of art termed here "iconic aesthetics." "Tolstoy's Image" thus refers both to the popular image of Tolstoy and to Tolstoy's theory of the image and representation, an aesthetic that revises Western bourgeois aesthetic philosophy by rejecting the traditional categories of the sublime and the beautiful. Instead, Tolstoy deconstructs Western philosophy to reveal the gender bias implicit in its bifurcated categories, and draws on his native Eastern Orthodox philosophical tradition to create a supersublime category, that of universal Christian love that transcends gender and individual difference in promoting a community of aesthetic response.

Many critics have observed that Tolstoy's views on art and aesthetics are "expressed more powerfully in the narration of *Anna Karenina* than in his theoretical statements on art."[3] While, as Gary Saul Morson has demonstrated, *War and Peace* is a work concerned with the failures of representation in the formation of narratives— histories and causalities—in *Anna Karenina* Tolstoy uses the visual— pictures, images, icons, female beauty—to interrogate the human need to aestheticize meaning. We look to narrative structures or frames to consolidate meaning, to square off and finish the pattern. We as readers are frustrated by unfinished business; we demand afterwords, like little tassels of bright, glossy thread at the tapestry's end, that signal the potential for continuity while satisfying our need for a feeling of closure. In fact, in life and in death, we cannot ever know the end of the story. The forces each individual sets in motion continue far beyond his or her physical presence in life, so that in sensing the limit—death—we also sense limitlessness.

The perception of the unrepresentable beyond the borders of representation is termed the experience of the sublime in aesthetic discourse. In its most widely accepted, Kantian definition, the sublime is understood as that moment of the intellect's failure to know and represent that thereby stimulates awareness of the unknowable sublime lying beyond the limits of consciousness. Since, according to Kant, it is only at the moment of confronting its own limitations that consciousness begins to apprehend what lies beyond it, the region of the boundary, the border, the frame, is valorized. In aesthetic philosophical discourse beginning with Burke, the category of the sublime is thus elevated over the more simple, mundane category of the beautiful. The sublime becomes invested with heroic, masculine attributes, while the beautiful is characterized as small, trivial, feminine. Furthermore, the model of aesthetic perception in the discourse of aesthetic philosophy establishes a male gaze directed at a female subject and thus injects prurience and eroticism into the play of disinterest and admiration. Tolstoy's treatment of these aesthetic categories in *Anna Karenina* and in his later treatise on aesthetics, *What Is Art?*, proceeds from his recognition of the engendering of aesthetics and the enslavement of beauty within that tradition of thought.

In *What Is Art?* Tolstoy characterizes the aesthetic category of beauty as the subjective response to the physically pleasurable. The implicit and traditional association of the aesthetic category of beauty with the feminine in Western aesthetic philosophy makes the representation of women in works of art problematic, since the category is devalued in contrast to the sublime. The representation of a woman as a work of art within a work of art therefore generates a *mise en abîme* that forces the reader's awareness of both the aesthetic question and the highly sexualized status of beauty. I read Tolstoy's depiction of Anna as constituting that moment in the literary tradition of treating heroines as objets d'art that exposes the fatal dangers of entrapment in physical beauty and draws attention to its own practice.[4] Chapter 4, "The Execution of Anna Karenina: Heroines Framed and Hung," compares Tolstoy to the modernists Proust and Joyce to demonstrate that Tolstoy shared their recognition of the Victorian blindness to the implications of beauty framed. Like Proust and Joyce, Tolstoy elaborated upon the Victorian literary convention of describing women as artworks whose beauty so often precipitated their ineluctable fall and execution. Even more than Proust and Joyce, Tolstoy indicts the pornographic modalities of the Western aesthetic tradition and recasts the portrait of the beautiful in iconic terms. The way in which he rewrites his heroine's end suggests that although Anna shares the fate that had come to be obligatory for the adulterous heroines of nineteenth-century literature, Tolstoy reinvested her suicide with a heroic and philosophical tenor usually reserved for male suicides. Thus, Anna's suicide figures both as an example of the victimization of woman and as a heroic step toward transcendence of the beautiful body in pursuit of a spiritual truth that cannot be contained.

The escape from the plane of the body to the spiritual is reflected in the concept of the sublime aesthetic response, the illimitable beyond limits that produces a sense of awe and wonder in the observer. The pursuit of such transcendence in art is characteristic of Romanticism or lyric poetry. It is not usually considered native to realist aesthetics. Yet the sublime, obliquely redefined by Tolstoy in *What Is Art?* in purely spiritual terms as the union of souls in aesthetic response, is arguably the keystone of Tolstoyan aesthetics and is a mode he often achieves in his greatest lyrical passages. Among the examples we might readily think of are Natasha's folk dance in "Uncle's" hut or Nikolai Rostov's feeling of transcendence at hearing his sister sing that transports him into a state of pure joy, despite his misery over his gambling debts. The ultimate example, Lyovin's[5] feelings of awe and compassion before Anna Karenina's portrait, will receive extended treatment in this study. It is no accident that characters in Tolstoy's novels experience the sublime in response to works of art or render their perceptions of life sublime by turning them into works of art. Tolstoy's own art is sublime in showing us the sublime powers of all great art. Indeed, his artistry and his aesthetic theory move beyond the sublime, working past the problematically engendered categories of traditional Western aesthetics toward what I term a lyrical, iconic aesthetics.[6]

The presence of lyric moments in Tolstoy's novels, especially moments that rely for their effect on stopping time and the flow of narrative via the description of artworks or of natural or feminine beauty framed and thus rendered artistic (the trope of *ekphrasis*), is one aspect of Tolstoy's iconic aesthetics. By iconic I mean that the framed image achieves the status of the visionary, and its elements become symbolic in a manner that reaches beyond the text to transport the reader beyond pictured reality. Although we may find lyric moments in many so-called realist novels, Tolstoy's employment of the lyric and iconic, combined with his stated contempt for most realist art, makes his usual literary-historical status as a high realist problematic.[7] In fact, I will argue in this book that Tolstoy should not be considered a realist at all; rather, I would call him a peri-modern, or presymbolist author. Nowhere are his proclivities for symbolism more apparent than in his manipulation of textual details in *Anna Karenina*. The random minutiae and telling details for which Tolstoy is celebrated indeed create the "effect of the real" but also, upon close reading, interact to reiterate, at the subliminal level, the thematic of the novel. Thus Tolstoy's details sharpen the reader's focus on the texture and warp of prosaic life while acquiring the status of legitimate symbols integrated into a larger pattern.

Parts II and III of this book, "Frame: Image and the Boundaries of Vision in *Anna Karenina*" and "Illuminations: Reading Detail and Design in *Anna Karenina*," examine four examples of sustained imagery sequences in the novel, to pursue the way in which each strand of imagery symbolizes the themes of the novel: the woman question, representation, illusion, and enlightenment. The themes of art, beauty, vision, and the visionary are addressed in chapter 5, "A Painted Lady: The Poetics of *Ekphrasis*," which notes those scenes and moments in the novel where artworks, artists, and aesthetic philosophy come under direct discussion. In chapter 6, "Knife, Book, and Candle: The Resisting Russian Reader," Tolstoy's concerns with representation are shown to be reflected equally in the topos of reading. Chapter 7, "The Woman with a Shadow: Fables of Demon and Psyche," follows throughout the novel the subtle use of a mythic and folkloric subtext that addresses the problems of vision as blindness, crime, and punishment determined by gender. With his evocation of the myth of Amor and Psyche, Tolstoy reiterates the theme of appearance versus reality in a mythological manner intended to explore the nature of female heroism. Chapter 8, "Picking a Mushroom and Escaping the Marriage Plot," suggests that Tolstoy creates a folkloric episode based on Russian folk customs and courtship rituals to counter the rhetoric of literary, especially Victorian, fictional courtship and to suggest an escape for women from the entrapment of that conventional courtship plot that leads either to the strictures of marriage or to the fatalities of passionate, adulterous love.

Thus, I will argue that in *Anna Karenina* Tolstoy rewrites the Victorian realist, domestic novel according to his own aesthetic principles, subverting mimesis and realist aesthetics by means of direct discussion and representation of art and artists in the novel, the insertion of subtexts drawn from the genres of myth and folklore, and the creation of an elaborate system of imagery that illustrates his themes and serves to elevate symbolism over verisimilitude, iconicity over conventionality.

This study contends that *Anna Karenina* expresses and exemplifies Tolstoy's iconic aesthetics; his exalted transcendent vision and his employment of linkages of symbolic detail raise his artistic theory and practice to a more mythological, symbolist, or postrealist register. His concern with the status of beauty—natural and human—as an aesthetic category and as a sociosexual construct informs both his aesthetic views and his sociopolitical views on the Victorian woman question, arguably the two dominating themes of *Anna Karenina*.

PART I

Passe-Partout: Tolstoy's Image

Portrait of Leo Nikolaevich
Tolstoy by I. E. Repin, 1901

14

The Myth of Misogyny:
De-Moralizing Tolstoy

The Image of the Author

We are concerned about the image of the author because it shapes
some of the preconceptions with which we approach a work of literature. Jacques Derrida has termed this area of reader response the
passe-partout; that is, the interior frame or matte used to block
and support the central canvas in painting.[1] The outer frame of the
artwork demarcates an interior world separated from the external
world and focuses our attention on the artistic status of what is enclosed; as Henry James characterizes it, the frame is "the charming
oval that helps any arrangement of objects to become a picture."[2]
Thus, the frame has been defined as a functional marker indicating
the "transition from the real world to the world of representation"[3] or
"the shift from the external to the internal point of view."[4] Yet the
frame has an existence that is separate from what it encloses, as Iurii
Lotman suggests:

> A picture frame may be an independent work of art, but it is located
> on the *other* side of the line demarcating the canvas, and we do not
> see it when we look at the picture. We need only to examine the
> frame as a kind of independent text in order for the canvas to disap-
> pear from the field of our artistic vision; it ends up on the other side
> of the boundary.[5]

The frame and the work of art do not interpenetrate and thus they visually exclude one another.

By contrast, the *passe-partout* conceived of figuratively could be understood as the critical consensus that defines the artwork in advance of our reading. To the extent that it establishes a set of expectations in the reader, it permeates and suborns the artwork, becoming an accretion of meaning on the meta level that in turn infuses the work with meaning. In Derrida's summation:

> Neither inside nor outside, [the *passe-partout*] spaces itself without letting itself be framed, but it does not stand outside the frame. It works the frame, makes it work, lets it work, gives it work to do. . . . *Between* the outside and the inside, between the external and the internal edge-line, the framer and the framed, the figure and the ground, form and content, signifier and signified. . . . What appears, then, . . . only appears to do without the *passe-partout* on which it banks.[6]

For example, what we have been led to expect about a work of art constitutes its *passe-partout*; we have already begun a dialogue with a text before we ever hear it. Just as the theater audiences of classical antiquity were well acquainted with the plots of Greek tragedy before they attended a performance, so many modern readers begin a novel like *Anna Karenina* well aware of the tragic outcome of the story. In the modern literary tradition where the author's persona is as important a mask as those we see on stage, we are also usually aware of the author's own biography and philosophy, what Boris Tomashevsky termed the "literary functions" of biography.[7] And we furthermore need to distinguish between the author's own masquerade and the critical mythologizing that follows upon it. Thus, the *passe-partout* for a Tolstoy novel engages us in a dialogue with Tolstoyan morality and ethics, while his Christian beliefs become constituting factors in our reading, determining our hermeneutic procedures and often demoralizing us by turning us off in advance to the sanctimony of a moralistic text. Yet, despite the dangers posed by the pitfalls of the "biographical and intentional fallacies"[8] and the unconscious abyss exposed by a psychoanalytically informed criticism, any reading of

Tolstoy's works must take into account the raw material of Tolstoy's biography. In addition, we must also consider the meta-biography, the myth or legend of Leo Nikolaevich, as it has been constructed to date.

The problems of literary biography and of creating a literary biography are themselves obscure. What are the links we would like to establish between the "life" and "works"? Between "theory" and "praxis"? What place do we give to the author's "unconscious" intention? Should authorial intention be a privileged category at all? Reading in a postmodern era when the author is considered to be dead and theoretical constructs based on linguistic indeterminacy are ubiquitous, shouldn't we liberate ourselves from the author and authority and simply revel in the *jouissance* of infinitely available textual nuances? Or must we deconstruct the text from the perspective of the author's own logocentrism, exposing or questioning ethics and choices so that we place ourselves in a position to forgive (or not to forgive) Tolstoy or Fyodor Dostoevsky or, in recent debate, Paul de Man? Often, the reader seems forced into the Solomonic procedure of splitting the author in two—man and artist—in order to prove how much we love him, a position resisted in Gary Saul Morson's discussion of Dostoevsky's anti-Semitism.[9] What kinds of critics will we be if we accept the convention of seeing double: Tolstoy the (poor) thinker as opposed to Tolstoy the (great) artist? The problem of measuring the distance between an author's extraliterary statements and his artistic works, or between his life and his art, is further complicated in the case of Tolstoy by his attempt at Christian reformation, the process of overcoming the gulf between *theoria* and *praxis* that tormented the great author throughout his life and precipitated his flight toward death.

We do not often question the extent to which we are influenced by reading within a community, the degree to which our readings may be predetermined by the *passe-partout* of critical reviews, the consensus of a reading body that has stamped its impress on the text before us and thus preempts our reading and directs our response. In responding to the critical community on the meta level, we create a meta-*passe-partout* that analyzes and interprets the *passe-partout* built around, beneath, through, and within the original text. The *passe-partout* is a halo of sanctified response that illuminates the text; the meta-*passe-partout* is our attempt to read the text separately from the critical interpretation that overlays it, like prying the painted wooden icon free from the gold, gem-encrusted filigree that conceals the figures beneath. Our meta-*passe-partout* must take into account the sociocultural context that created the *passe-partout*, as well as our own sociocultural frame and the types of mental habits that result from our ideological formation.

In approaching *Anna Karenina*, we necessarily question whether Tolstoy's novel is not misogynist based on our reading of Tolstoy's life as the biography of a sexist whose documented contempt for women engenders a misogynist representation of female characters in his oeuvre. It is not my intention in this chapter to resolve these questions or to reconsider every instance of alleged misogyny in Tolstoy's life and art in an exhaustive fashion.[10] Rather, I intend to question the framework within which such viewpoints have been formulated in order to liberate the novel and its heroine from a predetermined, automatic reading. I will begin by challenging the very meaning of the term *misogynist*, as it is understood within a late twentieth-century, postfeminist perspective, and will suggest that we ought to reconsider what may have constituted misogyny in Tolstoy's time as opposed to our own.

One failure of feminist deconstructionist criticism has been a reluctance to allow historical or cultural relativity to ameliorate the degree to which we perceive representations to be essentializing or stereotypical. Critical practice that seeks to expose gender bias might begin by exploring with greater precision what specificity of discourse or representation may be determined to be misogynistic. For example, changing the gender of the speaker in a text frequently changes our perception of bias. Or, to phrase it differently, a feminist poetics is needed that can locate misogynist elements in textual discourse with as much expertise as it does when following the course of much psychoanalytically and sociologically based feminist criticism that projects misogynist bias into the text on the basis of extratextual evidence. Feminist criticism of the latter variety often fails to discrimi-

nate between popular conceptions of misogyny and feminist definitions of misogyny. Is the opposite of misogyny necessarily feminism?
Are the two categories mutually exclusive? Is there any intermediate
mode of thought between the two extremes of misogyny and feminism, and how would the gradations be evaluated? Feminist psychoanalytic criticism rarely finds it necessary to consider the degree to
which misogyny may be conscious or unconscious: it assumes a male
chauvinism so profound that any sympathy for the opposite sex in an
author's writings could be controverted by the damning evidence of
his personal life.[11]

Although romanticism is partly responsible for creating the icon
of the artistic genius, and thus for elevating the literary biography—
as lived and as mythologized—to the level of an artistic creation, or
even allowing it to supersede artistic creation, romantic sensibility
also juxtaposes the life of the soul to the life of the body: as Rimbaud
proclaimed, "Real life is elsewhere." Much of modern criticism has
shied away from the kinds of questions posed here. It is only as a result of the poststructuralist sensibility that deconstructs all intention
and inscription according to its prosaic, practical failures that holding
a text accountable to its origins is again in vogue. Thus, feminist cri-
tiques of Tolstoy document and register his multiple verbal assaults on
his wife (and, by extension, women), his transformation of the married Natalia Rostova into a domestic drone, his "murder" of Anna
Karenina, his relegation of his heroines to endless childbirth, nursing,
and drudgery, and his hypostatization of the "ideal" woman into a de-
sexed, plain Madonna—Princess Maria, Dolly Oblonskaia.[12] Tolstoy
thus stands accused of painting grotesque deformations or repressions of the beautiful corporality we have come to expect from the
heroines of realist novels. And he is judged to have murdered those
creations whose beauty and vitality have escaped the descriptive mutilation of his pen.

These feminist criticisms[13] fit comfortably into the common
Western, twentieth-century resistance to Tolstoy the moralist; a resistance aroused by discomfort with tendentiousness and fanaticism,
and augmented by the usual Freudian reading of Tolstoy as guilt-
ridden oppressor and overcompensated orphan. The myth or "legend"

of Leo Nikolaevich as titanic moralist "monologizes" Tolstoy, painting him into the haloed shape of a formalized icon, a depiction that he himself was partly responsible for creating.[14] This study attempts to attenuate the rigidity of this monument by suggesting that Tolstoy's quest for the status and platform of wise man was his pursuit of a privileged *passe-partout* that would encourage his audience of readers to seek his hero, "truth," within his writings, and to apply what meaning they could find in his works to their own lives. His assumption of patriarchal form was by no means intended to box and shape the actual content of his thought, which, when read in the context of its own time, is radical, subversive, and, in many fundamental ways, feminist.

In exploring the interstices between the documents of an author's life and the artistic works, we often argue in favor of a literary work's polysemous evocation of a universally acceptable message that transcends the author's limited, human vision; as Schlegel put it: "Every excellent work, of whatever genre, knows more than it says and intends more than it knows." An author's extraliterary works, by contrast, are taken as representing the limits of the author's conscious mind, which cannot achieve the sublime, illimitable realm of his imagination. This is often the case, for example, in the criticism of Dostoevsky, whose journalism is usually ignored in the criticism because of its strident anti-Semitism. Curiously, the opposite situation obtains in criticism of Tolstoy's views of women, since Tolstoy, the artist who created *War and Peace* and *Anna Karenina,* seems to come closer to being a misogynist promoting the Victorian cult of domesticity than does Tolstoy, the thinker and essayist of the postconversion period who expresses a feminism central to his formulation of radical Christian asceticism. For both Tolstoy and Dostoevsky, the novels speak louder than their journalism. Much of Tolstoy's journalism on the woman question and his discussions of the problem in his diaries and letters have therefore been overlooked by critics seeking to establish his misogyny, who support their opinion with the standard set of well-cited examples. There have been few attempts,[15] feminist or otherwise, to appreciate the full complexity of Tolstoy's shifting views on the woman question. The following considerations cannot claim to lay the debate to rest, but they may at least challenge received notions of Tolstoy's views on the woman question and may suggest that we need to reconsider the very definitions of feminism and misogyny both in general and within the specific context of the Russian socio-historical tradition.

Tolstoy and the Woman Question

Tolstoy's thoughts on the various "accursed questions" connected with the woman question—the family question, the sexual question—were continually evolving. Although Tolstoy is usually compared to the French conservatives Alexandre Dumas fils, Michelet, and Proudhon, whose views undoubtedly influenced him, we might more profitably compare him to the feminist John Stuart Mill, author of the classic feminist treatise *On the Subjection of Women* (1869).[16] Mill, when challenged by Harriet Taylor in the first year of their courtship (1832) to compose an essay on women's emancipation, produced a stiflingly patriarchal portrait of the Victorian woman as ornament, helpmeet, and "Angel on the Hearth":

> The question is not what marriage ought to be, but . . . what woman ought to be,[17] . . . [and since] women in general . . . are more easily contented,[18] . . . it does not follow that a woman should *actually* support herself [through work] because she should be *capable* of doing so: in the natural course of events she will *not*. . . . there would be no need that the wife should take part in the mere providing of what is required to *support* life: it will be for the happiness of both [husband and wife] that her occupation should be rather to adorn and beautify it.[19] . . . Her natural task . . . will . . . be accomplished rather by *being* than by *doing*. . . . The great occupation of woman should be to beautify life.[20] . . . If . . . the activity of her nature demands more energetic and definite employment, there is never any lack of it in the world: . . . her natural impulse will be to associate her existence with him she loves to share *his* occupations.[21]

To these statements, Harriet Taylor responded: "The proper sphere for all human beings is the largest and highest which they are able to attain to. What this is cannot be ascertained without complete liberty."[22] Despite ten years of thought and research on women's rights stimulated by his long association with his feminist lover and wife, Mill, in his ultimate statement on women's emancipation, *still* continues to locate her sphere of activity in the home. In *The Subjection of Women*, he writes:

> It would not be necessary for her protection that during marriage she make . . . use of her faculties. Like a man when he chooses a profession, so, when a woman marries, it may in general be understood that she makes choice of the management of a household and the bringing up of a family as the first call upon her exertions . . . and that she renounces all [other objects and occupations] which are not consistent with the requirements of this. . . . But the utmost latitude ought to exist for the adaptation of general rules to individual suitabilities; and there ought to be nothing to prevent faculties *exceptionally* adapted to any other pursuit from obeying their vocation notwithstanding marriage, due provision being made for supplying any falling-short . . . in her full performance of the ordinary functions of mistress of a family.[23]

Since Mill's classical feminist treatise still confines woman to the home and limits her employment to the domestic sphere, her education and accomplishments amount either to decorative accoutrements or to hobbies that threaten to distract her from her only legitimate occupation.

Tolstoy's most conservative position as stated in *What Then Must We Do?* is far more radical than Mill's. First of all, far from placing married women gracefully in the drawing room behind the embroidery screen or the pianoforte—an objet d'art for men's pleasure in a de-eroticized depiction of the seraglio—Tolstoy appreciates, values, and empathizes with the oppressive work of pregnancy, childbirth, and domestic cares, which he considers to be far more difficult, strenuous, and important than men's work:

> You [women] alone know—not that false, showy kind of work in top hats and illuminated rooms that the men of our circle call work—

instead you know that genuine work given to people by God. . . . You know how, after the joys of love, you wait in agitation, terror, and hope for that tormenting condition of pregnancy that will make you an invalid for nine months, will bring you to the brink of death and to unendurable suffering and pain; you know the nature of true work . . . when, immediately after these torments, without a break, without a rest, you take on another burden of labors and suffering—nursing, during which time you renounce . . . the most overwhelming human need, sleep. . . . You do not sleep through a single night for years, and sometimes, often, you do not sleep at all for nights on end. (*PSS* 25:408–409)

Rather than merely extending latitude to those exceptional women who seek occupation beyond domestic activities, or "self-improvement" (*razvitie*), that buzzword of the Russian woman question debate, Tolstoy demands such development for *all* women, and, even more radically, he does not curtail such activity to what can be accommodated within the busy schedule of a wife and mother, but argues instead that extra considerations should be made to liberate women from drudgery, beginning with men's willingness to share the housework:

This is where the true emancipation of women lies—in not considering any line of work to be women's work, the sort that one is ashamed to touch, in helping them with all one's strength . . . and in taking from them all the work that it is possible to take upon oneself. Similarly with education—just because they will probably bear children and so have less leisure, for that very reason, we should organize schools for them that are not worse, but better than men's, so that they can build up their strength and knowledge in advance. . . . I thought about my churlish and egotistical attitude to my wife in this respect. I acted like everybody else, i.e., badly and cruelly. I gave her all the hard work, the so-called women's work to do and went out hunting myself. (Diary entry, 24 September 1894 [*PSS* 52:143])

Tolstoy's rejection of the terms of the woman question in his treatise *What Then Must We Do?* is often cited as proof of his misogynist outlook. In fact, Tolstoy radicalized the woman question in very pro-

found ways. In order to appreciate his polemic with the term, it is necessary to consider the way in which the term arose and became central to the Russian women's emancipation movement.

The woman question was initially formulated in Victorian England as the question of how to resolve the problem of the so-called redundant or superfluous woman; that is, the fact that in nineteenth-century English society, women considerably outnumbered men and constituted an unemployable, superannuated spinster population. Judging from journalistic publications, the woman question did not become the focus of active sociopolitical debate among the Russian intelligentsia until after the appearance of Mill's *The Subjection of Women* in Russian translations in 1869. For most of the nineteenth century, the issue of women's emancipation had been treated primarily in literary works, such as the novels of Ivan Turgenev, the plays of Alexander Ostrovsky, Alexander Druzhinin's *Polinka Saks* (1847), or Nikolai Nekrasov's "Sasha." Early Russian literary treatments of the theme of oppressed women were probably most influenced by the novels of George Sand, whose heroines suffer in the name of free love. Sand's novel *Jacques*, for example, provided the plot for the most read Russian novel on women's emancipation, Nikolai Chernyshevsky's *What Is to Be Done?* (1864).[24]

The course taken by the debate in Russian journalism after the translation of Mill's book perpetuated the concerns as stated in Victorian English journalism, with its emphasis on the superfluity of women rather than a focus on local Russian concerns.[25] Thus, the Russian debate was curtailed: the issue was not one of women's civil rights, or capacity to participate in public life, as women's rights and abilities were automatically presumed to be limited to the domestic sphere, following Victorian mores. According to this view, all women should marry and raise children, and the only problem posed by the woman question was how to dispose of those unfortunates who were unable to catch a husband. Thus, the strides already made toward women's education and liberation within the nihilist movement were overlooked in the journalistic debates or ridiculed in literary caricatures of the *nigilistka*. As evident from the debate at the Oblonskys' dinner party in *Anna Karenina* (a debate that clearly relies on Mill and Dumas fils' *L'homme-femme* as subtexts), the focus of Russian society remained on the plight of the superfluous woman—unmarried, without a place in a family—unable to earn a living because of her lack of education or access to the professions, and, as a last resort, forced into prostitution or poverty.

In both Europe and Russia, the number of single women increased rapidly in the second half of the nineteenth century as a result of socioeconomic factors. In an 1881 census entitled "The Prospects of Marriage for Women," the ratio of women to men in Great Britain was found to have increased in the course of the century from 102.9 to 100 to 149.8 to 100. Furthermore, the tendency of men to delay marriage as long as possible diminished women's chances for marriage to men of their own age group, since these men chose younger brides on average. A similar situation obtained in Russia after emancipation of the serfs, when, due to declining fortunes of the aristocracy, single women could no longer be supported within the extended family and became a "new 'female proletariat' of aunts, sisters, old maids, divorcées and widows, cut loose from the patriarchal family and left to their own economic devices."[26] In Petersburg, the number of unemployed women increased from 204,527 in 1858 to 320,832 in 1870. The number of prostitutes increased by 20 percent during the same period.[27] The ghettoization of women into "women's professions" paying less than subsistence wages was observed in such historical instances as the introduction of the telegraph to Russia and the instantaneous placement of thousands of working women in telegraph offices. The analogous situation in Victorian England was summarized in a pithy discussion in Anthony Trollope's *Can You Forgive Her?* (1864):

> Alice was glad to find that a hundred and fifty thousand female [telegraph] operatives were employed in Paris, while Lady Glencora said it was a great shame, and they ought all to have husbands. When Mr. Palliser explained that that was impossible, because of the redundancy of the female population, she angered him very much by asserting that she saw a great many men walking about who, she was quite sure, had not wives of their own.[28]

Despite women's demand for professional work and economic parity, the published debate on the woman question in Russia was in fact monopolized by men who defined the course of feminism in Russia and diverted attention from issues of woman's autonomy as these might have been determined by women authors. Jane Costlow has recently examined the woman question debate in Russia to recover those feminine voices that did participate. The main issue addressed was women's right to education, or development *(razvitie)*. The consequence of focusing on education rather than on socioeconomic status was that the initial impulse of feminism was tightly curtailed, as those women who were the first to obtain advanced degrees were to discover when they attempted to practice the professions they had qualified in. The classic example is Sofia Kovalevskaia, the mathematician and author who received a Ph.D. in Europe, wrote three dissertations, one of which won an international competition, and yet discovered on her return to Russia that the best job she could obtain was teaching arithmetic at an elementary school for girls.[29]

The two men considered to be the leading Russian feminists of their age, or the fathers of Russian feminism, were Pirogov and Mikhail Mikhailov. Both polemicists asserted that education was beneficial for women because it made them better wives and mothers. To quote from a leading left-wing journal of the day, the goal of emancipation was to transform every woman "from a simple nurse to a genuine mother, from a household servant to a free member of the family, from a harem odalisque to an authentic, loving wife."[30] In his book *The Physiology of Woman,* Pirogov asserted that education better enabled women "to share men's struggle. It is not the position of woman in society, but her education that needs to be changed." Mikhailov saw a need for education to "save [a woman] from unreal fantasies about sex and love." Neither man made any claims for the political rights of women in Russia.

Tolstoy's views on the woman question in the early 1880s, just after his self-proclaimed conversion, actually place him in the mainstream, if not the advance guard, of those in favor of women's rights at the time he was writing, and not to the far right as exemplified by the works of Michelet, Proudhon, and Dumas fils. As expressed

in the closing chapter of *What Then Must We Do?*, Tolstoy's position on men and women allows, first of all, for the education of all
women and for free and equal access to the professions for those
women who, because they are unmarried, cannot devote themselves
to domestic activity. As distinct from the conservatives, Tolstoy warns
against women seeking employment outside the domestic sphere, not
because he feels they are not capable, but because he feels they would
be demeaned by it, just as are men, who, in Tolstoy's view, should return to physical labor in the fields. Tolstoy in fact rejects the very
terms of the woman question: "The so-called woman question arose
and could only arise among men who had rejected the law of genuine labor" (*PSS* 25:407). In Tolstoy's opinion, women and men who
honestly fulfill their roles as wives and mothers, and fathers and labor-
ers, are infinitely more moral than bourgeois men engaged in vain and
trivial pursuits. Women's entry into the bourgeois, male-dominated
work force would only demean them by lowering them to the level
of men.

It should be noted that this point of view has been consistently
debated over the course of feminist history and still has its adherents
in the mainstream of feminism. For example, this same argument was
made by the suffragettes, who felt that entry into the male-dominated
public sphere would compromise female virtues and goals. The focus
of the suffragist movement thus centered on the vote, which allowed
women access to political reform without ejecting them from their
protected, domestic sphere of activity. In contemporary feminist debate, Betty Friedan's *The Second Stage* suggests a revision of the
"feminist mystique" that lured women into the marketplace as male
clones. Some feminist thinkers, such as Elshtain, argue that a return
to women-centered values such as motherhood should reshape feminism. Much postmodernist feminist French thought, as represented
by Cixous or Kristeva, is also directed to escaping male-dominated
models.

Tolstoy attributes the inequality between the sexes in the status
quo to the fact that men have abandoned the Old Testament precept
to labor in the sweat of one's brow, whereas women continue to bear
the full burden of the injunction to bring forth children in pain.

These women represent "the highest manifestation of a human being," and thus, Tolstoy concludes, the potential salvation of the human race lies in their hands:

> Such women who fulfill their mission reign over men, and serve as a guiding star to humankind; such women form public opinion and prepare the coming generation; and therefore in their hands lies the highest power, the power to save men from the existing and threatening evils of our time.
>
> Yes, women, mothers, in your hands more than in those of anyone else lies the salvation of the world.[31]

In the wake of the furor aroused by his exhortation to Russian women to be the saviors of humanity, to be the kind of mother who would not say no to another pregnancy, even after bearing twenty children, Tolstoy continued to work out his position on the woman question.[32] As a result, by the time he wrote *The Kreutzer Sonata* in 1889, his attitudes had undergone a significant shift to an antimarriage, antifamily position, advocating chastity, even within marriage. This belief was not idiosyncratic; there were quite a few movements in Europe, Scandinavia, and the United States, such as the Skoptsy, the "glove morality," and the Shakers, whose adherents held this view.[33]

Because of the changing status of single women at the end of the century, feminism of the time emphasized not the free love of George Sand but the valorous path of chastity and self-sufficiency through work. The autonomous working woman, one who was committed to service or to art and did not regard these as mere pastimes until she married, became the new heroine in literary works of this period. The late Victorians thus promoted an alternative to the rotund, matronly "Angel on the Hearth" and her fallen alter ego. Instead, the pre-Raphaelite, ascetic, pale, passionless heroine emerged, along with and sometimes in the same body as the hard-working, etherealized single woman. Sue Bridehead of Thomas Hardy's *Jude the Obscure* or Rhoda Nunn of George Gissing's *The Odd Women*, their very names indicating their virginal natures, are examples of heroines who find marriage confining or destructive and who pursue fulfillment and autonomy elsewhere. The heroines of Mrs. Humphrey Ward's novels of the 1890s, much admired by Tolstoy, also follow this formula.

These literary exaltations of the old maid, formerly an object of ridicule, transpose the unmarried woman from her previously dependent status (regarded with such horror by Kitty in *Anna Karenina*) into an ennobled emblem of independence and endurance. Thus, John Fowles, in his meta-textual rewriting of the Victorian novel, *The French Lieutenant's Woman,* was forced to offer two resolutions to the novel to reflect his critical awareness of two phases in the genre's development. The first high Victorian, traditional ending closes on the reunion and marriage of the two protagonists. The second, in which the heroine joins an artist's colony and rejects the hero's suit, represents the late, high Victorian, feminist resistance to the closure of wedlock.

This paradigm shift in social attitudes and literary representations of women and marriage is reflected in Tolstoy's postconversion rejection of the Victorian ethos, the institution of marriage, and the cult of domesticity. The charge of misogyny usually falls with some justice on this extremism in Tolstoy's views of woman as either earth mother or nun, whereas the woman who enjoys sex without bearing children is "unacceptable and an evil against humanity" (*PSS* 25:407). However, labeling Tolstoy a misogynist on the basis of this fissure says more about our stereotyping of men's thoughts about women than it serves to clarify Tolstoy's actual views. Tolstoy's attitudes reflect a rejection of all sexuality and sexual politics, not just female sexuality. If anything, in Tolstoy's writings male sexuality is attacked more viciously than female sexuality. Furthermore, the notion of a moral, Christian marriage that is sexually consummated is rejected entirely. Sex cannot be justified at all, even by procreation: Tolstoy now insists that all true Christians should refrain from having children. Instead of marrying to have children, "It is far more simple to abstain and, instead, to support and save those millions of children who are in need all around us. A Christian can only enter marriage without the consciousness of having sinned if he has seen and is certain that the lives of all living children are secure" (*PSS* 27:87). Instead of consummating their mar-

riage and being occupied in their children's upbringing, it is recom-
mended that husband and wife live together as brother and sister,
united in their common work for humanity. Tolstoy's views on chaste
Christian marriage bear a striking similarity to the nihilist experimental "fictitious marriages" of the 1860s. This affinity was noted at the
time;[34] Tolstoy himself did not reject the comparison. His view of a
nonsexual union is synonymous with radical social reform only to the
extent that early, radical Christianity is understood as a reformative
antisocial movement.[35]

Tolstoy and Radical Chastity

Tolstoy's revulsion from sexuality and domesticity is often interpreted
psychologically as reflecting his ambivalence and free-floating hostility toward women. To the extent that Tolstoy viewed the sex problem
as existing in both genders and in relationships between the sexes,
his doctrine should be seen less as a masculine fear of feminine sexuality than as a sincere form of what may be called radical chastity. Those
with a postmodern feminist,[36] post-Freudian perspective may question
views that equate the expression of sexuality with positive self-asser-
tion and creativity. Similarly suspect would be views that consider any
denial of sexuality to be neurotic, repressive, or sublimative. Because
of the prevailing attitude hailing the sexually "liberated" woman, radical chastity has often been overlooked or dismissed as a feminist position; asceticism is castigated as Victorian prudishness or excessive
modesty, calculated to soothe patriarchal anxiety about feminine sexuality. Misogyny is popularly considered to have engendered the
madonna/whore dichotomy, a bifurcation that valorizes female reproductivity while rejecting female sexuality. Within feminism, there
have been those, such as Andrea Dworkin or Simone de Beauvoir, who
prefer the single state or who, as Dworkin does, reject sexual intercourse altogether, arguing that such relations consign women to the
role of sex objects. There has been no voice raised more loudly in
anger at such consignment than Tolstoy's: "The greatest sin is to regard
a woman as a sex object."[37] Yet while some critics have noted Tolstoy's

apparent affinity for radical feminism, few critics allow him the courtesy of believing that he achieved such company deliberately.

Modern feminist critics have suggested that there can be no liberation, sexual or otherwise, until the misogynist perception of women as sexual objects is vanquished; feminine sexuality will not achieve autonomy "while patriarchy still exists and conditions female sexuality."[38] As Susan Sontag commented on the sexual revolution: "Without a change in the very norms of sexuality, the liberation of women is a meaningless goal. Sex as such is not liberating for women" ("The Third World of Women," 188). In *The Kreutzer Sonata*, Pozdnyshev queries the very process of women's emancipation on this same basis:

> Well, and they liberate women, give her all sorts of rights equal to men, but continue to regard her as an instrument of enjoyment and . . . there she is, still the same humiliated and depraved slave, and the man still a depraved slave owner . . . [This] can only be changed by a change in men's outlook on women and women's way of regarding themselves. It will change only when woman regards virginity as the highest state.[39]

Radical chastity might thus be viewed as a feminist attempt to reclaim the body by refusing to be the body men want. Certainly, the rejection of childbearing (Beauvoir), or its diminution to a secondary role in a woman's life, has become an accepted element of women's process of self-fulfillment in the late twentieth century, and women who choose such a path are not usually accused of repressed sexuality. By contrast, a feminist position that champions a woman's capacity to mother and nurture is considered suspect.[40] The notion of radical chastity, finally, returns us to the myth of the Amazon that lies at the basis of early twentieth-century representations of the new, strong working woman. Tolstoy himself gave us such heroines in Varenka in *Anna Karenina* and in the unmarried working women of *Resurrection*.

Tolstoy's shift from a Victorian cultivation of domesticity to a radical Christian asceticism is not as cataclysmic as it may appear at first glance. A profound ambivalence underlies the closing scenes of *War and Peace,* rendering the characters almost grotesque in their process of dissolution from heroic figures of potential to everyday mundane folk concerned with dirty diapers rather than war. Similarly, *Anna Karenina* ends as a "cry of despair," with the foundations of marital and family relations eroded. Lyovin's conversion does not bring him into closer harmony with his family, but rather into a temporarily benign heterophony where each sings his or her own tune without harmony or unison. In the final scene with Kitty, an unbreachable distance gapes suddenly between the thoughts of husband and wife, as Lyovin contemplates the starry night, filled with ecstasy at his newfound faith but fearing to tell his thoughts to Kitty, who is preoccupied with worries about bed sheets and dirty laundry.

Tolstoy's ultimate rejection of the family ideal—of sexual, romantic love, and procreation as its rationale—accompanied his rejection of the novel (together with all bourgeois art); indeed, the two are connected since the Victorian realist novel notably romanticizes domestic life and ends so gratifyingly with wedding vows. In a letter to a young unmarried girl, Tolstoy counseled her to choose the single life and, in order to strengthen her resolve, to avoid those pleasures of society that encourage girls to desire marriage: music, balls, novels.[41] "Novels," he wrote, "end with the hero and heroine married. Instead, they should begin with the marriage and end with the couple liberating themselves from it" (Diary entry, 30 August 1894 [*PSS* 52:136]). Tolstoy's observation has been echoed by the twentieth-century feminist literary critic Nancy Miller, who observes that the plot of the traditional novel only allows two endings for the heroine: marriage or death. Tolstoy would have been in sympathy with her conclusion: "Because the novel . . . is forced . . . to negotiate with social realities in order to remain legible, its plots are overdetermined by the commonplaces of the culture. Until the culture invents new plots for women, we will continue to read the heroine's text. Or we could stop reading novels."[42] This extremist suggestion might well be received with as much resistance as met Tolstoy's prescription for chastity within marriage. Tolstoy's wedding of narrative to sexuality renders abstinence a radical claim for sexual and textual liberation.

In this chapter I began by considering the ways in which the image of an author is constructed and the degree to which ideology complicates critical assessment of an author's biography and works. In the following chapter I continue to explore the problems of ideological criticism, in particular the issues central to feminist literary criticism and theory. This examination necessitates changing critical lenses in order to read Tolstoy as an artist and aesthetician, as well as the literary figure we considered in this opening chapter. The problematic of misogyny will then be considered within the framework of the novel *Anna Karenina,* whose heroine has suffered the vicissitudes of criticisms under the sway of ideologies and gender biases. The opening moves of this chapter were frankly played out on the *passe-partout;* in what follows our gaze will have to move back and forth between the *passe-partout* and the canvas.

The Judgment of *Anna Karenina*: Feminist Criticism and the Image of the Heroine

> The critic also, in his own way, *kills the woman,*
> while killing, at the same time, the question of the
> text and the text as question.
> Shoshona Felman, "Women and Madness"

Problems in Ideological Criticism: Criticizing Tolstoy

"If I were to try to say in words everything that I intended to express in my novel [*Anna Karenina*], I would have to write the same novel I wrote from the beginning."[1] These much-quoted words of Tolstoy's elevate the abstruse discourse of verbal art above critical exegesis, as he intended, and challenge any attempt at thematic or moral criticism. The repressive effect this comment has had on critics of Tolstoy's novels is attested to by as valorous a critic as Lionel Trilling: "There are times when the literary critic can do nothing more than point, and *Anna Karenina* presents him with an occasion when his critical function is reduced to this primitive activity."[2] In the past, Tolstoy critics have seemed to founder on the sense that the great novels are "Life, not Art"[3] and the belief that Tolstoy is to be placed in a category apart from that of other novelists, who are perceived as conscious and conscientious craftsmen. The infrequency of critical appreciations of Tolstoy's formal artistry seems to result from a perpetuation of Philip Rahv's early characterization: "Tolstoy is the exact opposite of those writers, typical of the modern age, whose works are to be understood only in terms of their creative strategies and design . . . Tolstoy was the least self-conscious in his use of the literary medium. There are no plots in Tolstoy, but simply the unquestioned and unalterable processes of life itself."[4]

In part this view must be attributed to a Western critical bias that barbarizes Tolstoy and Dostoevsky as crude Russians (or "Rooshians" [Ezra Pound]), "natural" untutored talents, or "genius in the raw" (Virginia Woolf). Dostoevskian iconography typically depicts the frenetic writer and tortured epileptic gripped by poetic madness and racing to complete his manuscripts against the overhanging threat of publishing deadlines and gambling debts. As for Tolstoy, legend poses him barefoot and clad in a peasant shirt, excoriating the conventionality and preciosity of all works of art treasured by Western bourgeois society; a writer whose own works were cleaved from life with one mighty blow by the Creator. As Vladimir Nabokov mythologized Tolstoy:

> Yet there remains
> one thing we simply cannot reconstruct,
> no matter how we poke, armed with our notepads,
> just like reporters at a fire, around
> his soul. It's to a certain secret throbbing—
> the essence—that our access is denied.
> The mystery is almost superhuman!
> I mean the nights on which Tolstoy composed;
> I mean the miracle, the hurricane
> of images flying across the inky
> expanse of sky in that hour of creation,
> that hour of Incarnation. . . . For, the people
> born on those nights were real.[5]

"When you read Tolstoy," Isaac Babel wrote, "you feel that the world itself is writing, the world in all its variety." This mythic view of an Olympian Tolstoy, the conflation of Tolstoy and God, pictured by

Maxim Gorky as "two bears in a den," simultaneously inspires awe and arouses the resentment of many readers at a rhetorical power that entraps them in a moral textual universe demanding a virtuous as well as a virtuoso criticism.

Gary Saul Morson attributes the didactic force of Tolstoyan language to Tolstoy's exploitation of what Mikhail Bakhtin terms "absolute language."[6] "Have you noticed Tolstoy's language?" Anton Chekhov wrote. "Enormous periods, sentences piled on top of each other. Those periods create the impression of power!"[7] And, for most readers, the "great chords" described by E. M. Forster "begin to sound."[8] In addition to being overpowered by Tolstoy's diction, sociologically oriented Soviet critics have also found problematic his engagement with moral issues, especially questions of religious faith or religious thought. This has also proven discomfiting to Western critics. As Richard Gustafson comments, "Much of what is central to Tolstoy seems embarrassing to Western critics. Often it is passed over in silence."[9]

The very notion of practicing a moral or ethical criticism is daunting since it exposes the critic to the dangers of the politics of interpretation. The critic may be accused of a doctrinaire lack of originality; conversely, he or she may be charged with a relativistic subjectivism, defined by deconstruction as "the problem that develops when a consciousness gets involved in interpreting another consciousness, the basic pattern from which there can be no escape in the social sciences."[10] Or can there be, as J. Hillis Miller argues, a moment of pure ethical critical response? Is there "a necessary ethical moment in the act of reading as such, a moment neither cognitive, nor political, nor social, nor interpersonal, but properly and independently ethical"?[11] Wayne Booth has recently pleaded for ethical and ideological criticism that treats those aspects of narrative that matter most at the same time that he recognizes the beleaguered status of this type of criticism.[12] How is ideological criticism to escape the twin pitfalls of the doctrinaire rejection, even censorship, of any ideologically flawed work or its obverse: the critical blindness that results from our own unconscious affirmation of the ideology implicit in a text?

Equally as problematic for those critics who attempt to engage

Tolstoyan morality as a necessary part of Tolstoyan artistry is the fact that the type of critical procedure that extracts a message or moral from the text is exactly the opposite of what Tolstoy demanded from literary criticism. In his treatise *What Is Art?* Tolstoy stated quite explicitly that the moral, theme, and topic of a work of art do not determine its value, even from the moral point of view. Rather, it is the effect of the work, its infectious capacity to knit together an audience in Christian love, that elevates even the most primitive secular work above an overtly Christian piece of iconography. These ideas were nascent even at the time Tolstoy was writing *Anna Karenina* some twenty years earlier. In the letter to Nikolai Strakhov quoted above, Tolstoy finds fault with the sociocriticism, or political criticism, practiced in his time and, by extension, all ideological or moral criticism: "People are needed for the criticism of art who can show the pointlessness of looking for ideas in a work of art and can steadfastly guide readers through that endless labyrinth of connections *(labirint stseplenii)* which is the essence of art, and towards those laws that serve as the basis of these connections."[13] In this passage, as the Russian formalists were quick to observe, Tolstoy rejects a criticism that would consider its task to be the elucidation and evaluation of a work of art's thematic content or message; instead he essentially calls for the practice of close readings: explications in which the critic would investigate the semiotics of a work of art, its signifying elements and structures and the laws or principles by which they are selected and combined. Furthermore, Tolstoy's invitation or challenge to a close reading is not meant to result either in a new or definitive interpretation or in the retrieval of authorial intention, but rather it is intended to reveal the "essence of art" and its "laws"; that is, he calls for an aesthetic, not an evaluative, telos for literary criticism.

Yet, particularly in the case of the novel, ethical criticism is not fully responsible for ideologizing or politicizing—affirmatively or subversively—an essentially neutral artwork. The novel itself, especially the novel of adultery, is already ideological. The goal in practicing an ethical criticism might therefore be to recognize that the ideological aspect of the work is necessarily part of its overall artistic design.[14]

Criticizing *Anna Karenina*

Feminist ideological criticism, therefore, seems a particularly appropriate tool for critiquing *Anna Karenina,* a novel that strenuously interrogates the gender implications of marital relations and romantic love. Because of the ambiguous characterizations of most nineteenth-century heroines, feminist criticism has undergone a paradigm shift in the last two decades. Feminist revisions of the canon and rereadings of major works about women resulted in a dead end rejecting all male characterizations of women as fundamentally ambivalent and hence misogynist. More recent feminist criticism poses the problem in a more sophisticated fashion as an issue in intentionality. If an author condemns his transgressing heroine to death, does this imply approbation of social conventions and mores, or does the author intend to provoke a sense of outrage and compassion for the victims of barbarous moral and social conventions?[15] As summarized by Higonnet: "Since certain values can be expressed only through their displacement and ultimate sacrifice in the figure of a tragic heroine, the novelist's critique of society may actually turn into a tacit confirmation of the existing order."[16]

Some recent feminist critics demand of novelistic heroines that they represent an unambiguous feminist ideal, even if it is only partially realized. Otherwise, according to their view, novelistic heroines remain the creations of a patriarchally structured desire, ambivalence, and anxiety. Twentieth-century readings of *Anna Karenina* follow this attitudinal shift and thus constitute a chronologically staged series of ideologically determined or culturally bound readings, ranging from Anna as victim to Anna as master of her own fate.

Since the novel's publication, Anna's transgression has been alternately universalized as "every man's tragedy" or trivialized as a Bovarian banality by a masculinist critical reading. When Anna's fall is read as universal, its specificity to the problems of gender is usually denied according to the perception that women's problems alone are insufficient to warrant the tragic mode unless they can be expanded to refer to both genders. Therefore, the specific problem of confinement within marriage must be de-gendered and read as the universal state of entrapment. By contrast, "men's problems," such as war or statesmanship, do not need to be rewritten in universal terms to include women's concerns; they are allowed to stand as fully significant in their own right. Iurii Lotman, for example, expresses this view: "The plot of *Anna Karenina* reflects, on the one hand, a certain narrow object—the life of the heroine. . . . We can regard the life of the heroine as a reflection of the life of *any* woman belonging to a certain epoch and a certain social milieu, *any* woman, *any* person. Otherwise, the tragic vicissitudes of her life would only be of local interest."[17]

Conversely, antifeminist readings assume that Anna's problems are too trivial for us to take her seriously. The power of Anna's rebellion is diminished even by feminist critics such as Mary Evans, who dismiss her as an inadequate role model for the task of women's liberation. Thus, in Evans's view, reading Anna as a victim of the patriarchy and bourgeois institutions only excuses her from being morally responsible. Evans accuses Anna of failing to act to subvert or resist the patriarchy: "Far from resisting conventions, Anna internalizes their constraints. Anna is a poor friend to other women, and she is left in no position to challenge others' judgements of herself as a fallen woman."[18] The fact that other women in the novel survive under patriarchal oppression, Evans argues, fulfills the reader's need for a viable alternative to Anna's ineffectual and self-destructive resistance. Evans concludes: "If there is a message in *Anna Karenina,* it is perhaps that domestic life and maternity save women from Anna's hideous fate of morbid jealousy and destructive introspection."[19]

Both masculinist and feminist readings, opposed as they are ideologically, impoverish the potential heroism of Anna's transgression and mute the mythological tones of her quest and fall. Judith Armstrong's recent feminist rereading of the novel relegates the mythos of Anna's fall to the unconscious, "unsaid" part of Tolstoy's novel. Armstrong's psychoanalytic reading suggests that it is Tolstoy's *unconscious* love for Anna and his repressed maternal attachment that invest his heroine with the power and meaning of a mythological hero, but this occurs only in the "unsaid" layers of the text: "The sub-

terranean forces at work in Tolstoy's novel affect every level of its
operation, subverting the norms of rhetoric and discourse as well as
those of morality, sexuality, and identity."[20] Thus, Armstrong concludes: "The hierarchy appears to win only if we read Anna's story
as one of retribution against an isolated individual who tried to pit
herself against the system; but in reality the triumph of the 'fallen
woman' is proclaimed in the power she exerts over author, reader,
and text."[21]

Both feminist and masculinist readings concur in finding Anna
guilty and in labeling her a bad, even an evil woman. Her failure
according to these interpretations is both proximate and ultimate
since she transgresses against the values of a patriarchal society, yet
fails to liberate herself and thus remains a compliant prisoner of the
patriarchy. In both views, Anna is an evil woman, and the compelling
and attractive features of her characterization are accounted for either by assuming that Tolstoy resists any shallow, two-dimensional
characterization or that he has failed to master his own psychosexual
drives and uncontrolled repressions. In the latter case, we are treated
to a Russian reprise of the Flaubertian *"Mme. Bovary c'est moi"*[22]
or to the type of Freudian psychoanalysis undertaken by Armstrong
to explain how Tolstoy's early traumatic loss of his mother resulted
in the compulsive projection of sexual anima onto a desired female
object whose resulting attractiveness and potential for cathexis is so
profoundly threatening that even her representation on paper must
be destroyed.[23]

Historically, the criticism has characterized *Anna Karenina* as a
conte moral or novelistic sermon using as a text the novel's epigraph,
"Vengeance is mine, I will repay." Despite recognition of the novel's
complexity and the ambivalence of Anna's characterization, the critical
consensus is that the novel condemns Anna with heavy-handed didac-
ticism. As Nekrasov observed, "Tolstoy, you've proved with patience
and with talent, / That a woman should not gallivant / With aide-de-
camp or adjutant / When she's a wife and mother."[24]

According to the usual reading of *Anna Karenina,* the novel reflects Tolstoy's conservative attitude toward the woman question.[25]
In commenting on Tolstoy's extraliterary discussions of sexual moral-

ity, marriage, and adultery, both feminists and nonfeminists automatically place Tolstoy among the archconservatives in the public debate on the woman question, despite the radical feminist implications of his postconversion writings on this subject (see chapter 1). If his postconversion views are discussed, they are only used to turn Tolstoy into the ridiculous, grotesque spectacle of a hypocrite preaching chastity within marriage while continuing to father children with his wife.[26]

Basing their conclusions on a cursory survey of Tolstoy's published views on the woman question and the unquestioningly damning evidence of his diaries and married life, critics usually assume that *Anna Karenina* supports traditional values and social roles based on gender stereotypes, even when they recognize that Tolstoy's aim is to expose the problematic nature of the institutions of marriage and family life. Even the most recent feminist rereadings of the novel follow this interpretation and thus perpetuate certain prefeminist attitudes.

For example, in some earlier critical accounts, the novel's heroines are denied consciousness of their own problematic status, and their desire for liberation is discounted as a psychological motivation. "The problem of family happiness and the meaning of life and death," writes a leading Tolstoy scholar in the 1960s, "is a man's subject. The Kittys, Annas and Natashas are not troubled by it."[27] What, then, is troubling Anna Karenina? According to René Wellek, she has "no interests" (as if *broderie anglaise* or visits to invalids would suffice!); she suffers from "boredom with her joint-cracking bureaucrat."[28] Even if the profundity of Anna's conflict is recognized, her emotional reaction is condemned: "A whole society, perhaps the species itself, is at stake, and here a wretched woman temporizes about it, numbs herself with opium, whimpers over her own precious individuality, and finally jeopardizes everything by suicide."[29] Alternately, Anna is castigated because she fails to assume responsibility for healing her own psychic conflicts and repressions:

> Anna's story is not a tale of social oppression or a drama of failed liberation. Tolstoy, it should be recalled, insisted that people have no rights, only responsibilities. . . . Anna abandons her flawed human

relatedness to which she is responsible. . . . But Anna is not destroyed
by others, and self-indulgence is not her fundamental flaw. Anna is
not punished by Tolstoy for her sexual fulfillment. In a fuller sense,
Anna's story is a moral tragedy of self-enclosure.[30]

Evans offers a related, if oversimplified, criticism: "[Anna] emerges
as guilty in the wider sense of a person who was unable to control and
discipline her passions and her inclinations."[31]

Anna's perceived inadequacy to the task of self-development and
social reform may be read in a different, less psychological way as
continuing the Russian literary tradition of the "superfluous man."
This literary figure, or type, represented by such characters as Eugene Onegin, Pechorin, and the Underground Man, finds his impulse
to social rebellion diluted by impotence and the special kind of Russian inertia that has come to be called Oblomovitis. When this problematic profile is embodied in Russian literature in the type of the
superfluous *man*, he earns our censorious sympathy and pitying contempt, but he is rarely labeled evil, even when he murders his best
friend or commits rape and other crimes. Rather, he is let off the
hook: "By implication, [the superfluous man] points to the inadequacy of a society incapable of assimilating such exceptional types."[32]
Tolstoy's maneuver of replacing the superfluous man with a superfluous woman whose incapacity is as much a result of her gender as is
her vital passion provokes a hostile, judgmental, response from both
feminist and nonfeminist critics of the novel. Is this response what
Tolstoy intended? Or is it a result of the inner workings of the novel to
condemn Anna? Or does the superfluous man draw less fire because
his Byronic lassitude, his cavalier destructiveness, and his refusal to
commit himself to human relations are implicitly approved of by a society with a masculinist code that considers these attributes the natural expression of male individualism? By contrast, a feminist critic
might argue, female rebellion involves disengaging from what are perceived to be a woman's natural occupations of housekeeping and
motherhood; therefore, she is considered to be monstrous and perverse in deviating from the natural parameters of her femininity. This

sexual stereotyping is common to both traditionalist male-dominated criticism and to the more recent feminist criticism. The following views expressed by nineteenth-century readers of the novel still seem to underlie contemporary judgments:

> [Anna]—*because she is frivolous and endowed with a superficial culture*—is bound to live the life of the emotions and to seek the joys of the heart which she cannot find in living with the man she married.[33]

Or:

> All the meaning of the family, all its potential and all its morality depend, do they not, on the wife and mother, and if she destroys the family will not the woman perish *along with the purpose of her life and any meaning she might have as a person?* . . . If only [women] could understand that in the self-denial and self-sacrifice of a wife and mother there is more value and more moral satisfaction than in the pursuit of their own appetites and fantasies![34]

The identical ideology may be found in twentieth-century criticism:

> A woman is the traditional repository of cultural values which she must convey to the young. Anna forfeits her responsibility to her own son and then, in hideous irony, presumes to write edifying books for children. I suggest that . . . when woman loses her proper role as culture-bearer, her society is dead.[35]

Even Evans, in her recent avowedly feminist reading of *Anna Karenina,* relies on the perpetuation of these attitudes in contemporary society when she subscribes to the notion that mothering is natural while fathering must be learned:[36]

> After all, the mother, a married woman, who deliberately chooses an adulterous relationship rather than her maternal responsibilities, would still today be labelled as a deviant and "unnatural" woman.[37]

Anna Karenina against Anna Karenina

The case against Anna, the "strategy of the novel" that "is directed against [her]" so that "Anna must be destroyed,"[38] is based on readers' perceptions of the inevitability of her suicide, which is construed as a death sentence, a form of divine or social retribution, prefigured in the novel's epigraph, "Vengeance is mine, I will repay." So common is the death of the transgressing heroine in nineteenth-century fiction that it has come to be seen as an obligatory sop thrown to conventional morality that gives the author the latitude to portray his or her heroine sympathetically or, alternately, reveals the author's discomfort in affirming deviance.[39] According to one feminist critic: "Anna, many feminists would remark, ends the novel dead: the inequalities between women and men that constitute a major feature of Western society are vividly portrayed in the novel—bourgeois heterosexuality kills women and ruins men."[40] Another feminist critic draws the same conclusion: "The overall message is to all intents unequivocal; in *Anna Karenina* Levin makes the right choices and so lives and flourishes beyond the back cover of the book; Anna chooses wrongly, and therefore must die even before the last chapter. Nothing could be clearer."[41]

However, most critics have found this aspect of the novel extremely problematic and far from clear. To begin with, Tolstoy's use of the biblical epigraph, especially in its incomplete form (omitting "saith the Lord"), creates a disconcerting uncertainty in the reader as to who is speaking: does Tolstoy quote God or speak for God or as his surrogate, or is Tolstoy God? Is authority equivalent or superior to divine nemesis? As Boris Eikhenbaum complains: "The point is not, of course, that Tolstoy makes the solution of guilt and criminality subject to the will of God, but that this God [is] now undoubtedly subject to the will of Tolstoy as the author of the novel."[42] According to an alternate critical tradition, Anna's death is not the result of God's vengeance on her, but is instead the culmination of the cruel and unforgiving treatment she received at the hands of her fellow man; "Society is the villain of the piece"[43] or, as Viktor Shklovsky proclaimed, "Genuine human morality contradicts the Biblical quotation, and it is not God, but people . . . who pushed Anna under the wheels of the train."[44]

These two readings reflect the distinction that needs to be made between the Old and New Testament judgments on sexual transgression and punishment. In Deut. 32:35, God reserves vengeance to himself and promises that punishment shall ensue without mercy whereas in Rom. 12:19–21, Paul exhorts his listeners to leave vengeance and punishment to God: "My dear friends, do not seek revenge, but leave a place for divine retribution." Since Tolstoy does not cite chapter and verse for his epigraph, it remains unclear whether he was referring to the Old or New Testament version of the edict or whether he intended to set up a tension between the two. Interpretations of the epigraph, therefore, have tended either to assume that it reflects an Old Testament morality and the punitive action of a wrathful God through worldly events or to follow the Christian precept that it is not for humanity to judge, but for God; and not on earth, but in heaven.[45] The latter is the view expressed by Dostoevsky: "There are not, and cannot be any healers or *final* judges of human problems other than He who says, 'Vengeance is mine; I will repay.' He alone knows the *whole* enigma of the world and the final destiny of man."[46] What we know about the origination of the epigraph in Tolstoy's novel argues for this latter interpretation. Eikhenbaum demonstrates that Tolstoy originally borrowed the biblical quotation from a passage in Artur Schopenhauer (*The World as Will*, Book 4, chapter 62) in which the philosopher demands the suspension of human judgment: "No person has the authority to set himself up as a moral judge and avenger, to punish the misdeeds of another with pain which he inflicts on him. . . . This would be, rather, presumption of the highest degree; hence the Biblical 'Vengeance is mine; I will repay.'"[47]

The biblical quotation may also be found in other novels of the period dealing with adultery, specifically in two works Tolstoy was known to have read and admired: Trollope's *Phineas Redux* (1876) and Mrs. Henry Wood's *East Lynne* (1861).[48] In *Phineas Redux* the eponymous hero attempts to soften the wrath of the abandoned husband by quoting this passage from Scripture. Similarly, in *East Lynne* the abandoned husband restrains himself from acting against his rival by quoting the same biblical passage. Within this literary tradition of adulterers and adulteresses spared punishment by the avenging husband, the scriptural passage becomes even more clearly associated with the other biblical text that is frequently repeated throughout *Anna Karenina*: "Let he who is without sin cast the first stone."[49] Tony Tanner suggests that the tension between Old and New Testament rulings on adultery constitutes the driving force of the novel of adultery:

> In the bourgeois novel we can find a strictness that works to maintain the law, and a sympathy and understanding with the adulteress violator that works to undermine it. . . . [T]he Old Testament and New Testament methods of confronting adultery may both be found operating within the same book. . . . Indeed, it is arguable that it is just such a tension between law and sympathy that holds the great bourgeois novel together.[50]

Other critics find the notion that Anna's suicide is a moral judgment to be "quite barbaric, a sort of divine judgement such as an author in the Middle Ages might have imagined,"[51] or a failure in artistic design, as in the case of D. H. Lawrence: "Imagine any great artist making the vulgar social condemnation of Anna and Vronsky figure as divine punishment!"[52] Or Anna's suicide is construed as a reprieve, her death "is meant . . . to be Anna's deliverance; it is out of pity for her that [Tolstoy] has granted her the favor of death."[53] Or it is out of pity for himself, as Harold Bloom suggests: "Tolstoy could not sustain the suffering it would have cost him to imagine a life [Anna] could have borne to go on living."[54]

Rarely, critics like Robert L. Jackson[55] have noticed the coloration of fatality in the details that overdetermine Anna's suicide and, like Martin Price, they regard Anna as a tragic heroine, "because for reasons that are admirable [she] cannot live [a] divided life or survive through repression."[56] "The tragic situation is a situation from which there is no escape," observes E. B. Greenwood. "[Anna's] fate has a contingency and yet a pattern that bears the marks, not of the author's vindictiveness, but of the poetic inevitability we associate with tragedy."[57] Other critics, perhaps following D. H. Lawrence's example, question whether there is the possibility for tragedy in over-stepping what Lawrence called the "smaller system of morality":

> Anna, Eustacia [Vye], Tess [Durbeyfield] or Sue [Bridehead]—what was there in their position that was necessarily tragic? Necessarily painful it was, but they were not at war with God, only with Society. Yet they were all cowed by the mere judgement of man upon them, and all the while by their own souls they were right. And the judgement of men killed them, not the judgement of their own souls or the judgement of Eternal God.[58]

If the novel has the tenor of tragic form, such that "destiny is the plot"[59] and "character is revealed as a determined shape, as an embodiment of an already existing fate,"[60] it is curious that most critics nonetheless deny Anna the status of a tragic heroine. Is this because they are reluctant to read an apparently ultrarealist novel as a tragedy or because there is something problematic in Anna's characterization that causes them to resist designating her fall as tragic? Or is it because the Tolstoyan *passe-partout* has blocked their critical judgment?

The issue of tragic form and the novel is discussed at greater length in chapters 3 and 7 of this study, where I explore the ways in which a realist text's celebration of the random and the prosaic may be subverted and sublated by its overarching poetic design. The more immediate questions that confront our attempt to evaluate feminist criticism of *Anna Karenina* make it necessary to defer these concerns in favor of formulating other theories of narrative, those having to do with feminist criticism and the concepts of heroism and heroinism.

Who Is a Heroine?

The notion of heroinism[61] is itself made problematic by gender, to the extent that one feminist critic feels it necessary to elevate Anna to the level of "hero, while leaving it to Kitty, Masha and Natasha to remain mere heroines. In other words, Anna transcends the constraints of her gender."[62] Although this statement is meant "to mount a feminist defense" of the novel, it is itself antifeminist. Anna must cross over gen-

der boundaries and cross-dress as a masculine hero since Armstrong
denies the heroic quality of the kinds of deeds that a heroine may be
called upon to undertake. Armstrong's statement implies that masculine heroism is superior to feminine heroinism and denies us a female
model for heroinic activity that we would recognize as morally and
spiritually equivalent to masculine heroism. Her claims for Anna's
heroism involve her "masculinization," for she notes that Anna, as a
writer, wields the pen, notorious emblem of the male member, and engages in the study of architecture, economics, and physics, traditionally male areas of knowledge. Armstrong further argues that Anna acts
like a male hero in the sense developed by Vladimir Propp and defined
by Lotman as the transgressor of boundaries. Thus, Armstrong overlooks the path taken by many feminist critics of searching for female-
based alternatives to male-defined patterns and paradigms; for example, maternal versus paternal models of "anxieties of influence" or, in
this case, a narrative model for female heroinism.

In considering the ways in which a paradigm of heroinism has
emerged in modern literature in tandem with heroism, Rachel
Brownstein comments: "The paradigmatic hero is an overreacher; the
heroine of the domestic novel . . . is overdetermined. The hero moves
toward a goal; the heroine tries to be it."[63] The hero ascends the
throne; the heroine marries another's destiny. The static and passive
role of the heroine in a hero-centered text was described in Lotman's
plot typology and was subsequently criticized for being phallogocentric by Teresa de Lauretis.[64] The Soviet semiotician Olga Freidenberg
has suggested that the basic mythological motif of heroic descent and
ascent is often overtly constituted in literary works as a figure of cop-
ulation and reproduction.[65] In all of the above typologies, the feminine principle constitutes the inert, spatial ground for the masculine
heroic action.

However, there are heroine-centered models of narrative that are
equally antique, classical, and mythological, as for example the myths
of Psyche or Persephone, whose activity, transgressions, and fulfillment of heroic deeds resemble those of classical heroes, yet who must
be interpreted differently because of their sex.[66] In her chapter,
"Women Heroes and Patriarchal Culture," Lee Edwards argues that

"the woman hero is an image of antithesis. Different from the male—her sex her sign—she threatens his authority and that of the system he sustains. . . . The woman hero uncovers fractures in the surface of reality, contradictions in its structure, gaps in its social ideology."[67]

Since the return of the hero signals the restoration of social order and balance, the hero must function as an emblem of authority and must combat his rebellious and subversive selves in the form of his shadow or demonic alter ego. A hero cannot represent the most menacing threat to patriarchal authority since, taken as an amalgam with his shadow, he (hero and shadow) already constitutes a figure of equilibrium. The heroine, however, is already constituted as "other" and thus represents the anarchic forces that threaten to undo order. This makes the heroinic acquisition of a shadowed "other" extremely problematic, as we shall see in chapter 7. Therefore, subversion is "a job for the woman hero, for in patriarchy, femaleness is the ultimate and ineradicable sign of marginality."[68]

What kinds of heroinic behavior can be fulfilled by a novelistic heroine? Evans argues that Anna cannot be elevated to the status of a heroine "since we might expect at best some evidence that a heroine attempts to rise above her fate," and Anna "offers no model of how women might resist the strictures of conventional patriarchal authority."[69] It is difficult not to feel that the kinds of feminist criticism that require that a heroine be a satisfactory role model have not evolved much beyond the views of Samuel Richardson, who in his 1759 preface to *Clarissa* demands that a heroine be an "exemplar to her sex." This prerequisite leaves it up to the critics' own moral code to define the exemplary: virtuous and compliant subjection to the patriarchy or militant and potent rebellion. Arguing against a similar judgment brought on Nora in Ibsen's *A Doll House,* Joan Templeton comments:

> Nora falls short according to unnamed, "self-evident" criteria for a feminist heroine, among which would seem to be one, some, or all of the following: an ever-present serious-mindedness; a calm, unexcitable temperament; . . . perfect sincerity and honesty; and a thoroughgoing selflessness. For *A Doll House* to be feminist, it would, apparently, have to be a kind of fourth-wall morality play with a

saintly Everyfeminist as heroine, not this . . . excitable, confused, and desperate—in short, human—Nora.[70]

The type of argumentation one would have to pursue to debate this issue further would curiously resemble discussions of Socialist Realist art, whose proponents demanded that perfectivized men and women of the future be depicted if there were no ideal role models to be found among the men and women of contemporary society.

Were there no candidates worthy to be represented as the heroine of a novel in Russian society of the 1870s? Is there no heroine therefore in *Anna Karenina*?

It may be argued that Anna's claim to heroism is denied because of her gender and the nature of the escape open to her in her attempt to "rise above her condition." Even if she is forgiven her sexual transgression, she is never excused for abandoning her son and ignoring her daughter. But is she judged by the same criteria as a hero who might act similarly? A hero who abandons his impoverished family in Ireland to pursue his muse in Europe (Stephen Dedalus), or who leaves his wife and children to seek higher education (Jude the Obscure), or who even sells his wife and child into bondage with no higher goal in mind (the Mayor of Casterbridge) will be read as having heroically shaken free of the mundane and will not be criticized as severely as a heroine who acts in the same way. Consider Irving Howe's (by now infamous) commentary on the opening of *The Mayor of Casterbridge*:

> To shake loose from one's wife; to discard that drooping rag of a woman, with her mute complaints and maddening passivity; to escape not by slinking abandonment but through the public sale of her body to a stranger, as horses are sold at a fair; and thus to wrest, through sheer amoral wilfulness, a second chance out of life—it is with this stroke, so insidiously attractive to male fantasy, that *The Mayor of Casterbridge* begins.[71]

Not only does Howe rank the criminal sale into slavery above the more common action of abandonment (which would at least have left the woman free, eventually even to remarry), but he does not even acknowledge the existence of the daughter, whose body is also sold. This oversight suggests the common prejudice that the power of the paternal instinct, if it exists at all, in no way resembles that of the maternal instinct. In the stereotyped view of parental roles, paternity is primarily seen as a condition of often oppressive responsibility that deprives the male of the freedom to pursue his true path in life, while maternity is considered to be the only fulfilling path in life for a woman, in whom maternal instinct presumably induces a state of selflessness and willing sacrifice.

In the continental tradition of the novel of adultery, motherhood is rarely a significant event in the heroine's life. Recall Mme. Bovary's indifference to her children once she realizes she cannot afford the pleasure of purchasing a lavish layette. Most continental novels separate the passion of the adulterous woman from the passion of the mother, and perhaps this represents a fissure in social perceptions of women's potential to fulfill multiple roles. As Tanner comments: "The wife and mother in one set of social circumstances should not, and cannot be, the mistress and lover in another. It is well known how bourgeois society tends to enforce unitary roles on its members. . . . From the point of view of that society, adultery introduces a bad multiplicity within the requisite unities of social roles."[72] Tolstoy's depiction of an adulterous heroine who is both passionately maternal (at least in the first half of the novel[73]) and sexual thus represents that threatening combination of maternity and sexuality that the Western Judeo-Christian ethic has sought to fragment. Within this ideology, a good woman is a good mother—that is, endowed with a proper maternal instinct that supersedes and eclipses all other drives. Evans poses the argument, in keeping with recent feminist theory,[74] that the experience of maternity automatically generates higher moral values, a "woman's way of knowing" and a "different voice of a caring morality."[75] This theorizing runs the risk of essentializing and biologizing the experience of maternity to a degree that many critics have seen as being virtually protofascistic. According to this view, taken to its extreme, it is not that a good woman is a mother, but rather that a mother is necessarily a good woman, one who, by mothering, automatically creates a higher moral sphere for her children without sub-

verting or threatening the patriarchal system within which she un-
avoidably exists.[76]

According to these criteria, Evans elects Dolly the true heroine
of *Anna Karenina,* because she endures her oppression in the patriarchy, because she is maternal to the exclusion of her own interests
and needs, and because she holds to a morality that is unconstrained
by social mores; for example, she visits Anna in spite of the social
stigma attached to such an act. In fact, the reader ought not to place
too much emphasis on this visit, since the familial relationship between the two women is sufficient to lift the social taboo against private visits between households. Ultimately, when Anna most needs
her, Dolly lets her down; she feels it more important to counsel Kitty
about breast-feeding than to respond to Anna's obvious distress.

For different reasons, Morson suggests that "Dolly Oblonskaya is
Tolstoy's moral compass"[77] and appoints her the "hero" of *Anna
Karenina,* "if by the hero of a book, we mean the character who best
exemplifies its governing values."[78] For Morson, however, the texture
and warp of Dolly's life is as significant as her social and moral status
as the embodiment of the Victorian ideal of the Angel in the House.
Morson reads *Anna Karenina* as a novel that exalts and exemplifies
the prosaic and "prosaics,"[79] and he finds Dolly's eventless, plotless,
and *"excessivement terre-à-terre"* existence to be the most prosaically
effaced testament to the quotidian and minute processes of life celebrated by the novel. In this sense, Morson seems to imply that Dolly
shares the features of the saintly Praskovia Mikhailovna of *Father
Sergius.*

While Dolly is unquestionably one of the positive characters of
the novel, one could certainly argue against Evans that she does not
succeed in creating a desirable moral atmosphere for her children.
They will grow up in a home that is based on a hypocritical, fictitious
marriage, and as they mature, they will increasingly recognize that
their mother is passively enslaved to a patriarchal society and an abusive husband. In fact, it is very difficult to read Dolly as a sister of the
exalted Angels in the House of Victorian fiction. Compared to those
warm, rotund, matronly queens, surrounded by a bevy of adoring
children who lovingly clasp their mother's neck and thick curls with

chubby fingers, Dolly is strikingly emaciated and worn, a hack dray horse among sleek thoroughbreds; she is surrounded not by plump cherubs, but by dirty, misbehaving urchins. The neat, tidy, and cozy domestic arrangements of the Dickensian or Trollopian matron—the bubbling teapot, lovingly netted slippers warming before a crackling fire, hearty but simple meals of clotted cream and home-baked scones—are reflected ironically in Dolly's desperate attempts to feed and clothe her children, in their reckless play with milk and jam, and in her moment of humiliation, when her patched bed jacket "of which she had been so proud at home" puts her to shame in front of the servants at Vronsky's estate.

Tolstoy's description of Dolly anticipates his subsequent journalistic accounts of the burdens of pregnancy, childbirth, and child rearing. Although he does homage to the indomitable spirit of woman, Tolstoy does not idealize or romanticize. He exposes the cult of domesticity for what it often becomes in a bad marriage: an oppression of woman and a denial of her selfhood perpetuated by the myth of the glories of maternity and housekeeping. In this sense, Morson's characterization of Dolly as the embodiment of the prosaic is closer to the truth. But does she represent the values that the novel espouses? If we assume, as Morson does, that the novel attacks the notion of romantic passion, a close examination of Dolly's own views on love and marriage, the same views that sustain her, makes this assertion problematic.

The positive perception of domestic life in the novel is presented by Lyovin, just as Dolly's idealization is achieved through Lyovin's eyes, for whom she represents "that picture of family life his imagination had painted"(282), an ideal of domesticity in which Lyovin is destined to be disillusioned. Fantasizing about his future family life, a vision clearly derived from Victorian literary models,[80] Lyovin "actually pictured to himself first the family, and only secondarily the woman who would give him a family"(101). The woman herself and the notion of an intimate relationship are irrelevant, so that any of the three Shcherbatsky sisters would have done for his wife. Thus, Lyovin's dreams are based not on notions of romantic love but on ideals of domestic life. And since Lyovin is disillusioned in his experience of family happiness, we might expect even greater disillusionment on

Dolly's part. Yet, humiliated and impoverished by Stiva's affairs, she still allows herself to be deluded as to the true nature of their marriage and thus colludes in the bourgeois myth of marriage, as it is recounted by Anna:

> "Such men are unfaithful, but their own home and wife are sacred to them. Somehow or other these women are still looked on with contempt by them, and do not touch on their feeling for their family. They draw a sort of line that can't be crossed between them and their families. . . .
> "I saw Stiva when he was in love with you. I remember the time when he came to me and cried, talking of you, and all the poetry and loftiness of his feeling for you, and I know that the longer he has lived with you, the loftier you have been in his eyes. . . . You have always been a divinity for him, and you are that still, and this has not been an infidelity of the heart . . ."(76)

That Dolly still believes in the bourgeois myth of romantic love and marriage, despite her awareness of its failures, is evidenced in her reactions to Kitty's wedding:

> [Dolly] was deeply moved. The tears stood in her eyes, and she could not have spoken without crying. She was . . . going back in thought to her own wedding . . . she glanced at the radiant figure of Stepan Arkadevich, forgot the present, and remembered only her own innocent love. She recalled not only herself, but all the women she was intimate with or with whom she was acquainted. She thought of them on the day of their triumph, when they had stood like Kitty under the wedding crown, with love and hope and dread in their hearts, renouncing the past and stepping forward into the mysterious future. Among the brides that came back to her memory, she thought too of her darling Anna, of whose proposed divorce she had just been hearing. And she had stood just as innocent in orange flowers and bridal veil. And now? "It's terribly strange," she thought. (479)

Dolly's description of the transition from maidenhood to married estate curiously echoes the romanticized narrative—complete with reference to the most romantic of *topoi*, the Alps—that Anna had spun to Kitty's wonder earlier in the novel: "'Oh! How good it is to be your age!' pursued Anna. 'I remember, and I know that blue haze like the mist on the mountains in Switzerland. That mist which covers everything in that blissful time when childhood is just ending, and out of that vast circle, happy and gay, there is a path growing narrower and narrower. . . . Who has not been through it?'"(79). Tolstoy contrasts Dolly's romantic, if disturbed, reverie at the wedding to the conversation of the peasant women who observe the ceremony from the doorway. Speaking as a united community of women, they speculate as to whether the bride is being married against her will or for money, and they flinch at "how the deacon rumbles, 'Fear your husband.'" No one asserts that the marriage is for love (perhaps an unconvincing notion). And the concluding comment, "'What a pretty dear the bride is—like a lamb all decked out [for the slaughter]! Well, say what you will, we women feel sorry for our sister,'"[81] expresses a folkloric wisdom in regard to the realities of married life that is starkly different from Dolly's sentimentalizing.

Dolly's seemingly heroic endurance is thus exposed as being sustained by the same dangerous bourgeois delusions of romantic love that drive Anna Karenina's passion. In fact, Dolly represents the "inauthenticity of maternal thinking" of which Evans, quoting Ruddick, accuses Anna. Maternal thinking is "a willingness to remain blind. . . . Maternal thought embodies inauthenticity by taking on the values of the dominant culture. . . . The strain of colluding in one's own powerlessness, coupled with the frequent and much greater strain of betraying the children one has tended [by raising them to perpetuate the patriarchy] would be insupportable if conscious."[82]

In depicting Dolly, Tolstoy drew yet one more portrait of the victimization of woman: in this case a spiritual rather than a physical death, a life based on lies, self-deception, dissimulation, and, ultimately, on cowardice.

In a novel whose author unceasingly worries the institutions of marriage and romance, the only genuine feminist heroine might be a woman who rejects the two familiar, fatal choices of marriage or passion to pursue her own autonomous path, who refuses to be the submissive partner in the patriarchal institution of marriage and similarly

resists being construed as the object of male desire. Only one character in the novel meets these criteria, and not only is her choice hard
and uncomfortable but she is too minor a character to be the heroine
of the novel. Nonetheless, Varenka's choice not to enter into marriage
with Koznyshev (discussed in chapter 8) and her constant occupation
with social service offer a glimpse of an alternate path for a heroine,
one that Tolstoy would increasingly valorize in the coming years.
Varenka is a heroine of the Florence Nightingale type, the Lady with
the Lamp rather than the Angel in the House or the fallen woman out
of the house.[83]

Does viewing Varenka as a heroine imply that genuine feminist
heroines must resist marriage? Or genuine Tolstoyan heroines? Are
there no happy families in *Anna Karenina*? Although Lyovin and Kitty's
marriage is usually seen as successful, some critics suggest that theirs
is a relationship of increasing estrangement, that by the end of the
novel "lack of communication has become a way of life for Kitty and
her husband."[84] The only unadulteratedly happy family in the novel
appears to be that of the Sviazhskiis, who are childless. It might be
suggested that their childless state implies the kind of Christian, fictitious marriage—an unconsummated connubial relationship like that
of brother and sister—that Tolstoy would later advocate.

Ultimately, recent feminist readings of *Anna Karenina* continue to
deny Anna's status as a unique woman: in one case because Anna does
not perform as the kind of maternal, sisterly woman the critic's ethical
code of feminism demands, she is supplanted by Dolly as the heroine
of the novel. In the case of Armstrong's reading, Anna is denied any
arena for heroinic action because she conceptualizes women's actions
as being potent only when they masquerade as men's. Since the critical view that Tolstoy is a misogynist is still well entrenched, a feminist
reading of the novel with that perspective must either develop a strategy for reconsidering the traditional values of domesticity within
feminist terms (the approach taken by Evans) or it must argue that
Tolstoy's unconscious desires granted Anna a force and vitality that
survive her textual extinction (the thesis submitted by Armstrong).

Perhaps we need a feminist reading of Anna that will liberate her from the sex-based roles and stereotypes that generate certain evaluative responses in both feminist and nonfeminist critics, without overlooking the specific differences in her experiences that her gender entails. Feminist criticism of Anna is needed that neither sutures femininity to maternity nor masculinizes it.

Among the first words we hear Anna speak in the novel are that she takes "not the Petersburg view, but a woman's view." We might realize that she means not just "women's views" but "*a* woman's view," a woman who follows her own, proximate, and imperiled experience of motherhood, marriage, passion, and death. Even though her trajectory through the novel is highly plotted according to the narratives of romance and ruin, her failures and her sufferings are unique.

If ideological criticism of this novel has foundered on any one problem, it is on the need to take Anna on her own terms, of which her gender is an essential element but an element that should not be allowed to essentialize her or the meaning of her narrative.

By shaking Anna Karenina loose from the standard critical frame that views the novel as a misogynist text exalting the values of domestic life, we are now in a position to reconsider and reinterpret the context and intertext of the novel: the woman question and Victorian fiction. In the next chapter I will examine how Tolstoy's ambivalent emulation of the Victorians and his polemic with the canon of the nineteenth-century realist novel motivate his assault on aesthetic philosophy. Tolstoy rejects his framework—the established canon of realist literature—as a fundamental failure of representation. His aesthetic vision unfolds both on the margins of his oeuvre—in his essays and other writings—and in the creative work itself. In the next chapter, still on the borders of *Anna Karenina,* we will consider these issues from a theoretical perspective before turning to the artwork itself.

Beyond the Motivations of Realism: Tolstoy, the Victorian Novel, and Iconic Aesthetics

> When we appraise a work according to its realism, we only show that we are talking, not of a work of art, but of its counterfeit.
> Tolstoy, *What Is Art?*

"English Happiness": *Anna Karenina* and the Victorian Novel

Tolstoy's admiration for the Victorian novel is well known: Dickens' portrait hung over his desk at Yasnaya Polyana; Anthony Trollope "killed him with his mastery."[1] Tolstoy's admiration for George Eliot, William Thackeray, Charles Dickens, and Trollope is attested to in numerous diary entries and in his correspondence, and he included Dickens, Eliot, Lady Braddon,[2] and Mrs. Henry Wood on his list of important literary influences. He particularly admired the writing style of Victorian women authors for the "naturalness of [their] way of writing."[3] Finally, according to his wife, the English novel served him as a source of inspiration: "I know that when Lyovochka turns to reading English novels, then he will soon turn to writing."

In his earlier life, Tolstoy's admiration for English novels had been accompanied by a view of English society as a kind of utopia.

When contemplating the possibility that he would be exiled in 1872, he planned to take his family to England, which he considered to be the only civilized country in Europe. Yet by the time he was writing *Anna Karenina*, his anglophilia was being undercut by xenophobia, as evidenced in the acidic description of Vronsky's English-style estate and the mild sarcasm with which he characterizes as "English happiness" the fulfilled desires of the hero of the English novel Anna reads on the train from Moscow to Petersburg. Indeed, the brief synopsis of the English novel in Anna's hands could almost serve as a parody of the standard conventions of Victorian, especially Trollopian fiction, complete with parliament, hunt, illness, marriage, and estate.

Furthermore, despite Tolstoy's avowed admiration for the Victorian family novel, whose structures he openly borrows in *Anna Karenina*, the Victorian novel becomes a source of anxiety for his heroine, whose subsequent cognitive dissonance is described in a passage that could never be contained in a conventional Victorian novel. While Victorian heroines are given to blanching, blushing, or fainting with emotion, their thoughts are rarely expressed in the kind of psychological interior monologue developed by Tolstoy. For example, Edith Dombey, oppressed and harassed by her husband, expresses her conflict and anger in immobility:

> Far into the night she sat alone, by the sinking blaze, in dark and threatening beauty, watching the murky shadows looming on the wall, as if her thoughts were tangible, and cast them there. Whatever shapes of outrage and affront, and black foreshadowings of things that might happen, flickered, indistinct and giant-like, before her, one resented figure marshalled them against her. And that figure was her husband.[4]

By contrast, Anna Karenina's shadows reveal the profundity of her despair as she contemplates suicide:

> She lay in bed with open eyes, by the light of a single burned-down candle, gazing at the carved cornice of the ceiling and at the shadow of the screen that covered part of it, while she vividly pictured to herself how he would feel when she would be no more, when she

would be only a memory to him. "How could I say such cruel things to her?" he would say. "How could I go out of the room without saying anything to her? But now she is no more. She has gone away from us forever. She is . . ." Suddenly the shadow of the screen wavered, pounced on the whole cornice, the whole ceiling; other shadows from the other side swooped to meet it, for an instant the shadows flitted back, but then with fresh swiftness they darted forward, wavered, mingled, and all was darkness. "Death!" she thought. And such horror came upon her that she could not realize where she was, and for a long while her trembling hands could not find the matches and light another candle. . . . "No, anything—only to live! Why, I love him! Why, he loves me! This has been before and will pass," she said, feeling that tears of joy at the return of life were trickling down her cheeks. (781)

The plot of the Victorian novel Anna reads on the train is a prolepsis that determines the trajectory of her future life. While the topos of the heroine seduced by romance and the novel is common to the novel of adultery (viz. *Mme Bovary*), Tolstoy, by introducing a Victorian novel at this critical juncture, makes clear that he is invoking Victorian narratives of acquisition (wife and estate) rather than continental narratives of fall in adultery. Moreover, by beginning Anna's fall with the reading of a Victorian novel, he reverses the source of danger from the continental romance to the Victorian novel and thus locates the source of seduction in the Victorian domestic ethos rather than in the illicit passion of the continental romance.

There are Victorian novels of adultery, but the French theme of the fallen woman as it appears in Victorian literature is de-sexed; as Matthew Arnold observed, the English mentality is unsympathetic to the French novelist's "service to the goddess Lubricity."[5] In contrast to the French femme fatale, the English adulteress is curiously passionless; in fact, there often is no adultery committed at all (see *Dombey and Son, Can You Forgive Her?, Middlemarch*). In *Anna Karenina*, Tolstoy parodies Victorian prudery in representing the consummation of an affair by laying bare the conventional ellipsis: he draws a pointedly dotted line *between* chapters to emphasize the enormity of the omitted episode.

When a Victorian heroine does in fact commit adultery (e.g., *East Lynne, Lady Audley's Secret*), the emphasis of the narrative is usually on the enormity of the fall and the loss of estate and children rather than on the sweetness of seduction or the adulterous liaison. The melodramatic chords of the Victorian sensation novel are usually struck on the theme of maternity and maternal sacrifice rather than on passion and its vicissitudes. In the Victorian novel of adultery, it is the loss of children and real estate that constitutes the fallen woman's punishment. Thus, the famous apostrophe to the reader that was the high point of any theatrical performance of *East Lynne*:

> Lady—wife—mother! Should you ever be tempted to abandon your home . . . Whatever trials may be the lot of your married life, though they may magnify themselves to your crushed spirit as beyond the endurance of woman to bear, *resolve* to bear them; fall down upon your knees and pray . . . rather than forfeit your fair name and your good conscience; for be assured that the alternative, if you rush on to it, will be found far worse than death!
>
> Poor thing! poor Lady Isabel! She had sacrificed husband, children, reputation, home, all that makes life of value to woman.[6]

Lady Isabel repents her adultery almost immediately and, yearning desperately for her children, takes advantage of the erroneous report of her death to disguise herself as a governess in her husband's employ in order to be near them. The climactic, melodramatic scene of the novel where she struggles not to reveal her true identity to her dying son could easily have inspired Tolstoy's creation of the passionate surreptitious reunion between veiled mother and son in *Anna Karenina*.

Anna's grief over the loss of Seryozha places her within this Victorian tradition. What most distinguishes Anna's narrative from that associated with the continental tradition of adulteresses is precisely the conflict she experiences between her maternal love for Seryozha and her sexual love for Vronsky. Anna is thus unique in literature in that she combines the maternal aspect of the Victorian fallen woman with the passionate sensuality of the French mistress. By giving Anna two

Poster for *East Lynne*. Courtesy of the Harvard Theatre Collection.

love stories, Tolstoy reinstantiates the narrative of passion into the Victorian paradigm and questions the objects of desire erected by the Victorian ethos.

The desire for an English happiness may be seen as motivating all of the main protagonists in *Anna Karenina,* even Lyovin, whom Stiva describes somewhat disparagingly as a "Dickensian gentleman." In-

"Anna Visiting Her Son" by M. A. Vrubel, 1883

deed, the accretion of English phrases, words, and details in the novel, in tandem with certain plot conventions of Victorian literature, have provoked a critical consensus of praise for the novel as a continuation or culmination of the Victorian tradition. Indeed, as Morson observes, "It is easier to read *Anna* according to the conventions of the English novel."[7] In fact, so potent is this effect that the editors of one translation of the novel refer to "Victorian Russia."[8]

Many critics have noticed the English touches in *Anna Karen-ina*:[9] in addition to the English names Annie, Kitty, Dolly, Hannah, and Betsey, there is Vronsky's English groom, Cord; the Oblonskys' English governess, Miss Hull, Anna's dressmaker, Wilson, and various unnamed English nurses; Kitty works at *broderie anglaise,* Lyovin and Stiva dine at the Anglia, Vronsky belongs to the English Club; the horses at the race are mostly English racers, the riders sit their horses "in imitation of English jockeys," and others besides Vronsky have English grooms; Princess Betsey drives an elegant English carriage; Sir John is lionized in the Russian salons; Vronsky refers to the Russian elections as "our Parliament." English books are read throughout the novel: in addition to Anna's Victorian novel, Lyovin reads Tyndall; the English fairy tale of the three bears is applied to the three Shcherbatsky girls and Kitty's nickname is Tiny Bear (a bilingual pun was intended since Tolstoy's wife's maiden name was Behrs); Lidia Ivanovna reads two English Sunday School tracts aloud: "Safe and Happy" and "Under the Wing." English expressions and phrases are quoted throughout the novel in suggestive ways for characters and events: Karenin is disliked for his "sneering," Anna has a "skeleton in the closet," Vronsky's horse, Frou-Frou, has "the blood that tells," and, ironically, Vronsky considers that he has the "pluck" that is nec-essary for good horsemanship and winning the race. Vronsky is fond of the expression "not in my line," and Anna thinks of their dying rela-tionship that "the zest is gone." An ominously significant English proverb is quoted:

> "No, I imagine, joking aside, that to know love, one must make mistakes and then correct them," said Princess Betsey.
> "Even after marriage?" said the ambassador's wife, playfully.
> "It's never too late to mend," the attaché quoted the English proverb. (125)

Most important, the estate where Vronsky and Anna live after her separation from Karenin is English in custom, manner, and style and thus represents the fulfillment of Anna's desire, aroused by the English

novel she read on the train, to "accompany the hero to his estate."
Anna rides an English cob wearing an English-style riding habit, and
this behavior, like that of Lady Mary in the English novel, scandalizes
her sister-in-law, Dolly. In the nursery are "little carts ordered from
England, and appliances for teaching babies to walk, and a sofa after
the fashion of a billiard table, purposely constructed for crawling, and
swings and baths . . . They were all English" (645–46). The guests
play billiards and lawn tennis and *"toute-à-fait à l'Anglaise"* they meet
at breakfast and separate for the day. Yet the estate is obviously not
truly English, but English as it is perceived by Russian readers of English novels. For example, Dolly's view of the estate gives her an "impression of wealth and sumptuousness and of that modern European
luxury of which she had only read in English novels" (644). Thus,
Anna Karenina does not merely cite or bow to the English tradition;
the English novel is the novel within the novel that represents the fantasies and desires of the major characters, including Kitty and Lyovin,
and scripts the future anglophile life of Vronsky and Anna. In this capacity, the English novel in *Anna Karenina* represents values that are
alien, false, illusory, and ultimately dangerous.

It has become common in recent criticism to treat the Victorian
novel as a "palimpsestic" text[10] that reveals various strata that subvert
the very institutions the text overtly supports. Thus, Victorian novels
are seen as especially structured on ambivalences, so that, despite
plot events and treatments that support the status quo, some critics
discern "symbolic structures opposed to the sexual values of the direct narrative gradually form and emerge, often constituting a distinct
'counterplot' to the overt handling of theme and characterization.
The authors' ambivalence is expressed through narrators who mingle
desire, fear, and hostility toward female characters in a way that both
represents and exposes Victorian sexual values.[11]

The critic's task becomes that of retrieving the unconscious text
through the analysis of verbal symbols, textual images, and other clues
that lead us either to the author's unconscious, repressed drives, or to
a view of the larger repressions of an entire society or era. As discussed in chapter 1 and chapter 2, recent criticism of Tolstoy has fol-

lowed a similar directive. Yet it is necessary to remember that Tolstoy
was a non-native reader of Victorian literature and not himself a Victorian; he does not read well as a bundle of repressions since, far from
being unconscious, Tolstoy was hyperconscious of his psychic drives
and conflicts and subjected himself to a self-analysis that is equal to
any undertaken by Freud.[12] Furthermore, the conflict Tolstoy experienced between his love for aristocratic life and art and his critical
awareness of the exploitative and exclusionary practices associated
with these institutions was well ventilated in his oeuvre. There is no
need to analyze his work for repressed meanings: Tolstoy's texts do
not subvert themselves; they are themselves overtly subversive. My
intention in advancing this argument is to assert the power of Tolstoy's
artistry *(masterstvo)* rather than leave his texts at the mercy of critical
blindness and refocusing. Without relying too heavily on the idea of
authorial intention, I argue that rather than assuming textual repressive returns that ultimately jettison the text out of Tolstoy's control,
we should champion his powers, victories, and subtleties. In assessing
Tolstoy's possible indebtedness to the Victorian novel, therefore, we
might conclude that he borrows Victorian social and textual conventions in order to expose them; he does this by criticizing the ethos and
morés of bourgeois society and by rewriting the Victorian novel so
that it transcends the boundaries of its conventions.

In his later writings, Tolstoy quite explicitly denounces Victorian
fiction:

> In the majority of cases, the men, who are supposed to represent
> something noble and elevated, from Childe Harold to the latest he-
> roes of . . . Trollope are in fact, nothing but depraved parasites, who
> can be of no use for anything or anyone, while even the heroines, one
> way or another, are nothing more than objects of pleasure for the
> men, mistresses, similarly idle and addicted to luxuries.[13]

In addition to attacking the basis of marital relations and the
foundations of bourgeois Victorian society, Tolstoy increasingly
directed his criticism against the very form of Victorian fiction. In

his earliest diary entries on the English novel, he is impelled to move beyond the constraints of convention as he notes that Trollope relies on "too much that is conventional"[14] and that "to tolerate [conventional] mannerisms [in novels] means to follow the times: to correct them means to be in advance of them."[15] While the Russian novel afforded him the freedom of working in an unconventional mode and genre (as he was proud to note, "We Russians in general do not know how to write novels in the sense in which this genre is understood in Europe"[16]), he nonetheless capitulated to the genre in its European form by characterizing *Anna Karenina* as a "novel, the first [novel] I have ever written." The mastery with which Tolstoy works within the genre is so great that he is usually considered "grandly representative of that time, as if George Eliot, Thackery, Trollope and even John Stuart Mill had been rolled into one."[17] Or, in Georg Lukacs's assessment, Tolstoy redeems realism: "Tolstoy saved the traditions of the great realists and carried them on and developed them further in concrete and topical form in an age in which realism had degenerated . . . He is the last great classic of bourgeois realism, the last worthy link in the chain that stretches from Cervantes to Balzac. He is a classic of realism."[18] The combination of this standard assessment and a tendency for criticism to reject interpretations of Tolstoy's novels that seem to verge on the allegorical and symbolic have resulted in a view of Tolstoy that overlooks the very profound distinctions between Tolstoyan realism and European, especially Victorian, realism.[19] *Anna Karenina* is not a realist novel, although it has come to be read that way. Rather, it reflects on every level, both thematic and formal, Tolstoy's polemic with realism and with Victorian literature, and his quest for mythopoesis as an alternative.

The Motivations of Realism

Tolstoy's treatment of art, realism, and the Victorian novel in *Anna Karenina* presages his later condemnation of the Western canon of great art and reveals his lifelong quest for a native Russian art that would achieve the universal appeal and status of myth. Although myth in the realist novel in the form of archetypal imagery is often read as irrepressible projections from the author's unconscious, Tolstoy's mythopoesis was conscious and intentional; it was crafted from his use of the transparent language of impersonal authority, his rewriting of legendary plots, and his attention to the symbolic value of textual details. His aesthetic demanded the creation of a new art, a fusion of the universal accessibility of popular genres with the profundity and elegance of belles lettres. He would later reject his novel *Anna Karenina* for being an inadequate step along the path toward true Christian art, and the criticism has respected Tolstoy's own bifurcation of his thought and oeuvre into pre- and postconversion phases. However, Gustafson's recent work on Tolstoy argues for reading this self-appointed conversion as a slow evolution in thought and artistry rather than as a cataclysmic shift.

In the standard assessment of Tolstoy, he is supposed to have fulfilled the demands of realism in his preconversion works and then to have reacted against them following his conversion. Dmitry Mirsky summarizes the process:

> In his early work [Tolstoy] was a representative man of the Russian realistic school, which relied entirely on the method of "superfluous detail" . . . that gave the particular and individual convincingness that is the very essence of the realistic novel. The general effect of such detail is to bring out the particular, the individual, the local, and the temporary at the expense of the general and the universal. . . . This particularity which excludes a universal appeal and emphasizes social and national differences was what the old Tolstoy condemned in the methods of realistic fiction. In his early work he had entirely adopted them and carried them farther than his predecessors.[20]

Thus, following his conversion, Tolstoy explicitly rejected the elitism of a novelistic discourse that depends for its effect on the reader's familiarity with details of privileged social groups[21] and termed realism *provincialism*.[22] His views are conveyed as an unrestrained antirealist, antinaturalist program in *What Is Art?*:

The essence of [mimesis] consists in supplying details accompanying the thing described or depicted. In literary art, this method consists in describing, in the minutest details, the external appearance, the faces, the clothes, the gestures, the tones, and the habituations of the characters represented, with all the occurrences met with in life. . . . This abundance of detail makes the stories difficult of comprehension to all people not living within reach of the conditions described by the author. . . . Strip the best novels of our times of their details and what will remain?[23]

In the case of the realist novel of the nineteenth century, the affluence of textual detail, especially when unmotivated by plot considerations or participation in a symbolic system, reflected the aesthetic preference for mimesis of the trivial and random in the pursuit of verisimilitude. In his essay "What is Realism in Art?" Roman Jakobson places Tolstoy within the European realist tradition when he notes that Tolstoy, "describing Anna's suicide, primarily writes about her handbag"[24]; this forms an intrusion of what Jakobson considers extraneous or "unessential" detail, introduced to create a heightened sense of verisimilitude. Jakobson ascribes Tolstoyan detail to the desire to achieve realistic effects, in keeping with the theories of Tolstoy's fellow Russian formalist critics, especially Shklovsky and Tomashevsky; the latter critics' concepts of motivation *(motivirovka)* endure in the debate on realism, which has been reargued, for example, by Roland Barthes in his essay *"L'effet du réel."*[25] These formalist elements of motivation may be defined as follows:[26]

1. Realistic motivation *(bytovaia, realisticheskaia)*,[27] where the textual element is motivated by the intention to create effects of verisimilitude, as in the example cited by Jakobson above.
2. Psychological motivation *(psikhologicheskaia)*,[28] where the device is employed to reveal the psychology of a character or social group.
3. Compositional motivation *(kompozitsionnaia)*,[29] where the device is needed to advance the development of the plot or characterization or to elaborate some aspect of the artistic design.
4. Artistic motivation *(khudozhestvennaia)*[30] or, in some cases,

meta-aesthetic motivation, where the device is utilized because the conventions of the genre require it. Artistic motivation may also occur as the parodic deployment of conventional
elements or the refusal to motivate an element, in which case,
the artistic structures may appear unmotivated; however, they
are in fact motivated by the desire to "lay bare the device" of
artistic convention.

The absence of a psychogenic motivation in formalist theory—
what psychoanalytic criticism would consider a device motivated by
the author's need for ego mastery of a problem projected onto the
text—may be accounted for by the lack of the development of
Freudian psychology in the Soviet Union. Just as psychoanalytic criticism might account for all textual elements through a subconscious
motivation, so structuralist-semiotic criticism might account for all elements in a text in terms of a more broadly understood compositional
motivation. Such co-optation of every detail in service to an overarching poetic design or intention has been termed *semiotic totalitar-
ianism* by Morson.[31]

Prosaics versus Poetics

Morson's alternative proposition, a theory of prosaics, would allow
textual detail the same unmotivated status as random detritus in real
life and everyday experience. Morson's notion of the prosaic makes
use of Bakhtin's theory of the novel (although it extends beyond
Bakhtin), and Morson thus enthusiastically affirms the novel's realist
proclivities, in the sense that it is large, loose, and messy. But if it is a
mistake to read life as a novel (a mistake especially common to novelistic heroines)—that is, to invest every event and detail with significance or motivation—surely it is just as dangerous to read the novel as
life; to denude textual details of significance. This approach suggests
either loss of faith in the omnipotence of a creative intelligence or at
least posits the inattention or lack of unity of this intelligence.[32]

The theory of prosaics suggests that the author is an entropy-producing entity who generates as much useless text as meaningful text; thus, Tolstoy in writing *War and Peace* "did not set out with a plot already mapped out; rather, he sought to scatter potentials, some of which would be realized, many of which would not."[33] Yet where is the authority that can separate the two? Although the development of realism in art may be seen as accompanying the secularization of culture, it is still important to recall that the death of God is not coterminous or coterminal with the death of the author. A creative intelligence *does* pull the puppet strings of the fictional world within the covers of the novel. Thus, Morson with his theory pulls at the seams between conscious and unconscious artistic control that bind the text's plethora of details.

To illustrate his principle of "creation by potential,"[34] Morson takes as an example the scene in *Anna Karenina* where the artist, Mikhailov, finding his drawing accidentally transformed when a drop of wax spills on the paper, is newly inspired. Morson comments: "One completely random event redefines the relations of all the elements of the painting. The same is true of history. Mikhailov is a good painter for the same reason that Rostov is a good soldier: each is aware that configurations change rapidly and unexpectedly, and is alert to the opportunities presented in a world of uncertainty."[35] Morson thus draws an analogy between the processes of life and creativity, and he valorizes the artists of life who improvise around the unexpected and random, as opposed to the more rigid characters who must rely on maps and models. Tolstoy, according to Morson, is an artist like Mikhailov; he creates without models or predetermined plans, according to the inspiration and needs of the moment. Yet Morson's reading does not account for the differences between the universe of life and the universe of the artist's creative endeavor. Mikhailov's drop of wax originated not in the real world but in the imagination of Tolstoy, who utilized that particular example to illustrate his notion of creativity.

Tolstoy's anecdote about Mikhailov and his sketch of "a man in a rage" was probably inspired by Pliny the Elder's legend about Protogenes, "the artist in a rage."[36] In the legend Protogenes is frustrated by his failure to represent the froth of saliva on the face of a dog:

In the picture there is a dog marvellously executed, so as to appear to
have been painted by art and good fortune jointly: the artist's own
opinion was that he did not fully show in it the foam of the panting
dog, although in all the remaining details he had satisfied himself,
which was very difficult. But the actual art displayed displeased him,
nor was he able to diminish it, and he thought it was excessive and
departed too far from reality—the foam appeared to be painted, not
to be the natural product of the animal's mouth; vexed and tormented, as he wanted his picture to contain the truth and not merely
a near-truth, he had several times rubbed off the paint and used another brush, quite unable to satisfy himself. Finally he fell into a
rage with his art because it was perceptible, and dashed a sponge
against the place in the picture that offended him, and the sponge
restored the colours he had removed in the way that his anxiety had
wished them to appear, and chance produced the effect of nature in
the picture![37]

In this fable, the artist's hand remains in creative control. The drop of
wax and the water from the sponge demonstrate that the artist, far
from generating entropic waste, actively recycles and recoups everything into his work—any detail may be worked into the artistic design. Or, to return to the notion of motivation, any textual element *is*
motivated; or a motivation may be found for any textual element.

Semiotic theory has treated the notion of motivation as essential
to forming discriminations about the very nature of signification; the
concept of the "arbitrariness of the sign" (*l'arbitraire du signe*) posits
that verbal symbols are unmotivated, that is, they are purely conventional. Motivated signs, or icons, to borrow Peircean terminology, by
contrast find their elements—the vehicle and the referent—essentially wedded; that is, there is a natural cohesion or isomorphic resonance posited between signifier and signified. Thus, the concept of
iconicity implies a belief in an Edenic or philosopher's language,
where there is a natural and necessary relationship between word and
referent. While this relationship is presumed lost in modern languages, it is often suggested that poetic discourse retrieves or exploits
its vestigial potentialities.[38]

If the movement toward iconicity as a natural, preverbal harmony between sound and sense is a tendency of poetic discourse, then one of the distinctions between poetry and prose might be that prosaic discourse is conventional, arbitrary, and oriented to representation while poetic language is oriented to itself (the Russian formalist notion of "orientation on the expression," *ustanovka na vyrazhenie*). Since the conventions determining arbitrary meaning in language are formed socially, prose texts can claim greater immediate accessibility than poetic texts. Since realist prose claims to represent with a minimum of discursive and textual conventions, it is therefore the mode that exalts the notion of a consensual collectivity. The collective (author and audience) that imposes its own values and meanings on language all the while maintains a belief—or delusion—that the manner of representation is objective. A belief in pure arbitration of the sign suggests a humanist naïveté, or, as Elizabeth Ermarth has characterized it, realism as a historical moment sustained a communal "linguistic innocence," a referentiality "innocently pointing toward an objective world beyond it. . . . To the extent that all points of view summoned by the text agree, to the extent that they converge upon the 'same' world, that text maintains the consensus of realism."[39] Yet this consensus is erected upon the transient formation of a community—a construct as ephemeral as the linguistic indeterminacy that undermines its practices. J. Hillis Miller locates the blindness of Victorian literature in precisely this problem:

> Perhaps the power behind language is only brought to the surface in the gaps between words, in the failures of language, not in its completed articulations. Correspondingly, human beings, it may be, are characterized by unappeasable desire and consequently, by permanent alienation from their deepest selves. Any replacement of desire by fulfillment is only temporary and illusory. For the Victorian novelists, on the other hand, the existence of an authentic satisfaction of desire makes the happy ending possible.[40]

Prosaics therefore skirts the dangers of a naive realism, just as poetics risks investing language with a mystical lyricism.

Lyrical Motivation

Since the formalists base their theories of motivation on prosaic models, and their theories of literature on a stringent division between poetic and prosaic discourse, they overlook the potential for a self-reflexive motivation in prose that is extratextual rather than intertextual. In other words, the formalists bind most reflexivity in prose to parody and evolution, and they overlook the moments in prose that are stilled or arrested, that exist for themselves and not to advance the plot, and that are in some sense transcendent, lyrical, or even mystical, as exemplified by symbolist or modernist prose. The formalists thereby promote the concept of artistic motivation at the expense of other kinds of textual dynamics that might have an affinity with the aesthetics of Symbolism, from which the formalists were anxious to distance themselves. Thus, there is an absence in formalist theory of a framework for what we might term *lyrical* motivation.

The notion of a lyrical motivation is not introduced here to characterize the involvement of textual details in a larger symbolic system (Symbolism); that function might better be termed *tropological* motivation and could be accounted for in formalist theory by the notion of compositional motivation. The very term compositional—related to the plot *(siuzhet)* of the story-plot *(fabula-siuzhet)* distinction—provides a model based on prose, plot formations, and plot devices, where symbolic details and tropes might serve as foreshadowings, leitmotifs, and the like. But a different use of detail, to create a heightened effect through rhetorical devices or lyrical evocations, seems less well accommodated within this category, if only because of the affinity of this use of detail with poetry and Romanticism.[41] Categorizing detail in a prose work in this way would furthermore have the effect of moving the realist work closer to Romanticism or, at the very least, toward Symbolism, thus making the boundaries between prose and poetry problematic.

Indeed, if we evade the direct, referential signification implied by the needs of the *siuzhet* and strain toward a more abstruse referentiality, we find the very notion of a lyrical motivation demanding a specific discussion of textual symbolism, imagery, and rhetoric that expects greater play in its extratextual parameters. In other words, such elements are motivated not by the needs of the composition but by those of its effects. To put this distinction in functional terms based on Roman Jakobson's communication schema: compositional motivation implies a twin orientation on the reference and the message; lyrical motivation suggests an orientation to the receiver.

Lyrical motivation therefore is intended to transcend the boundaries of the text or composition and to transport the reader beyond the local understanding that the text or composition had provided. Lyrical motivation thus reveals its basis in poetry and especially in the Romantic, neo-Romantic, or Symbolist lyric. Therefore, it should presumably be a category that is irrelevant for realist prose. This is certainly the way Bakhtin dismisses concepts of lyricism from his characterization of double-voiced prose discourse:

> [N]o matter how one understands the interrelationship of meanings in a poetic symbol [a trope], this interrelationship is never of the dialogic sort; it is impossible under any conditions or at any time to imagine a trope [say, a metaphor] being unfolded into the two exchanges of a dialogue. . . . The entire event is played out between the word and its object; all of the play of the poetic symbol is in that space.[42]

It is this aspect of Bakhtin's thought that de Man finds most problematic and refers to as a "metaphysical *impensé*": "[F]or Bakhtin, the trope is an intentional structure directed toward an object, and, as such, a pure *episteme* and not a fact of language; this in fact excludes tropes from literary discourse, poetic as well as prosaic, and locates them, perhaps surprisingly, in the field of epistemology."[43]

De Man's relocation of Bakhtin's trope within the field of pure epistemology on the basis of its object orientation is perhaps a result of the inherent difference in the philosophical systems of the two thinkers. Traditions of Russian thought and their bases in Eastern Orthodox religious philosophy posit an iconicity that does not founder on the same subject-object existentialist crisis that plagues modern Western thought. Thus, the problem of *mimesis* needs to be reconsidered in a non-Western, perhaps more genuinely Greek way—in the terms expressed by Dostoevsky when he claimed to be a realist "in the higher sense." Realism as a prosaic mode would thus appear to be impure, and the boundaries erected in critical theory between realist prose and Symbolist verse would appear to be less than impermeable. Perhaps it would be useful to create a category of post-realism for writers like Tolstoy who work within realism to push beyond it. More accurately, Tolstoy should be considered a peri-modern whose prose experiments point in the direction of symbolist and modernist innovations.[44] Most important, Tolstoy's differences with Western realism can be shown to be based on the Eastern Orthodox foundations of his aesthetic theories.

Tolstoy's Iconic Aesthetics and Eastern Orthodoxy

Gustafson has recently shown that the theological basis of Tolstoy's thought and artistry encompasses "a range of thought from ontology to epistemology to aesthetics, ethics, and political theory."[45] Suggesting the principle of iconicity[46] as the fundament of Eastern Orthodox theology, Gustafson proposes that Tolstoy's prose be read as motivated throughout by the impetus to emblematize, to replicate a world that is itself a replica, permeated by divine signification. Since Eastern Orthodox theology conceives of reality as not being separate from God, "Reality reflects the Divine, because God is in the world and the world is in God. Thus, everything in the world speaks of the Divine. . . . Reality is God's language, His word and His world. Life is revelation, and reality is emblematic."[47] Tolstoy's realism, in Gustafson's view, is thus not "verisimilitudinous, but baldly emblematic."[48]

Within the belief system of Eastern Orthodoxy, the icon, whether it is verbal or visual, is directly carnate—a window opening onto the celestial plane. If we characterize poetic tropes as "verbal icons" in Tolstoy's creative universe within the larger context of Eastern theology, the anxiety of representation and nostalgia for divine absence that de Man sees at the heart of lyrical emblems and tropes becomes irrelevant. As de Man's asserts, "The existence of the poetic image is itself a sign of divine absence, and the conscious use of poetic imagery an admission of this absence. . . . Poetic language seems to originate in the desire to draw closer and closer to the ontological status of the object, and its growth and development are determined by this inclination."[49] By contrast, in Gustafson's characterization of poetic images within the Eastern Orthodox understanding, verbal icons "transcend their material bounds and [disclose] the spirit,"[50] thus affirming divine presence and unifying object and reference.

The debate sketched here between East and West seems to hinge on the Neoplatonic "extreme realist" conception of vision and representation, that, in its profound skepticism of perception and reality, informs the problematic epistemological status of linguistic versus visual epistemes. Or, to put it in other terms, the "picture theory of language" and the "language theory of pictures"[51] both presuppose that cognition intercedes in perception to create a linguistically constructed field of meaning that ruptures the union between the real and the real-as-perceived. In the Western philosophical tradition, this gap is never closed. In the Eastern philosophical tradition, the gap is not problematic. Instead, the attempt to suture is valorized as a continuing process not of impossible straining toward a perfect state and an unattainable Godhead but as the experience of daily life. To understand the concept, it is necessary to adopt the Eastern Orthodox value placed on a kenotic Christ—a Christ incarnated, whose path through earthly existence may be followed in the simplest processes of living itself.

The division between East and West may also be historically conceived of as occurring during the iconoclast controversy, such that the bifurcation in theological and aesthetic thought results in a mistrust of representation in Western culture, as opposed to a belief in the power of iconic representation in Eastern thought. In *Anna Karenina* Tolstoy treats the visual and the verbal as equally compromised; yet while he explores the ambiguous field of vision in the Platonic sense, he recognizes its promise of transcendence through an iconic veracity.

In *Anna Karenina* Tolstoy employs the themes of vision, the visionary, visual art, and framing to address the problems in aesthetics sketched above. He would later examine and critique these issues directly in *What Is Art?*

The Prison House of Sight:
Iconicity and the Beautiful versus
the Sublime in Tolstoy's Aesthetics

Tolstoy's aesthetics as laid out in *What Is Art?* essentially constitute
a Christianized version of the Kantian distinction between the beautiful and the sublime. In *What Is Art?* Tolstoy, citing authorities from
Baumgarten to Darwin, rejects all possible definitions of art constructed on a notion of beauty and charges that the very attempt to define beauty must founder on the problem of taste and relativism as debated in the English eighteenth-century school of aesthetic philosophy:

> There is and can be no explanation of why one thing pleases one man
> and displeases another, or vice versa. So that the whole existing sci-
> ence of aesthetics fails to do what we might expect from it. . . .
> namely, it does not define the qualities and laws of art or of the beau-
> tiful . . . or the nature of taste. . . . So the theory of art founded on
> beauty, expounded by aesthetics, and in dim outline professed by the
> public, is nothing but the setting up as good of that which has
> pleased and pleases us, i.e., pleases a certain class of people.[52]

Yet Tolstoy is curiously silent on that other pole of aesthetic perception, the category of the sublime. Although he mentions the sublime
as a category in Burke's aesthetics, he completely excises the concept
from his discussion of Kantian aesthetics, which he limits to the notion of "pleasure without desire . . . so that art may be called a game,
not in the sense of an unimportant occupation, but in the sense of a
manifestation of the beauties of life itself without other aim than that
of beauty."[53]

For Kant, the categories of the beautiful and the sublime are ar-
ticulated comparatively: "The beautiful in nature is connected with
the form of the object which consists in having definite boundaries.
The sublime, on the other hand, is to be found in a formless object, so
far as in it or by occasion of it *boundlessness* is represented, and yet its
totality is also present to thought."[54] Yet Kant is careful to reiterate that
sublimity is an effect that resides in the viewer's sense of the limits of
his or her own imagination, such that it is "our attitude of thought,

which introduces sublimity into the representation of nature."[55] Since the viewer cannot comprehend the magnitude of the unbounded, "this very inadequateness for that idea in our faculty for estimating the magnitude of things of sense excites in us the feeling of a supersensible faculty. . . . Nature is . . . sublime in those of its phenomena whose intuition brings with it the idea of its infinity. This last can only come about by the inadequacy of the greatest effort of our imagination to estimate the magnitude of an object."[56]

This concept of the sublime emerges in Tolstoy's treatise in the defining function of art he proposes to replace the sensual and pleasurable effects of the beautiful. The sublime response, understood as the experience of limits and the sensation of awe provoked by the intimations of what lies beyond them, is reworked by Tolstoy into Christian terms: as the transcendent reception or "infection" of overpowering emotion, which transmutes selfish, material, impulses into *caritas* and forms a universal collective of Christian brotherhood.

The same distinctions are operative in Tolstoy's use of vision, visual experience, and the visionary in *Anna Karenina,* as will be discussed in chapter 5. In the experience of the beautiful—for example, in Vronsky's infatuation with Anna's beauty—the viewer is seduced by the beautiful and loses the sense of an enclosing frame that indicates sheer physicality and the veneer of embodiment. In other words, the sublime spirit is not envisioned once the seductive force of the beautiful body holds sway. In this sense, Tolstoy rigorously rejects the Kantian notion of aesthetic disinterest.

We can take Tolstoy's description of Anna reading on the train as a textual illustration of his critique of Kant's pure beauty: as she reads Anna desires to put into action every event described in the text. The aesthetic response as Tolstoy describes it in this passage is far from disinterested; the work of art, whether for good or evil, does not simply please, it infects, and its capacity to do so is not affected by its moral status. Thus, emphasis on the frame (the index of sublimity as the sensation of limits) is essential to remind the reader that what is viewed is a representation and to activate the sense of limits that extends the text's meaning into a more abstract realm, beyond the impulses generated by its seductive, infectious representation.

Thus, throughout *Anna Karenina* Tolstoy exalts the perception of
borders, boundaries, frames, and limits by characters in the novel.
For example, when Lyovin views peasants working through a doorway
that frames his vision into a genre painting, the beauty of the healthy,
physical bodies of the working peasants strikes him as temporary and
ephemeral. The body itself is a frame of life; the sublimity of death is
what is suggested by his viewing of the scene. A similar moment occurs in *War and Peace* when Prince Andrei views his soldiers bathing
in a stream and transforms their flesh into "cannon fodder."

An emphasis on the frame is a modernist move that sets up the experience of the sublime and signals that the viewer must access
ultimate vision through an aperture leading from the earth-bound into
a transcendent realm. This is the function of icons as they are understood in Eastern Orthodox theology: icons are not representations but
rather direct windows into heaven. Thus, the frame sets a limit that we
recognize as the field of our own vision while we never lose sight of the
fact that what is shown expands far beyond the borders that enclose it.
Such an aesthetic challenges and reworks the realist conviction in regard to adequate representation that characterizes the Victorian novel.
Tolstoy thus departs from the realist camp and affiliates himself with
the modernists, as will be shown in the following chapter.

Tolstoy's aesthetics thus offer a reworking, or a mirrored translation into Eastern terms, of the Western philosophical distinction between the beautiful and the sublime, while he simultaneously turns
the ontology of perception away from the crisis in epistemology toward a metaphysical resolution. The Western category of the beautiful is understood in Tolstoy's terms as the seduction of representation,
the failure of Plato's cave dwellers to recognize their enclosure and
hence their blind acceptance of the shadow play they witness and
prize as real. Tolstoy's Easternization of Kant's notion of the sublime
retrieves the other aspect of Plato's thought and saves vision from the
prison house of sight by exalting the moments when vision knows its
own bounds, the only way in which it can know the unbounded.

PART II

Frame: Image and the Boundaries
of Vision in *Anna Karenina*

The Execution of Anna Karenina: Heroines Framed and Hung

> It is only after my death that another can begin to
> aestheticize my personality.
> Mikhail Bakhtin

Beauty Framed

In *Anna Karenina* Tolstoy uses framing and frame devices to thematize and illustrate the views on representation and aesthetics that he would later state explicitly in *What Is Art?* He thus engages the aesthetic debate over beauty and figures it in his novel in the framed beauty of the female body of his heroine, Anna Karenina. In adopting this strategy, he may be compared to other writers of symbolist prose, such as James Joyce or Marcel Proust, whose treatments of female beauty represent a conscious and reflexive variation on the traditional narrative strategy of depicting novelistic heroines as artworks and, by extension, a problematicization of the fields of representation and symbolization.

Verbal presentations of heroines in artworks—portraits, busts, miniatures—occur with great frequency in the novelistic tradition; usually they serve as surrogates for the actual female body. The modernist response to this tradition is represented by Joyce and Proust, who exploit the symbolic power of such doubly coded descriptions. Tolstoy's textual delineations of Anna as objet d'art fall between the (postindustrial) modern and the (historically avant-garde) modernist;

by juxtaposing Anna's portraits and art of self-portraiture to Lyovin's habit of viewing nature as a symbolic landscape painting, Tolstoy succeeds in thematizing the categories of the beautiful and the sublime as an issue keyed to gender and to sexuality. By creating a series of framed portraits of Anna—texts within texts—he repeatedly arrests his narrative flow in order to frame his heroine and alert the reader to the existence of the frame of beauty, corporality, and the marketplace of both, that confines her. Tolstoy thus conflates the aesthetic question and the woman question in a manner that places him among the Symbolists rather than the realists. *Anna Karenina* thus marks a shift from the approved and probably unconscious mechanism of describing women as works of art so common in realist prose to the modern anxiety over the possible meanings of such representations. In the modern crisis of reading and interpretation, Tolstoy even exceeds such symbolists as Proust and Joyce in his greater awareness of how the gaze is engendered, and in his redesignation of the power of beauty from its entrapped, pornographic role in Western bourgeois art to a transformative, even redemptive role in Eastern iconic representation. The viewers in Proust and Joyce experience a failure of interpretation and transmute their sense of the limitation of seeing into sublime experience; Tolstoy's viewers respond in another mode altogether: in the realm of iconic perception. What I suggested on a theoretical plane in chapter 3, I will demonstrate in chapter 5 through close textual analysis of the moments in the novel where Anna is framed. Before turning to Tolstoy's portraits of Anna, however, I will consider in this chapter what such framing prefigures: Anna's ultimate enclosure—her death. I will do so by considering the literary tradition of the pictorialization of female characters to which *Anna Karenina* may be compared.

Frame as Foreclosure:
The Pictorialization of Women in Literature

> He stood still in the gloom of the hall . . . gazing up at his wife. There was grace and mystery in her attitude as if she were a symbol of something . . . If he were a painter he would paint her in that attitude.[1]

In this central, time-stopping scene from Joyce's "The Dead," Gabriel's gaze casts a framing net around a living woman, rendering explicit the hypostatization of the picturing mode of describing women that is so common in nineteenth- and twentieth-century literature. The topos, an extended *ekphrasis* (a verbal description of a visual art form), transforms the female form into a tableau vivant and renders her natural beauty intentionally and artificially artistic. In premodern novels such as *La Princesse de Clèves* it is often an actual portrait or reflection that serves as a pretext for this type of description; in the modern and modernist novel the heroines themselves are posed against scenic or framing backdrops, and this allows the author to elicit the full effect of the picturesque.[2] That depictions of feminine beauty most often arouse a prurient interest rather than a transcendent vision constitutes the agon of Joyce's narrative since Gabriel's desire for his wife as the artistic object he has made of her is denied, just as the composition he had created, *Distant Music,* proves to be a hermeneutic failure. In fact, Gabriel's creations and representations are always failures, as exemplified by his memory of an early love letter to his wife: "Why is it that words like these seem to me so dull and cold? Is it because there is no word tender enough to be your name?" (232). These words, "Like distant music . . . were borne toward him from the past" (232). The phrase "distant music" thus refers to both of Gabriel's representative crises and failures in love. The distant music of his wife's portrait has an entirely different meaning for her; it evokes the memory of a love that scorned embodiment and pursued the purity of disembodied emotion in death. Transcendence for Gabriel, in Joyce's story, is inspired by a different kind of painting—the landscape, the dehumanized, dead world framed behind the window panes at the story's close. It is the vision of falling snow covering the "living and the dead" that expands Gabriel's eros into agape—his sexual desire for his wife is replaced by a universalized empathy for all humanity.

Epiphanies produced by viewing nature suggest the romantic notion of the sublime, the evocation of an invisible world that is exalted over the tangible, the visible, and the present. Luce Irigaray suggests that the realm of the invisible is invested with a superior valuation of masculinity resonant with the nostalgia and awe produced in infancy by the absent father. Conversely, the category of the beautiful may be associated with the ever-present maternal body, an image of enclosure.[3]

Thus, the apparent superiority of landscape over portrait and of the beauty of the natural world over feminine beauty in the Western novel establishes a literary tradition where the beauty of the female body has lost its status as a natural category, as a result of the economics of marriage and sexual transaction, which forced feminine design and conscious intent to produce the effect of beauty. Women have lost their status as beautiful objects of the phenomenal world and become, instead, objets d'art. Beauty as signifier (body of soul) becomes unstable and charged with anxiety in the male gaze as the would-be purchaser fears being duped by mere appearance. So Seldon muses in *The House of Mirth*:

> He was aware that the qualities distinguishing her from the herd of her sex were chiefly external, as though a fine glaze of beauty and fastidiousness had been applied to vulgar clay. Yet the analogy left him unsatisfied, for a coarse texture will not take a high finish; and was it not possible that the material was fine but that circumstances had fashioned it into a futile shape?[4]

For Proust and Joyce, the momentum of this tradition culminates in the crisis of representation and interpretation characteristic of Symbolism and modernism, when vision focuses on its own blindness and generates the moment of the sublime. Therefore, both Proust and Joyce abandon the beautiful as a dangerous and impenetrable aesthetic. Both turn to the romantic sublime as the solution: in Joyce's final landscape of snow-covered Ireland and in the vision of Proust's narrator of church spires rising from the valley.

As discussed in the preceding chapter, Tolstoy would ultimately reject this duality and argue for a different action of representation altogether, one that unerringly unites the viewer and the viewed and produces a community of response in empathic brotherhood. If the gallery of the aesthetic philosophical category of the beautiful is constituted of portraits, the sublime enlists landscapes. Tolstoy makes rogues' galleries of both of these, as the next chapter will illustrate. Anna's final visions—portraits of humanity in the vanity fair—alienate her from humanity and drive her to death while Lyovin's symbolic landscapes transport him to a sublime isolation. It remains for the iconic power of great art to create the Tolstoyan moment of supersublime harmony and transcendence.

Tolstoy's novel reflects the author's formation within a different, non-Western philosophical and theological tradition and anticipates his creation of an original category within both Western and Eastern aesthetic philosophy. The visionary and visual moments in *Anna Karenina* illustrate the dangers of envisioning within the categories of the sublime and the beautiful established by Western aesthetics and literature, and they offer an alternative view that revives the beautiful, the embodied, and the feminine. The romantic sublime, hinging as it does on intellectual effort and recognition of its own failures, is deconstructed when the symbolic systems Lyovin construes from his landscapes are overturned by visions of framed feminine beauty that work directly and intuitively. As I will demonstrate in the next chapter, these visions are iconic in that they live or seem to live—they are directly carnate embodiments of the spiritual force of love. Reading feminine beauty in any other way dooms the female body to death.

The type of portrait described above occurs almost compulsively within a literary tradition where beauty evokes extraordinary anxiety that can only be assuaged through the destruction of feminine beauty and the superimposition of a masculine disembodied sublime. Literary works that participate in this tradition present portraits within texts and offer texts as portraits, thus creating a tail chase of artifice pursuing the real, the natural, and the genuine (the clay beneath the glaze). By contrast, the landscape—whether a windowed view or insetting, a framed vision, or even the mirrored interior or setting bracketed by door posts and entryways—acquires the status of the "real" world, adequately represented. The portrait, on the other hand, becomes a figure of reproduction and evokes the ambivalence and anxiety attendant on the exclusively feminine mysteries of human creation.

For example, in Proust's *Combray,* a pregnant kitchen girl is compared to Giotto's etching of Charity, and this provides the pretext for an extended disquisition on the disjunction between the emblem and the emblematic:

> [M. Swann] it was who pointed out the resemblance, and when he inquired after the kitchen-maid he would say: "Well, how goes it with Giotto's Charity?" And indeed the poor girl, whose pregnancy had swelled and stoutened every part of her, even including her face and her squarish, elongated cheeks, did distinctly suggest those virgins, so sturdy and mannish as to seem matrons, rather, in whom the Virtues are personified in the Arena Chapel. And I can see now that those Virtues and Vices of Padua resembled her in another respect as well. For just as the figure of this girl had been enlarged by the additional symbol which she carried before her, without appearing to understand its meaning, with no awareness in her facial expression of its beauty and spiritual significance, as if it were an ordinary, rather heavy burden, so it is without any apparent suspicion of what she is about that the powerfully built housewife who is portrayed in the Arena Chapel beneath the label "Caritas" . . . embodies that virtue, for it seems impossible that any thought of charity can ever have found expression in her vulgar and energetic face.[5]

The fact that the motto of the emblem *caritas* provides an explanation for the composition that would otherwise fail to convey its meaning, "that Charity devoid of charity,"[6] is reproduced in the conception of pregnancy itself. Pregnant with a meaning that is indiscernible and incomprehensible to the male gaze, filled with a mystery that is, on the one hand, only tangential to the figure herself, but of which she, on the other hand, is the opaque embodiment, Giotto's Charity symbolizes anxiety in representation and a failure of interpretation: "[I]n later years I came to understand that the arresting strangeness . . . of these frescoes derived from the great part played in them by symbolism, and the fact that this was represented not as a symbol (for the thought symbolized was nowhere expressed)."[7] The exegesis of Proust's narrator's makes explicit the unease generated by the mysteries of the female body and reproduction and recalls Joyce's narrative of failed visualization. Thus, Gabriel notes that his wife stood on the stair "as if she were a symbol of something. He asked himself what is a woman standing on the stairs in the shadow, listening to distant music, a symbol of?"[8] She is a symbol of symbolization as well as the failure of symbolization. Gabriel cannot hear the music she hears, but only sees its effect, which, like the effect of beauty itself, is external and arresting, but indeterminate, subject to misreading. The difficulty in reading woman is transferred into a textual strategy of creating a fixed and forever stilled portrait, where style and immobilization combine to provide the semblance of available meaning. Yet both Gabriel and Proust's narrators are blind—denying the female body its sublime potentials while imprisoning the framed woman in the mode of an icon or emblem. The portrait, whether actual or invented, thus participates in the tradition of Mariolatry, in that its sublimity depends on an external—arbitrarily symbolic rather than innately iconic—investiture of meaning.

The pictorialization of women in fiction is accompanied by the theme of eroticism and acquisition. In some novels, beginning with *La Princesse de Clèves* and following folkloric formulas, portraits arouse desire and act as surrogates of the desired object or as charmed substitutes. Thus, Prince Myshkin of Dostoevsky's *Idiot* is doomed to fall in love with Nastasya Filipovna once he has seen her portrait and recognized the suffering in her face.[9] In the nineteenth-century novel the concept of marriage as the sale of a beautiful object creates the "double bind" in the "temptation to be a beautiful object" described by Judith Fetterley: "Marriage is deadly because it is an economic transaction in which the beautiful object becomes the possession of the man who has money enough to buy her."[10] Or, as Wendy Steiner comments with regard to *The House of Mirth*, "[Lily Bart] has fallen under the spell of the ideology that most empowers her beauty—the literary romance—and in that system of values she cannot be a transcendent love object if her beauty is merely the coin that buys her wealth and station."[11]

Resisting any reduction of self to a beautiful object for sale results in death for Lily Bart, or destruction for the Victorian heroine, as is the case for example with Edith Dombey, whose beauty is described in explicitly economic terms by Dickens:

It was a remarkable characteristic of this lady's beauty that it appeared to vaunt and assert itself without her aid and against her will. She knew that she was beautiful: it was impossible that it could be otherwise: but she seemed with her own pride to defy her very self.

Whether she held cheap attractions that could only call forth admiration that was worthless to her, or whether she designed to render them more precious to admirers by this usage of them, those to whom they *were* precious seldom paused to consider.[12]

During Edith's courtship by Mr. Dombey, hers is "the face of a proud woman, engaged in a sordid and miserable transaction."[13] She rebels against the fate she cannot resist: "There is no slave in a market, there is no horse in a fair, so shown and offered and examined and paraded . . . as I have been."[14] A similar feeling is at the basis of Kitty Shcherbatsky's illness:

> Father began saying something to me just now. . . . It seems to me he thinks all I want is to be married. Mother takes me to a ball: it seems to me she only takes me to get me married off as soon as possible. . . . Eligible suitors, as they call them—I can't bear to see them. It seems to me they're taking stock of me and summing me up. Before to go anywhere in a ball dress was a simple joy to me, I admired myself, now I feel ashamed and awkward. (134)

Woman's beauty is thus appropriated, acquired, and framed as the object of the male gaze and desire and as the subject of economic transactions. Sometimes possession is taken through the portrait rather than the actual body, as in *La Princesse de Clèves*. Alternately, feminine beauty creates the desire for the creation of a work of art, as in *Emma* or *Middlemarch*. In the latter examples, the creation of a portrait is based on a deception or delusion, as when Emma paints an idealized portrait of Harriet for her own suitor, who is much more intrigued by the "portrait" of Emma painting, or when Vaumann pretends to take Mr. Casaubon's likeness for a painting of Thomas Aquinas in order to paint Dorothea.

The viewing of portraits, like the describing of them, constitutes a form of textual art criticism, just as Swann's comparison of Odette to a Botticelli painting becomes another example of one of his unfinished essays in art criticism and thus another failure in his approach to aesthetics—he cannot complete his work, and he falls in love with a woman who is "not his type." Alternatively, painterly styles may be used to frame character, as is the case with the demonic, pre-Raphaelite portrait of Lady Audley:

> No one but a pre-Raphaelite would have painted, hair by hair, those feathery masses of ringlets with every glimmer of gold and every shadow of pale brown. No one but a pre-Raphaelite would have so exaggerated every attribute of that delicate face as to give a lurid brightness to the blonde complexion and a strange, sinister light to the deep blue eyes. No one but a pre-Raphaelite could have given to that pretty pouting mouth the hard and almost wicked look it had in the portrait . . . it was as if you had burned strange-colored fires before my lady's face, and by their influence brought out new lines and new expressions never seen in it before. The perfection of feature, the brilliancy of coloring were there; but it seemed as if the painter had copied medieval monstrosities until his brain had grown bewildered, for my lady, in his portrait of her, had the aspect of a beautiful fiend.[15]

The portraits of women in Western novels, and the tendency of the novel to describe women in pictorial terms, establishes a tradition for making the notion of beauty and corporality figure as the problematic moment of blocked signification and ultimate transcendence in aesthetics and representation.[16] *Anna Karenina* participates in this tradition, deconstructs it, and offers an alternative vision.

Frame as Finality: The Death of the Heroine

For Mikhail Bakhtin the issues discussed above are endemic to all portraiture, regardless of the subject's gender:

> Individuals in painting (including portraiture) are finalized or "closed." [Paintings] present man exhaustively; he is already com-

pletely there and cannot become other. The faces of people who
have already said everything, who have already died [or] may as well
have died. The artist concentrates his attention on the finalizing,
defining, closing features. We see all of him and expect nothing
more (or different). He cannot be reborn, rejuvenated, or transformed—this is his finalizing (ultimate and final) stage.[17]

In this passage, one of Bakhtin's rare descriptions of a visual
rather than a verbal text, his unacknowledged bias against the static,
the spatial, and the lyrical emerges as the flip side of his valorization
of the modes of narrativity and temporality. Bakhtin's perception of
the problem of characterization that is raised by the notion of portraiture seems to suggest that any verbal description of character (as
in a novel or other prose work) is superior to any pictorial representation; the novelistic characterization permits the character to be en-
folded in a series of dialogic events and encounters that are unfolded
over time and thus permit the evolutionary and developmental shifts
in character and chronotope that Bakhtin valued so highly.[18] Yet such
a viewpoint ignores the ultimately cyclical nature and framing force of
the prose work itself, whose beginnings and ends and episodic selec-
tivity ultimately close off character as firmly as any frame. Furthermore, Bakhtin minimizes the tendency of prose toward the pictorial,
as for example the "spatial configurations" and lyricism realized in the
topos of *ekphrasis*: the use of actual or virtual portraits that become
framed moments within the verbal text given over to description.
These arrest readers and alert them to the problem of embodied and
represented character.

The issue of the verbal representation of visual art and visual
illustrations of verbal texts received its classic treatment in Gotthold
Ephraim Lessing's *Laocoön*. It should be recalled that Lessing's discussion of the differences between visual and verbal representations
is a response to tendencies in aesthetic philosophy that assume the superiority of one or the other mode. What seems to be true in the case
of both painting or verbal art is that the action of framing, enclosing,
and outlining seems in itself to impose an absolute perspective; the
frame serves not so much as a break between the real and the repre-

sented worlds as an indexical arrow directed inward. Drawing a frame thus draws a conclusion, as if what has been chosen to be framed is intended to serve as the absolute symbol of itself.

Bakhtin's concern in the passage cited above seems to reflect a certain anxious conviction that the process of framing is so finalizing a movement that it will ultimately denude the painting or portrait of its potential meanings. But how does the death of multiple meanings become translated into the death of the person represented? Surely the viewer's sense of object permanence (understanding that the subject's life continues beyond the moment represented) constitutes a secondary frame around the original utterance, a porous and continually changing frame that allows for numerous re-visions of the original? Bakhtin seems to be concerned not with a general truth about painting but with the kind of painting that considers that it has told the truth; in other words, an "official" mode of portraiture in which the moment framed is believed to be a distillation of the ultimate truth about the subject. And since this ultimate truth about any living subject can only be constituted after death, the frame of the painting assumes the status of the black border of the obituary. The assumption that everything that needs to be told about an individual has been told in a portrait accomplishes the reduction of the self to the physical and thus ends the "inner" spiritual life.

As thus sketched, the portrait or bust becomes a death mask most clearly in the description of novelistic heroines, for whom beauty more often than not foretells doom. *Anna Karenina* may be read according to this overdetermined plot of beauty and fatality, yet the very fact of Anna's suicide forces us to confront the questions raised in chapter 2: does Anna's end reflect Tolstoy's enactment of divine punishment and participation in a judgmental gaze or does it represent his chastisement of a world and plot that allows no other conclusion? In comparison to the deaths of other literary heroines, Anna's suicide is distinctive both in terms of its placement in her narrative—she is not, in fact, abandoned by her lover—and in terms of her chosen means. Indeed, the literary antecedents for her leap beneath the train are male protagonists driven by shame and ruin: Dickens' Carker in *Dombey and Son* and Trollope's Lopez in *The Prime Minister.*

Viewed against this tradition, Anna's suicide acquires a masculine, even a heroic character and no longer seems to belong to that register of pathetic, fallen women who die for love or its lack.

As Nicole Loraux has observed, in classical literature, heroines met their death (whether it was murder, sacrifice, or suicide) in the throat: either by hanging, decapitation, or cutting of the throat.[19] Thus, in a textual movement of figural and literal decapitation, the portrait of Anna Karenina serves to prefigure her final enclosure in finitude. The action of severing the body from the head, the ornamental proclivities of a knotted rope or beading of blood, and, most important, the preservation of Anna's severed head from damage all suggest a form of framing—the heroine is transformed into a mute bust of immobile marble; she is ultimately seen as an inanimate objet d'art. Such an event occurs literally in *War and Peace,* where the statue executed to adorn the grave of the "little Princess" uncannily resembles her and seems to have the expression Prince Andrei had seen in her dying face.

In Victorian literature, heroines commonly lose their heads before dying. When Anna Karenina in the delirium of postpartum complications comments, "How badly painted those violets are, not like real flowers at all," she recalls those dying heroines who, like Ophelia, spend their last delirious hours counting and naming flora and fauna. In a similar way, Catherine Earnshaw Linton, dying during complications of labor, pulls feathers from her pillow and names the birds of the moor above Wuthering Heights. It is often the deathbed scene that offers the best subject for a dramatic pictorialization of the dying or condemned heroine, as Hardy well knew when his last view of Tess had her laid out like a sacrifice on the stones of Stonehenge, or as Flaubert capitalized on by having Emma Bovary's last act be that of contemplating her face framed in a mirror. Mirrors offer a natural opportunity to frame the heroine; Emily Brontë thus frames Catherine by having her look in a mirror that she takes to be the black press of her childhood room at Wuthering Heights. Like Anna Karenina who, before her last ride to suicide, looks in the mirror and does not recognize herself, Catherine does not understand that the "face in the press" is her reflection in the looking glass.

The death of criminals and adulteresses condemned to decapitation or hanging is usually deferred or concealed in Victorian fiction. The death of Tess of the D'Urbervilles is an example of an execution that is not witnessed but is instead signaled by the mounting of a black flag. Her dead body is not seen; it is only prefigured in the Stonehenge scene. Hetty Sorrel, the infanticide, is sentenced to be hung but is reprieved and her sentence is commuted. The bigamist and would-be murderess, Lady Audley, is spared capital punishment and confined in an asylum for the insane. Even for those adulteresses who engineer their own execution through suicide, public mutilation is usually avoided and death is courted through planned self-destruction à la Camille: exposure to the elements (Lady Dedlock), fasting prior to childbirth (Catherine Earnshaw Linton), murder invited (Nastasya Filipovna),[20] or illness not fended off (Lady Lynne). The latter heroines' demise could almost be construed as actual suicide, the chosen end of Emma Bovary or Anna Karenina.

Literary suicides can be divided into those that are driven by the plot and those that are ideological. Plots that require suicide involve ruin, failure, loss, or self-denial; ideas that require suicide involve existential crises, commitment to an ideology requiring suicide, or noble self-sacrifice. The former have come to be feminized, either according to the protagonist's gender or by reason of the failure of manhood. The latter are masculinized, even valorized, as a kind of warfare, as the courageous and willful resistance to destiny, plots, and social conventions. In the first instance the character succumbs to plot, but in the second the character rises above it.

A variety of types recur among plotted suicides in the nineteenth-century novel:[21] (1) the sensational suicide, the almost supernatural variety of self-destruction that overtakes Dickens' characters for example, propelling them under trains or into spontaneous combustion; (2) anorectic suicide, the self-willed death through inanition or exposure that is so common to the Victorian heroine; (3) the escapist suicide, committed in the face of social ruin, shame, or loss; (4) the romantic suicide, like the suicide of Werther, for example. By contrast, we might designate a nonplotted, or ideological suicide,[22] a suicide committed in service to a higher ideal, a heroic act of self-sacrifice offered in war or revolution, such as Sydney Carton's "far, far better thing" or Kirillov's suicide to prove a point. Akin to an ideological suicide would be a fictitious suicide, such as that staged by Sand's Jacques or Chernyshevsky's Lopukhov, who pretend to commit suicide in order to allow their wives to remarry the men they love. Within this last tradition is the hero of Tolstoy's *The Living Corpse*, who stages a pseudosuicide to allow his wife to marry her lover, Karenin.

Cultural attitudes toward suicide, whether real or fictional, tended to shift in the course of the nineteenth century as a result of the increasing treatment of suicide attempts as a medical problem. In popular representations on stage and in penny romances, suicides are prevailingly of the Ophelia variety, where the dying woman is seen as deranged or mentally ill or psychologically broken. An important example for *Anna Karenina* is Ostrovsky's play *The Storm*, where the adulterous heroine, although sympathetically portrayed, becomes hysterical prior to her suicide. Barbara Gates considers this tendency in the popular conception of suicide to be a "medicalization" or "feminization" of suicide, or, as Higonnet puts it, cultural attitudes began to "shift from a moralistic but potentially heroic vision of [suicide ideological suicide] to a more scientific yet demeaning acceptance of the act as illness."[23] Within this framework, it is has been easy for critics to read Anna's suicide as a weak, impulsive, and vindictive act. The shift from a view of suicide as a masculine heroic act to a view of it as an irrational, hysterical act resulting from feminine weakness or medical pathology emerges in a dichotomous literary representation of romantic versus ideological suicides.

The ideological suicide was not always masculine, as classical examples from Antigone to Joan of Arc suggest. Despite the fact that men's suicides outnumbered women's suicides in the nineteenth century,[24] the popular perception of the typical suicide as reflected in literature was of a woman crossed in love or fallen. In addition, according to Gates, "Many Victorians wanted to believe that 'redundant women' had really no place to go but toward death."[25] In part, this reflected a general perception in Victorian society of women as being afflicted by vapors, hysterics, female ailments, or a weaker nature.[26]

While there has been no study corroborating a similar phenomenon in Russia, popular literature in Russia perpetuated the same European stereotypes, beginning with Nikolai Karamzin's *Poor Liza*. Even Kitty in *Anna Karenina* succumbs to a wasting illness, an undiagnosable "female malady" ascribed to her broken heart. Although her illness is deconstructed by Tolstoy as a physical symptom of shame and distaste for the marriage market, Kitty comes close to accomplishing the kind of anorectic suicide that afflicted and carried away many a less resilient Victorian heroine.

Because the heroine's suicide is seen as plotted, inevitable, and in some sense natural to her sex, this very action of woman's suicide acquires a somatic, involuntary character. The heroine is drawn to her suicide as Dickens' suicidal heroine is drawn to the murky waters of the Thames. As Higonnet comments, "The voluntary act often appears involuntary; the quest for autonomy is replaced by breakdown of identity."[27] Thus, a heroine's suicide loses any ideological quality it may have had even as a form of social rebellion, which it was implicitly recognized to be. As Florence Nightingale wrote of women "starving for work" but trapped in the idle idyll of Victorian domesticity, "Some are only deterred from suicide because it is the most distinct way to say to an indifferent God: 'I will not, I will not do as Thou wouldst have me.'"[28] Alternately, suicide is the only possible closure for a life of disobedience or deviance, for it expresses the heroine's remorse for her sins. In this sense, the heroine's suicide reflects primitive cultural taboos, apparently still practiced, that require a woman to commit suicide following rape or dishonor. Thus, Higonnet concludes: "[E]ven those 19th century male writers most sympathetic to women's plight in bourgeois life subvert the heroism of women's voluntary deaths in their focus on social and masculine victimization; the reliance on social explanation which climaxes in the realistic novel . . . underplays the heroine's choice."[29]

The Execution of Anna Karenina

"The marvel," one critic has commented a propos of Tolstoy's "execution" of Anna, "is that Tolstoy had the patience and compassion to stay his hand as long as he did."[30] Anna's is generally considered a romantic and a plotted suicide that is essentially impulsive. As Konstantin Leontiev writes, "Anna leaves the house without any plan or decision; her decision is made almost instinctively, under the influence of chance impressions."[31] In fact, Anna contemplates suicide continuously and obssessively from the time of her final visit with her son and her appearance at the opera, which can be read as a scene of public execution and social death. Long before she even plans to leave the house, suicide is in the back of her thoughts:

> "I want love and there is none. So, then, all is over." She repeated the words she had said, "and it must be ended."
>
> "But how?" she asked herself, and she sat down in a low chair before the mirror.
>
> Thoughts of where she would go now . . . and many other ideas . . . came into her head; but she did not give herself up to them with all her heart. At the bottom of her heart was some obscure idea that alone interested her, but she could not get clear sight of it. Thinking once more of Aleksey Aleksandrovich, she recalled the time of her illness after her confinement, and the feeling which never left her at that time. "Why didn't I die?" and the words and the feeling of that time came back to her. And all at once she knew what was in her soul. Yes, it was that idea alone which solved all. "Yes, to die!" (774)

Anna's suicide is also ascribed to baser motives since she thinks, "And he will feel remorse; will be sorry; will love me; he will suffer on my account" (774). Yet this particular passage may also be understood, as Higonnet reads it, as Anna's attempt to create her own meaning for her life. In fact, her first thoughts are to eliminate the "shame and disgrace" experienced by her husband, son, and herself: "it will all be saved by my death."

Tolstoy himself did not characterize Anna's suicide as romantic in his caustic parody of the novel that was meant to reproach Katkov for suppressing the final part and publishing only a paragraph summarizing its events. Tolstoy suggested that Katkov might have spared himself the cost of printing the entire novel by publishing only an abstract: "Upset with things in Moscow, Anna Karenina commits suicide." Tolstoy's synopsis tellingly does not mention Vronsky, love, or Anna's status as a fallen woman. Furthermore, Anna's romantic plot does not demand that she commit suicide since Vronsky has not abandoned her—her fantasies about Vronsky's potential infidelities and abusive treatment of her create a motive for suicide from literary models, almost as though the suicide were her goal and the loss of her lover its necessary pretext.

Because of the philosophical reflections and observations that precede it, Anna's suicide has an ideological quality and it is not unreasonable to conclude that she commits suicide for the same reasons that Lyovin hides guns and ropes from himself at the novel's end. Both characters are aware of the existence of a senseless evil, as exemplified by Lyovin's thoughts:

> "In infinite time, in infinite matter, in infinite space, is formed a bubble-organism, and that bubble lasts a while and bursts, and that bubble is I."
>
> It was an agonizing fallacy. . . . But it was not merely a fallacy, it was the cruel jest of some wicked power, some evil, hateful power, to whom one should not submit.
>
> He must escape from this power. And the means of escape every man had in his own hands. He had but to cut short this dependence on evil. And there was one means—death. (822)

In this sense, Anna's pursuit of death begins as the culmination of her plot of rebellion and fall, but it continues as a presaging of modern existential despair, fear and trembling.

Anna fails at her attempt to die the death of the Victorian heroine—her puerperal fever is not fatal—nor does she succeed at the French route of poison through an accidental overdose of morphine, despite her addiction. Although Tolstoy's original intention was for Anna to commit suicide by drowning (a choice that would have been more in keeping with the traditional manner of women's suicide[32]), her death beneath the train is a more potent emblem of the theme of beauty and fatality. The viewing of the body by Vronsky gives us some indication of what Lyovin would have seen: "On the table shamelessly sprawled out among strangers, the blood-stained body so recently full of life; the head unhurt, thrown back with its weight of hair, and the curling tresses about the temple, and the exquisite face, with red, half-opened mouth, the strange, frozen expression, piteous on the lips and awful in the fixed open eyes" (813). Thus, Anna's suicide constitutes in some sense her final self-portrait. When we recall that in earlier drafts Lyovin's philosophical conversion was to proceed after he had viewed Anna's body at the station, the scene where he views her portrait can be read as a clear substitute. In the final version, it is an artist's portrait of Anna that Lyovin views but one no less transformative.

The moment of this viewing, which we are about to consider in the following chapter, is the site that unites the many themes of the novel: the issue of forgiveness and judgment, the framing that prefigures death and the enclosure of meaning, the iconicity of aesthetics that discloses meaning. The figure of the framed woman regarded by a viewer in the text sets up the mise-en-abîme for our viewing of Tolstoy's novel, itself a portrait, and makes our choice in the paradigm of judgment and execution a critical and inescapable one. In his discussion of painting, Roland Barthes comments that "the included observer is metonymic for our own observation . . . [and our] . . . follies of pattern hunting and obssessive frame mongering."[33] The interpretive failures of Joyce's Gabriel and Proust's narrator are indicative of the modernist response to a recognized symbolism and mirror our response to a doubly framed image, a text within a text. In the next chapter, we view Lyovin viewing Anna—woman and portrait—and thus are made aware of the direction of our own gaze and the degree to which the novel presents Anna as spectacle and implicates us in its specularity.

A Painted Lady: The Poetics of *Ekphrasis*

The Poetics of *Ekphrasis*

In *What Is Art?* Tolstoy discusses a play in which "the author wishes to transmit to the spectators pity for a persecuted girl. To evoke this feeling in the audience by means of art, the author should either make one of the characters express this pity in such a way as to infect everyone, or he should describe the girl's feelings correctly."[1] Instead, Tolstoy complains, most authors fail because they do not utilize these techniques but rely on verisimilitudinous or extreme effects. In *Anna Karenina* there is a spectator in the text who reflects the audience's act of viewing and judging the heroine we are meant to pity. The scene where Lyovin and Anna meet is preceded by Lyovin's viewing of Mikhailov's portrait of Anna. Lyovin's response to the artwork and to the actual woman infects the reader and simultaneously directs our gaze to Anna as a represented character, and to art—the portrait, the novel—as the means for infecting us with pity and compassion. Thus, the description of Lyovin's act of gazing and the verbal description of the visual work of art constitute an *ekphrasis* (the term is used here in the sense developed by classicists, that is, the verbal description of a visual work of art).[2] This moment allows Tolstoy the opportunity for meta-aesthetic commentary.

Roland Barthes describes *ekphrasis* as "a brilliant detachable morsel [of description], sufficient unto itself," and introduced solely for the "pleasure of verbal portraiture."[3] His surprisingly limited definition disregards the potential for *ekphrasis* to function not just as a description of art but as art criticism and meta-aesthetic discourse. For example, it is possible to read Homer's description of the shield forged by Hephaestus for Achilles as a pretext for describing the customs of the day; however, no one could read Virgil's description of Aeneas's shield in this fashion. Because of its intertextual relationship to Homer's description, the passage expresses a reflexivity and awareness of the value of art and description that Virgil employs to valorize Rome; as Lessing comments: "Homer makes Vulcan devise decorations because he is to make a shield worthy of a divine workman. Virgil seems to make him fashion the shield for the sake of the decorations."[4]

Similarly, since John Keats's extended *ekphrasis* in his "Ode on a Grecian Urn" exalts the classical ethos in its visual inscription, it also necessarily comments on form and on the apparent superiority of visual over verbal or aural representation: "Heard melodies are sweet, but those unheard /Are sweeter; therefore, ye soft pipes, play on; / Not to the sensual ear, but, more endear'd, / Pipe to the spirit ditties of no tone." On the one hand, the visual form is superior to other media because it preserves forever the ecstatic moment: "Forever panting, forever young." On the other hand, the ode comments on the representational conventions and constraints of that "Cold Pastoral." *Ekphrasis* thus establishes a tension between narrativity and stasis: in the ekphrastic moment, the stilling of the narrative flow required for ekphrastic exposition is renarrativized in the course of the temporally elaborated descriptions of the visual work of art. This paradox of modes returns us to the problem referred to in aesthetics by the term *ut pictura poesis* ("poetry is like painting"). This notion developed from a casual analogy in Horace's *Ars poetica* into a precept of aesthetics and literary theory that poetry *should* be like painting. The classical emphasis on *mimēsis* or imitation as the ultimate goal of a work of art informed the critical debate on the limitations of representation within and between the two media. The accepted notion, as stated by Longinus in his treatise *On the Sublime* and later developed by Burke in his *Philosophical Inquiry into the Origin of Our Ideas of the Sublime and Beautiful,* exalted the capacity of painting to represent things themselves. Poetry, on the other hand, could only "affect by sympathy rather than imitation; to display rather the effect of things on the mind of the speaker, or of others, rather than to present a clear idea of the things themselves (172).[5]

Ut pictura poesis thus engages the phenomenological issue of traditional aesthetics as to whether or not poetry constitutes thinking in images. This latter view implies that the contemplation or creation of images facilitates the primary cognitive processes associated with the preverbal or extraverbal states of childhood, mysticism, and ecstatic visions. The association of literary pictorialism with primal vision and epiphany privileges ekphrasis and, by extension, other descriptive moments in a text that organize visual perceptions in a pictorial manner. Such "framed" and "frozen" moments reflect the degree to which art is taken to inform and form our vision, and the extent to which vision is exalted as the conveyer of untranslatable and unnameable spiritual grace. The capacity of verbal texts to create vivid pictorial effects is seen as a fulfillment of energeia, expressed by the term hypotyposis, which Barthes claims may serve to place things right beneath the eyes of the listener, not in a neutral way but in a manner that releases into the representation all the force of desire ("mettre les choses sous les yeux de l'auditeur, non point d'une façon neutre, constative, mais en laissant à la representation tout l'éclat du désir").[6] When the hypotyposis is self-conscious, that is, aesthetically framed (ekphrastic), literary pictorialism becomes a commentary on all visual practice. Thus, as Mary Ann Caws suggests, this technique "makes a statement of coherence against the narrative flux and against the flux of our own time, so that our reading of frames and of the framed passages . . . is the model of not just reading, but of what, while reading, we live."[7]

The fact therefore that we organize our life experiences into narratives and our views of the world into pictures exposes us to the risk of being poor storytellers and mediocre artists. At worst, we are victims of the clichés and conventions that tell us how to make pictures; at best, our artistic structuring of experience lends coherence and epiphanic illumination to otherwise random and chaotic experience, and a sense of aesthetic closure weaves together the loose and unfinished, raveled threads of life. The danger is that we risk the enclosure that constricts, the form that deforms, or the representation that misrepresents.

A desire for coherence in the presentation of self or the quest for psychic unity and meaning in existence, the urge to contextualize life experiences, increases our desire for the end of the story or the frame of the picture. Thus, ominously, the desire for a finished self-portrait or a comprehensive icon is subtended by the death instinct, as critics like Mikhail Bakhtin and Peter Brooks have noted. As Jean-Paul Sartre commented about the process of writing his autobiography, "I became my own obituary."[8] Both the main protagonists of *Anna Karenina,* Anna and Lyovin, pursue meaning through visions, both rely on frames to secure understanding, and both find themselves drawn toward death. Their desire to frame and compose their views of self and their interpretations of life according to artistic models suggests that we may read them as artist figures.[9] Anna willfully completes her self-portrait by committing suicide while, in the essential contrast of the novel, Lyovin leaves his narrative unfinished and open ended and "goes on living." This contrast is overdetermined by the exigencies of plot and gender: many novelistic heroines, whose only two choices are oppression in marriage or liberation through death, "choose to die in order to shape their lives as whole."[10] Lyovin's vision of Anna, occurring at a critical moment in the novel when the intersecting trajectories of the two protagonists' lives emphasize their essential kinship and differences, is doubly marked as the viewing of a woman and the viewing of a representation of a woman. It is a great work of art, Mikhailov's portrait of Anna, that occupies central view.[11]

Lyovin's *Laocoön*

The power of the ekphrastic moments in *Anna Karenina* motivated John Bayley to draw the conclusion that Tolstoy's views on art "are expressed more powerfully in the narration of *Anna* than in his theoretical statements on art."[12] Certainly, the passages in *Anna Karenina* dealing with the artist Mikhailov and the other moments where art is discussed by the novel's characters allow Tolstoy to delineate the creative process and to comment on aesthetic theory. Thus, Lyovin's observations while attending a concert of modern music become a disquisition on aesthetics in general. In this episode, Lyovin attends a concert of Balakirev's *King Lear in the Steppe*,[13] a piece "in the modern style" of the Wagnerian *Gesamtkunstwerk*. During the entr'acte, Lyovin enters into a debate with his friend:

> Lyovin maintained that the mistake of Wagner and all his followers lay in their trying to take music into the sphere of another art, just as poetry goes wrong when it tries to paint a face, which is what should be left to painting, and as an instance of this mistake he cited the sculptor who carved in marble certain shadows of poetical images flitting around the figure of the poet on the pedestal. "These shadows were so far from being shadows that they were positively clinging to the ladder," said Lyovin. The comparison pleased him, but he could not remember whether or not he had used the same phrase before. (714)

Lyovin is right to question the originality of his statement. In fact, his habit of unconscious quotation overtakes him in this section of the novel, where the pressures of urban social life seduce him into a constant theft of bons mots in pursuit of the appearance of wit. For example, earlier in this chapter, Lyovin quips that punishing a revolutionary by exiling him to Europe is like casting a pike back into the water. Lyovin later realizes that he had "borrowed" the bon mot from an acquaintance who had read it in a newspaper article that in turn quoted from Krylov's fables. Lyovin's indictment of the sculptural (material) representation of poetic (intangible) ideas is similarly not original but derivative: it strongly echoes, at several points, Lessing's *Laocoön* (1766), the classic polemic on the Horatian precept of *ut pictura poesis*.

Lyovin wants to argue against the doctrine of *ut pictura poesis*; yet his sculptural example as he describes it does not serve as an apt illustration to support the separation of painting (specifically, portraiture) from poetry. The sculptural example is only effective when read against the intertext of *Laocoön*. Lessing's discussion focuses on the critical controversy over whether Virgil's description of the agony of Laocoön antecedes or is derivative of the classical sculpture of Laocoön being devoured by serpents, and it concludes with his famous theses on the need to modify the subject to accommodate different modes of representation. Imitating Lessing, Lyovin employs a

Statue of Laocoön in the Vatican Museum. Courtesy Alinari/Art Resource, New York.

sculptural work for his example, but he replaces the figure of the high priest Laocoön with the figure of a poet.[14] Lyovin describes the sculptural work as hampered by clinging shadows that were meant to represent "poetic ideas." We may see the shadows in terms of the Laocoön sculpture as a recasting of the serpents that encircle Laocoön and whose different positions in the two works (poem and sculpture) form the basis for much of Lessing's argumentation. In *The Aeneid* (2. 11. 305–307), the serpents mount Laocoön's body and engulf him totally: "Twice round his waist their winding volumes rolled, / And twice about his gasping throat they fold. / The priest thus doubly choked,—their crests divide, / And towering o'er his head in triumph ride" [Dryden]. As Lessing points out, a literal rendering of this description would have obliterated any visual expression of Laocoön's agony; therefore, the sculptor winds the serpents about Laocoön's wrists and ankles, "parts which might be concealed and compressed without injury to the expression . . . [and which] also convey the idea of arrested flight."[15]

Lyovin's clinging shadows illustrate the problem of the embodiment of the spiritual in the material: the indefinite, cerebral creative ideas of the poet are invisible mental constructs that manifest themselves only in the artist's own work and appear ridiculous when represented as concrete objects attendant upon it. Lyovin's image evokes Lessing's indictment[16] of the artistic conventions employed for representing the cloud of invisibility cast over the hero by the deus ex machina in classical canvases: the solution, a "cloud" painted to one side of the "invisible" figure, Lessing argues, is beyond "the limits of painting. His cloud is a hieroglyphic, a purely symbolic sign, which does not make the rescued hero invisible, but simply says to the observers, 'You are to suppose this man to be invisible.' It is no better than the rolls of paper with sentences upon them which issued from the mouths of personages in the old Gothic pictures."[17] The echo of *Laocoön* in Lyovin's brief treatise on aesthetics is enhanced by the subject of Lyovin's statue: a poet, surrounded by his poetic ideas; the creator about to create and seeking an appropriate embodiment for his artistic vision. The choice of flitting shadows to represent creative inspiration suggests a demonic rather than a divine source and raises the question of good and evil in creation.

Thus through Lyovin's illustration Tolstoy subtly debates the question of how or whether art may achieve its theurgic potential. This is an issue of central importance in the most sustained *ekphrasis* in *Anna Karenina*, the description of Mikhailov's painting *Pilate's Admonition*. Mikhailov's problem, as Anna, Vronksy, and Golenish-

chev perceive it, is how to represent a human, real Christ, or whether
such a representation is possible or even desirable; whether a spiritual
entity can be materially embodied or represented; whether divine or
demonic inspiration is required for such a manifestation; whether the
material representation deforms or profanes the spiritual.[18] Tolstoy's
indebtedness to Lessing is again discernible in the Platonic distinction he draws between Vronsky's dilettantism and Mikhailov's genius.
In *Laocoön* Lessing differentiates between artworks that imitate nature directly and those that imitate other artworks (imitations of imitations); the latter category, Lessing argues, utterly degrades the
artist; primacy of *mimēsis* is thus the criterion by which genius is distinguished from talent. Therefore, Vronsky is automatically indicted
as an epigone who cannot discriminate between truth and illusion (recall the memorable analogy of a man caressing a doll as if it were a
real woman) and who therefore paints after the style of other artistic
schools: "He appreciated all kinds [of art], and could have felt inspired by any of them; but he had no conception of the possibility of
knowing nothing at all of any school of painting, and of *being inspired
directly by what is within the soul,* without caring whether what is
painted will belong to any recognized school" (489) (emphasis
added). In contrast, Mikhailov paints directly from the heart: "I cannot paint a Christ who is not in my heart" (499), drawing inspiration
from "inner vision" (painting is "removing the coverings" from the
true insight) while "[Vronsky] drew his inspiration, not directly from
life, but indirectly from life embodied in art" (489). Thus it is that
Vronsky's portrait of Anna ("in Italian costume in the French style")
fails and remains unfinished while Mikhailov succeeds in creating a
portrait that "impressed everyone, especially Vronsky, not only by its
likeness, but by its characteristic beauty," and by its revelation of "the
very sweetest expression of [Anna's] soul" (501).

The Portrait

In his study of *ekphrasis* in the European novel, Mack Smith determines that Mikhailov's portrait is successful because it lives and

"stands out from its frame."[19] This organicist valuation of the creative process, which invests the created object with a life of its own, is exemplified in Mikhailov's experience with his sketch of a "man in a violent rage" onto which a drop of wax falls. The new shape lent to the figure by the drop of wax inspires Mikhailov. As he works, "(t)he figure, from a lifeless imagined thing, had become alive and could not be changed. The figure lived, and was clearly and unmistakably defined" (463). Mikhailov's view of the creative process, "removing the coverings from already existing figures," is counterpoised to Vronsky's belief in "technique." Victor Terras has glossed this passage as "a classical statement of the Neoplatonic organic concept of the creative process."[20] In his study of *War and Peace,* Gary Saul Morson terms this process "creation by potential," a notion opposed equally to the classical, programmatic/algorithmic principle of composition and to the romantic conception of poetic madness or the frenzy of inspiration caused by divine or demonic possession. The autonomous, organic status of the artwork suggests that the artist is not in full control of his text and that the work of art evolves autonomously and organically, developed by the artist's delicate manipulations, as Plotinus's sculptor "liberated" his vision of Beauty from the prison of the unformed block of marble.

Mikhailov's struggle to uncover the true forms within his art might be considered as exemplifying of the mode of sincerity Tolstoy would demand of the great artist in *What Is Art?* Tolstoy characterized art according to three main precepts:

1. An artist is successful if he or she succeeds in conveying through the force of his artwork his own genuine feelings (the work's "sincerity" and its capacity for "infection").
2. Art is successful only if it is universal; that is, if it is accessible to all people, regardless of their class, education, formation, culture, and any other characteristic.
3. A work of art succeeds as Christian art not necessarily because of its choice of Christian or biblical subject matter but because of its ability to inspire brotherly love and to unite humanity with divinity.

If we evaluate the three paintings by Mikhailov that we are shown in *Anna Karenina* according to Tolstoy's own aesthetic principles, we find that the painting *Pilate's Admonition* fails, despite its biblical subject matter and Mikhailov's sincerity, because, by Mikhailov's own admission, it requires education to understand it; even then Vronsky and Anna do not fully appreciate it. By contrast, the less ambitious secular painting of two boys fishing in a stream is a success, not merely because it infects the viewers with the bucolic mood of a lazy afternoon fishing expedition but because it appeals to a wide audience and, most important, stimulates the viewer's desire to share the thoughts and experiences of another: "Two boys were angling in the shade of a willow tree. The elder had just dropped in the hook and . . . was entirely absorbed in what he was doing. The other . . . was lying in the grass leaning on his elbows, with his tangled, flaxen head in his hands, staring at the water with his dreamy blue eyes. What was he thinking of?" (500).

By Tolstoy's own criteria, Mikhailov's portrait of Anna is the most successful artistic creation in the novel, and as such it is contrasted to the various other portraits of Anna presented in and by the text. In addition to the three painted versions and the verbal portraits sketched by other characters, there are Anna's own ekphrastically presented self-portraits; that is, Tolstoy's framings of Anna's presentations of herself as an art object. The most notable scenes in which Anna is overtly framed and aestheticized are her first and last public appearances at the ball in Moscow and at the opera in Petersburg. Anna's presentation of herself as spectacle and art object (portrait or bust) meant to be admired and desired for its beauty alone is contrasted in the novel to Lyovin's sublime visions of the world (landscapes) that become iconic emblems of his spiritual development. Thus, Tolstoy appears to perpetuate the romantic tradition of elevating the category of the sublime over that of the beautiful and preferring the landscape to the portrait.

Although described briefly in the section of the novel in which it is painted, Mikhailov's portrait of Anna receives its most sustained ekphrastic treatment in the scene where the novel's two leading protagonists meet, when Lyovin is coerced by his brother-in-law, Stiva, into visiting Anna. Tolstoy has been criticized for failing to exploit the full dramatic potential of this scene; for example, Boris Eikhenbaum characterizes the connection established at Anna's and Lyovin's meeting as a "light dotted line" having no significance for the plot.[21] In fact, their meeting inaugurates Lyovin's education or *Bildung*, which is achieved through his contemplation of an image.[22] So powerful and crucial is this scene that Joan Grossman has argued that the episode be regarded as the keystone in the arch of *Anna Karenina*,[23] although, on purely architectural grounds, the placement of the keystone in this chapter would make it asymmetrical to the novel's balanced structure, as elegantly diagrammed by Elisabeth Stenbock-Fermor.[24] If the scene is not the keystone, it is nonetheless highly demarcated and circumscribed in the text. Lyovin's viewing of the portrait is multiply framed and deeply imbedded in the narrative; the ornate setting of the portrait and its viewing similarly frame Anna's entrance, which is in turn framed by Lyovin's vision of her. The most exterior frames of this episode, the two occasions on which Lyovin and Stiva dine together, neatly bracket the novel structurally and thematically since both occasions serve as Platonic symposia where the various types of love are discussed, defined, and, on the second occasion, witnessed. Novelistically, and proleptically, the placement of the chapter in the plot serves as an additional frame. As has often been noted, Anna is contiguously and metaphorically located in a brothel, or women's quarters *(teremok)*.[25] In terms of temporal sequence, Stiva and Lyovin fulfill the novelistic convention of having dinner, drinks, playing cards, and then going off to _____ ; a notion that is rendered explicit by Kitty in her subsequent argument with Lyovin: "You were drinking at the club, drinking and gambling, and then you went . . . to her of all people!" (732). The setting of the scene is itself seductive: dark lighting, soft carpets, even the treillage reminiscent of the trellis work in the traditional Islamic *teremok,* from behind which Anna emerges. It is this context, in addition to what Lyovin knows of Anna's history, that informs his sense of guilt and embarrassment and predisposes him to a harsh judgment of Anna as a fallen woman.

In the dialogue with Stiva when they are en route to Anna, Lyovin reaffirms his attitudes toward fallen women and his negative expectations of Anna as he frames and stereotypes his projected image of her.

The reader is reminded of his disquisition on fallen women in the symmetrically opposed first dinner scene with Stiva: "I have a loathing for fallen women. You're afraid of spiders, and I of these vermin . . . those who know only the nonplatonic love have no need to talk of tragedy. In such love there can be no tragedy" (46).

As in their first dinner discussion, on this occasion Stiva tries again to solicit Lyovin's tolerance for human imperfection. As Stiva and Lyovin ride in the carriage to Anna's, Stiva attempts, in three short narratives, to win Lyovin over with his descriptions of Anna. Stiva's sketches are dialogized by Lyovin's resistance and by Stiva's own sense of verbal incompetence, as well as by their lack of fitness to frame the subject. Not only does Stiva fail to draw a portrait of Anna to his own satisfaction (he concludes each sketch by falling back on, "but you'll see for yourself. . . ."); the pictures of Anna he presents are unrecognizable even to the reader since they introduce events and actions that are new in the narrative. The resulting sense of estrangement (ostranenie) has the effect of distancing and renewal, so that we, like Lyovin, seem to be hearing about a stranger and anticipate seeing Anna as if for the first time. Stiva begins by describing Anna as "calm and dignified," when the reader last saw her in a state of psychic disintegration, rebelliously flouting social convention at the opera. Stiva then seeks to arouse Lyovin's sympathies by describing Anna's writing of childrens' books, but then he immediately negates this portrayal: "But are you imagining she's an authoress? Not at all." Finally, he attempts to present Anna as a "woman with a heart" who has adopted a protégée and her family, a description he proceeds to deconstruct: "It's not philanthropy. . . . She saw them, helped them, . . . But not by way of patronage. . . . But you'll see for yourself" (724). But prior to seeing for himself, Lyovin is aided by another, more accurate interpretation of Anna's character: Mikhailov's portrait.

Upon entering Anna's house, Lyovin's first action is to examine his face in the mirror. His face is red, but he denies to himself that he is drunk.[26] Lyovin's second action is to contemplate Mikhailov's portrait of Anna. The juxtaposition of the two portraits—one real in a mirror, the other so real it seems to step from its frame—reinforces our sense of Anna and Lyovin as alter egos, a view buttressed by the novel's structure, which continually juxtaposes parallel events from these two characters' lives. In psychoanalytic terms,[27] the act of viewing the "other" necessarily involves the projection of self; the conflation of portrait with reflection is emphasized linguistically by the description of a reflector lamp *(lampa-refraktor)* that overhangs Anna's portrait and suggests the double function of illumination and reflection. Lyovin's presence as the observer in the text mirrors the reader's role as voyeur and introduces the implicit comparison of Mikhailov's painted portrait with Tolstoy's verbal one. The ultimate effect of the framing of the heroine is to focus our attention, and to estrange us from our familiar interiorized relationship to Anna in order to see her through others' eyes. This makes Lyovin's mental and spiritual transformation before the painting all the more effective.

Lyovin's *Bildung* consists in his acceptance of human, specifically feminine imperfection, as expressed in his attitude toward "those vermin," fallen women, whom he has traditionally and conventionally stereotyped as vulgar, lower-class, uneducated, and lacking in the capacity for suffering or consciousness. His Victorian ("Dickensian," in Stiva's term) prejudice is well described by Anna, who thus defines Stiva's similar views on women to Dolly: "I know how men like Stiva look at it. . . . Their own home and wife are sacred to them. Somehow or other these [fallen] women are looked on with contempt by them. . . . They draw a sort of line that can't be crossed between them and their families" (76). Lyovin's encounter with Anna, an educated woman of high society with a complex, sensitive character, necessarily breaks the frame of his own expectations and provokes in him not the feeling of disgust he had anticipated but "a tenderness and pity which surprised him" (729). What brings about the birth of compassion and tolerance for human frailty and imperfection, a capacity for forgiveness that is the beginning of true faith on Lyovin's part? It is not simply a case of physical attraction, although Lyovin is by no means immune to Anna's attempt to "arouse in [him] a feeling of love" (733); yet even in this response we must ask if the resulting feeling is that of *erōs* or *agapē*. Lyovin's first examination of the portrait of a fallen woman of high society, coming immediately on the heels of his glimpse of his own guilty face "caught in the act," undermines his self-righteousness and harsh judgment of others and produces the requisite sense of humility. And then the portrait itself immediately enchants Lyovin:

> He could not tear himself away from it. He positively forgot where he was and not even hearing what was said, he could not take his eyes off the marvellous portrait. It was not a picture, but a living, charming woman, with black curling hair, with bare arms and shoulders, with a pensive smile on lips covered with soft down; triumphantly and softly she looked at him with eyes that baffled him. (725)

Lyovin is captivated not only by the exceptionally lifelike quality of the portrait, or by its beauty, but by the mysterious expression of Anna's eyes, a mystery that perhaps implies the inner life of the subject, which can only be represented enigmatically.[28] In its act of framing, the portrait paradoxically shows what cannot be framed. The viewer's response to beauty framed is to sense the sublimity of spirit that escapes those borders. Thus, Lyovin's vision of Anna is expanded rather than contained by the portrait, although when Anna first appears to Lyovin, she appears as "the very woman of the portrait . . . with the same perfection of beauty which the artist had caught" (725). But it is when Lyovin recognizes the disjunction between the Anna before him and the character of the ideal Anna in the portrait that he begins to appreciate and to commiserate her agony:

> [H]er face, suddenly taking on a hard expression, looked as if it were turned to stone. With that expression on her face she was more beautiful than ever; but the expression was new; it was utterly unlike that expression, radiant with happiness and creating happiness, which had been caught by the painter in her portrait. *Lyovin looked once more at the portrait and at her figure* . . . and he felt for her a tenderness and pity which surprised him." (729) (emphasis added)

By the end of the evening during which he "all the while was thinking of her inner life, trying to divine her feelings . . . though he had judged her so severely hitherto, now *by some strange chain of reasoning* he was justifying her and also sorry for her" (730) (emphasis added).

It is the portrait that leads Lyovin to wonder at the mysteries of

Anna's spiritual or inner life and thus to recognize the conflict and agony she endures. Lyovin achieves this understanding by "some strange chain of reasoning," because it is not by reason at all but by intuition and empathy, stimulated by contemplation of a true work of art that gives him insight. In a similar way, Vronsky had earlier marveled that Mikhailov, without knowing Anna, had managed to portray her soul: "'One has to know and love her as I have loved her to discover the very sweetest expression of her soul,' Vronsky thought, though *it was only from the portrait that he had himself learned* the sweetest expression of her soul" (501) (emphasis added).

Lyovin's revelation before Anna's portrait initiates the spiritual conversion he will achieve by the close of the novel: his acceptance of an intuitive faith that is not based on reason; his recognition of and tolerance for the imperfection of human life and his resulting compassion. Lyovin thus plays the role of Christ asked to judge the fallen woman. In response to the Pharisee's demand for judgment, Christ bent down in silence and began to write in the dirt, as if revising Mosaic law. While seeming to perpetuate the tradition of scribal elitism, Christ tempered its dicta by maintaining oral silence, thus drawing a distinction between the abstract realm of the logos and the real plane of human response. Forgiveness transforms even Kitty, who, although she condemns Lyovin for his compassion for Anna, will herself instantly forgive her when she sees her. Thus, Mikhailov's portrait fulfills Tolstoy's requisite for true Christian art as stated in *What Is Art?*: that it unite people in compassionate love.

Lyovin's viewing of Mikhailov's portrait of Anna is contrasted to an earlier scene where a portrait of Anna is also contemplated by a man sitting in judgment of her. In the chapter that follows the one in which Anna reveals to Karenin her liaison with Vronsky, Karenin attempts to pursue his usual evening's diversions after having written his wife a letter requiring her to continue their married life as before. He attempts to read a French work on the Eugubine Tables but finds himself unable to concentrate and instead contemplates his wife's portrait:

> Over the armchair there hung in a gold frame an oval portrait of Anna, a fine painting by a celebrated artist. Aleksey Aleksandrovich

glanced at it. The *unfathomable eyes* gazed ironically and insolently at him. Insufferably insolent and challenging was the effect, in Aleksey Aleksandrovich's eyes, of the black lace about the head, admirably done by the painter, the black hair and handsome white hand with one finger lifted, covered with rings. After looking at the portrait for a minute, Aleksey Aleksandrovich shuddered, so that his lips quivered, and uttered the sound "brrr." (301) (emphasis added)

Karenin proceeds to solve not the mystery of his wife's "unfathomable gaze," which he now interprets as insolence, nor the (for him) unsolvable mystery of the Eugubine Tables, but "a complication that had arisen in his official life" (301). Anna, like the Eugubine Tables, remains a cipher.[29] The effect of the black lace about the head and the "insolent" expression both recall Anna's earlier appearance at the ball and predict her later fatal appearance at the opera. In both public appearances, Anna is depicted as an aesthetic object, framed by her attire.

At the ball:

Anna was not in lilac, as Kitty had so urgently wished, but in a black, low-cut, velvet gown, showing her full shoulders and bosom that looked as though *carved of old ivory,* and her rounded arms, with tiny, slender wrists. The whole gown was trimmed with Venetian lace. In her black hair, all her own, was a little wreath of pansies, and there were more of the same in the black ribbon winding through the white lace encircling her waist. Her coiffure was not striking. All that was noticeable were the little wilful tendrils of her curly hair that would always break free about her neck and temples. Around her finely *chiseled,* strong neck was a thread of pearls. . . . Now [Kitty] understood that Anna could not have been in lilac, and that her charm was just that *she always stood out from her attire,* that her dress could never be conspicuous on her. And her black dress, with its sumptuous lace, was not conspicuous on her; *it was only the frame and all that was seen was she.* (85) (emphasis added)

In contrast to Anna, who is presented both as a chiseled ivory statue and as a work of art within a frame, Kitty appeals in such a way that her attire is part and parcel of her character, "as if she had been born in that tulle and lace, with her hair done up high on her head and a rose and two leaves on the top of it" (83). Despite the apparent "natural" quality of Anna's coiffure and toilette, the reader recognizes, with some irony at Kitty's expense, what the more experienced Dolly will later understand as she examines Anna's gown: "Anna had put on a very simple batiste dress. Dolly scrutinized that simple dress attentively. She knew what it meant, and the price at which such simplicity was obtained" (645). It is a supreme artistry that creates the impression of being natural whereas only genuine innocence could render the frills and furbelows of Kitty's attire natural.

Anna's conscious presentation of herself as an aesthetic object is even more pronounced in the later scene where she attends the opera. As in the ballroom scene and in the portrait contemplated by Karenin, lace is again the framing feature. In fact, this scene becomes an enactment of the features Karenin sees in the portrait, while Vronsky's role and reactions throughout this chapter parallel those of Karenin in the earlier scenes between Anna and her husband. Vronsky now assumes Karenin's role as Anna becomes a "closed book" (or cipher) to him:

> He looked at her with searching eyes, but she responded with that defiant, half-mirthful, half-desperate look, *the meaning of which he could not comprehend.* . . . Anna was already dressed in a low-necked gown of light silk and velvet that she had had made in Paris, with costly white lace on her head that *framed her face* and was particularly becoming, *setting off her dazzling beauty.* (569) (emphasis added)

In the following exchange, Vronsky, "appealing to her exactly as her husband once had done" (570), feels an increasing hostility toward Anna as his respect for her diminishes, "although his sense of her beauty [is] intensified" (570). After pursuing her to the opera, Vronsky watches as Anna, framed by the proscenium of her opera box, upstages the diva:

> Vronsky . . . caught sight of Anna's head, proud, strikingly beautiful, *and smiling in the frame of lace. The setting of her head* . . . reminded

him of her just as he had seen her at the ball in Moscow. But he felt
utterly different toward her beauty now. In his feeling for her now
there was no element of mystery, and so her beauty, though it at-
tracted him even more intensely than before, now offended him too.
(573) (emphasis added)

Vronsky feels no sense of mystery, although he has never understood
Anna less than at this moment, when he is ignorant of her tragic
meeting with her son and cannot comprehend her behavior. What
Vronsky sees in Anna's self-portrait is the presentation of beauty without barriers to the sexual knowledge he has of her; as a result, his
aesthetic experience of Anna is empty and superficial, virtually pornographic, and therefore offensive.

Such a reading is defensible when we recall Tolstoy's later dictum
in *What Is Art?* that true art requires no ornament or technique
while false art relies on convention and decorations. In his famous
analogy, Tolstoy argues:

> However strange it may be to say this, the art of our time and circle
> has undergone that same thing that happens to a woman, whose fem-
> inine charms, destined for motherhood, are sold for the satisfaction
> of those who lust after such satiations.
>
> The art of our time and circle has become a fallen woman. . . .
> It is just as made-up, just as commercialized, just as deceptive and
> ruinous. . . .
>
> True art does not require any adornment, like a wife beloved of
> her husband. False art, like a prostitute, must always be adorned.[30]

Anna as a fallen woman, is contrasted in the novel to Dolly, who is
concerned about her appearance only as the mother of her children:
"Now she did not dress for her own sake, not for the sake of her own
beauty, but simply so that, as the mother of those exquisite creatures
[her children], she might not spoil the general effect" (278). Despite
her lack of feminine vanity, however, Dolly is no stranger to the impulse to be aestheticized in a picture, although in her case it is as the
mother of "exquisite creatures" that she desires to be framed. Thus,
meeting Lyovin as she is bathing with her children, "she was espe-

cially glad he should see her in all her glory. No one was able to appreciate her grandeur better than Lyovin. Seeing her, he found himself face to face with one of the *pictures of family life his imagination painted"* (282) (emphasis added). When Dolly exclaims, "How glad I am to see you!" the reader easily discerns that her pleasure is not in seeing but in being seen by Lyovin in a flattering picture.

In contrast to Dolly and Anna's narcissistic self-portraits, Mikhailov's portrait of Anna is transcendent. The revelatory effect of Anna's portrait on Lyovin is reminiscent of his response to a vision of Kitty earlier in the novel: a vision that, like the portrait of Anna, constitutes an *ekphrasis* and radically revises his world view. Following a night spent with the peasants after the harvest, during which Lyovin experiences a false epiphany and considers marrying a peasant woman, he catches a glimpse of Kitty traveling to her estate, framed by the window of her carriage: "At the window, evidently only just awake, sat a young girl holding in both hands the ribbons of a white cap. With a face full of light and thought, *full of a subtle, complex inner life* that was remote from Lyovin, she was gazing beyond him at the glow of the sunrise" (293) (emphasis added). Lyovin, struck by this portrait of Kitty, realizes the full falsity of his previous night's epiphany and acknowledges that the solution to the mystery of his life rests with her.

Whenever Lyovin attempts to find solutions to his philosophical dilemmas, he creates pictures by framing the vision of the real world before him and using it as an emblem or icon of his thoughts and experience. Thus, in his rodomontade in the passage preceding his vision of Kitty, Lyovin observes a "strange mother-of-pearl shell of fleecy white cloudlets" (293) in the sky that he "takes as a symbol of [his] ideas and feelings" (294) concerning the formation of his new views of life: "Just now I looked at the sky and there was nothing in it—only two white streaks. Yes, and so imperceptibly too my views of life changed!" Similarly, on the morning of his betrothal to Kitty, "what Lyovin saw then he never saw again" (424): a fortuitous, synchronic composition of birds, freshly baked loaves and children at play, drawn into a visual composition that crystallizes his spiritual state of ecstasy.

In the earlier passage, after Kitty's carriage disappears over the horizon, Lyovin glances at the sky to find that the shell has gone: "There in the remote heights above, a mysterious change had been accomplished. There was no trace of a shell, and there was stretched over fully half of the sky an even cover of tiny and ever tinier cloudlets" (294). Both images, the shell and the cover, suggest containment, physical exteriors that embody spiritual essences, and thus incorporate the theme of representation. Lyovin makes his vision stand as an emblem of the natural law of flux, of constant change and variation, of the impossibility of fixing the world and himself in an eternal state of perfection. This recognition makes possible his later acceptance of life as spiritual struggle in an ongoing process, and of himself as an imperfect creature with the intent of perfecting himself and the knowledge that this intent is as sufficient as the achievement of perfection. At the close of the novel, he accepts not only these facts but also his own flawed nature that resists process and seeks finalization by attempting to stop time and to preserve moments in a "frozen," "framed" state.

Thus, at the novel's conclusion, Lyovin acknowledges both the dangers of framing and, paradoxically, the salvific potential of such visions. Once he recognizes the limitations of earthbound vision, he can allow his tendency to organize the world into symbolic landscapes to enhance his nonrational, intuitive approach to faith without falling prey to the dangers of trusting his insight too much. Lyovin's sense of limits and acceptance of the bounded field of bodily experience that cannot contain transcendence constitutes Tolstoy's restatement of the Kantian definition of the sublime, as discussed in chapter 3. Lyovin's final epiphanic picture of the sky is bordered and framed by his awareness of his narrow scope of sight and his appreciation of the value of the sensation of limits:

> Lying on his back, he gazed up now into the high cloudless sky. "Do I not know that that is infinite space, and that it is not a rounded vault? But, however I screw up my eyes and strain my sight, I cannot see it but as round and finite, and in spite of my knowing about infinite space, I am incontestably right when I see a firm blue vault, far more right than when I strain my eyes to see beyond it." (833)

Tolstoy closes Lyovin's narrative on an exaltation of the experience of the sublime realized through the traditionally romantic vehicle of the awe-inspiring landscape. Yet this is an experience of the sublime that carries Lyovin away from human relations, which now irritate him as distractions from his spiritual growth. Indeed, he finds the mood of ecstasy difficult, if not impossible, to reconcile with the daily events and human interactions of prosaic existence, which "momentarily overshadow" his state of grace. By contrast, his viewing of Anna's portrait brought him into harmony with humanity and made it possible for him to empathize even with someone completely different from himself. Anna's portrait thus belongs in the category of the iconic and is superior to the mode of the sublime; it is a transcendent portrait that implies the continual process of perfectivization through living experience.

Lyovin's final vision is contrasted to the series of streetscapes Anna views through the frame of her carriage window en route to her suicide: she interprets these pictures as profane projections of the vanity fair and cartoonish illustrations of unmitigated human greed and self-delusion. The hyperrealist, almost naturalist, depictions of dirty ice cream and grotesque visages are neither sublime nor iconic. Instead, Anna is seduced by an implacable realism and a photographic objectivity into making these scenes stand as accurate portrayals or "physiological sketches" of the human condition. Unaware of her own hermeneutic action of framing and reading, she accepts her frame of mind as the objective truth and the candlelight by which she reads her "book filled with troubles, falsehoods, sorrow, and evil" (799) as the ultimate and final illumination.

PART III

Illuminations: Reading Detail and Design in *Anna Karenina*

"Tolstoy Resting in the Forest" by I. E. Repin, 1891

Knife, Book, and Candle:
The Resisting Russian Reader

> [The] picture of her holding but not exactly reading a
> book is both memorable and significant. It is the
> conscious heroine's characteristic posture.
> Rachel Brownstein, *Becoming a Heroine*

> Seeing herself as a creation—
> Clarissa, Julie, or Delphine—
> by writers of her admiration,
> Tatyana, lonely heroine,
> roamed the still forest like a ranger
> sought in her book, that text of danger.
> Pushkin, *Eugene Onegin*

> There is no happiness in love, except at the end of
> an English novel.
> Trollope, *Barchester Towers*

> The best books are English.
> Tolstoy

Anna's Novel

A major criticism often leveled at the author of *Anna Karenina* is that
he failed or refused to provide the reader with the biography of his
heroine, as is traditionally expected of the nineteenth-century novel:
we are denied, complained Percy Lubbock, the information we need
about "Anna's past and present, the kind of experience that has made

her and that has brought her to the point she now touches. Without this her action is arbitrary and meaningless."[1] While many novels open in medias res or delay the introduction of the main protagonist for several chapters, the seventeen chapters that precede Anna's appearance strike many readers as excessive, especially as the author ignores the opportunity to offer any biographical information at all, either through indirect or authorial discourse. A similar delaying tactic confused the first readers and critics of *War and Peace* who were uncertain as to the identity of the main protagonists.[2] In contrast to *War and Peace,* the title *Anna Karenina* clearly identifies the novel's heroine and places the work within a tradition of biographical novels that often begin with an account of generations of family history preceding the hero or heroine's birth and childhood. This makes Tolstoy's silence about Anna all the more striking. The adultery plot, the problematic epigraph, and the novel's thematic concerns with the woman question heighten many readers' desire for the very information denied them: specifically, how Anna came to be married to Karenin, easily the single most important moment in the heroine's biography, what George Eliot called the "determining act of her life."

Summarizing the plot of *Anna Karenina,* Vladimir Nabokov could not resist the novelist's habit of improving on a tale in the retelling of it and thus begins his outline of the novel with precisely the information and chronology Tolstoy denied it: "Married off as a very young girl by a well-meaning aunt. . . ."[3] As Nabokov no doubt intended, certain qualifiers leap into the comfortable syntactic slots prepared for them by years of syntagmatic associations, prodded by the "very" of "very young girl": "Married off *against her will* as a very young girl by a well-meaning *but misguided* aunt. . . ."

In fact, Tolstoy began his notes for the novel with this rather different account of Anna's marriage: "She marries under good *auspices.*" The word *auspices* is in English in Tolstoy's notes, so that in the first sentence of his first draft outline, Tolstoy evokes the Victorian novelistic tradition within which he will place his heroine and suggests the kind of "good auspices" that in the Victorian English context might imply wealth, status, estate, but not romantic love. The reader is deprived of this information in the final version of the novel: we never learn the precise circumstances of Anna's courtship by Karenin except in rather vague, poetical terms from Anna when she is speaking to an admiring Kitty, and in a bitter moment from Karenin, who now rewrites his entire experience of courtship and marriage as a plot that victimized him.

The reader experiences the desire to hear Anna's story in the scene where Anna is romanticized by Kitty: "Kitty felt that Anna was perfectly unaffected . . . but that she lived in another, higher world full of complex poetic interests beyond Kitty's reach" (65). Like Kitty, the reader views Anna as a heroinic figure, an angel of mercy who has reconciled Stiva and Dolly, who wins the affection of all who meet her, and who is beloved by children. Anna encourages Kitty to exalt her by offering her a mystifying, fragmentary autobiography concocted out of conventional, novelistic discourse, complete with the romantic alpine topography of mountaineering as biography and heroic destiny: "I remember and I know that blue haze like the mist on the mountains in Switzerland. That mist which covers everything in that blissful time when childhood is just ending, and out of that vast circle, happy and merry, there is a path growing narrower and narrower . . . and you enter the corridor gladly yet with dread, though it seems bright and beautiful. . . . Who has not passed through it?" (79).

Kitty's thoughts express the reader's own curiosity: "'But how did she go through it? How I would like to know the whole romance novel [*roman*] of her life,' thought Kitty, remembering the unpoetical appearance of Aleksey Aleksandrovich, her husband" (67).

Tolstoy does not give us Anna's past history to read because he considers her story *"déjà lu,"* already cast in the predetermined plot of the nineteenth-century European novel, a plot that is invoked by Anna's reading of a highly conventional English novel at the crucial moment in her own story. Tolstoy intended his reader to write Anna's story according to the intertext of the Victorian novel that she reads. Furthermore, Anna's attraction to the Victorian reality presented in the realist novel she reads reveals the seductive power of those fictions that promise a coherent and fulfilled life buttressed by social and moral structures. Anna's desire to be the heroine in an English novel is thus the desire to occupy a fixed social role or position,[4] represented as offering total fulfillment. In the world of the Victorian novel, there is no dysphasia or slippage between the inner and the social self. Anna's yearning for fixity is replicated in her desire to be inscribed heroini-cally and in her impulse toward aestheticization, with the act of read-ing suggesting self-determination. As J. Hillis Miller observes, the Vic-torian novel thus specifically negotiates the issue of the containment of the irrational self within a suture of social position and social role:

> Victorian fiction raises for the 20th century reader the dark question of whether the assimilation of the protagonists into the community by way of a happy relation to another person is a valid resolution, or whether, to our deeper insight, it should appear as a covering over and forgetting of the fundamental fact of human existence so perva-sively dramatized in the body of the book—in the drive for some "il-limitable satisfaction."[5]

Anna Karenina responds to the type of realism that demands that the "end of the novel, like the end of a children's dinner-party, must be made up of sweetmeats and sugar-plums,"[6] rounding off with an epilogue wherein the characters find themselves neatly paired off and settled down.

As Nancy Miller argues, although the Victorian novel may appear feminocentric in plot structures, the standard plots in fact, allow the heroine only two viable choices—marriage or death. Thus, the Victo-rian novel is actually phallogocentric in ethos.[7] These tendencies in Victorian fiction inform Tolstoy's description of Anna's anxiety in reading. Tolstoy depicts the blocks in Anna's process of identification with the text she reads to point to the exclusionary practices of Victo-rian realism.

The Resisting Russian Reader

The English novel first appears in Anna's hands when she assumes a position that is privileged throughout the novel, riding in a moving vehicle, a carriage, or train with a view onto the world through a win-dow.[8] In addition to the framing function of her carriage windows, the novel Anna reads provides an additional frame or view onto a textual world that she illuminates with her candle. The movement of the train is isomorphic to her progress through the text and through life, and predictive of its end. Anna thus takes up the now familiar pose of the heroine succumbing to the dangerous or pernicious influence of literature, a topos that dates back in the European tradition to the transgressing lovers in Dante and the originary deluded consumer of chivalric romances, Don Quixote. Among Quixote's many successors, the women have seemed to outnumber the men. Barthes comments in *S/Z*: "This is a vast commonplace of literature: the Woman copies the Book. In other words, every body is a citation: of the 'already-written.' The origin of desire is the statue, the painting, the book."[9]

Feminist criticism has made us aware of the ways in which the literary figure of women reading literature is complicated by their immersion in an alien or other ("phallogocentric") discourse: "In such fictions the female reader is co-opted into participation in an experience from which she is explicitly excluded; she is asked to identify with a self-hood that defines itself in opposition to her; she is required to identify against herself."[10] Reading an other's discourse has its parallel in the Russian literary tradition, where "otherness" is built into the reading experience; where reading has generally meant reading a strange, foreign text, usually in a foreign language. The diglossic situation of the Russian nobility, who used French for literary purposes and conversation and who, as a result, often had a poor command of their native tongue, was a complicating factor in the development of Russian belles lettres and was ridiculed by Tolstoy in *War and Peace*. Thus, gender issues aside, the image of a Russian reading a European work of literature already presents a problematic awareness of a literary tradition that has been characterized by an agonizing self-consciousness of its own derivative nature and a struggle for originality. The absence of a developed, native Russian literary tradition and, indeed, of a developed literary language aggravated the Russian attitude of condescension toward what was perceived as the decadent, moribund Western artistic tradition, which Russian artists were eager to borrow from in order to supersede.[11] The situation has often been compared to that of American letters: Henry James, for example, commented that to be an American entailed the "responsibility of fighting against a superstitious valuation of Europe."[12] It is against this background that we understand Dostoevsky's triumphant acclamation of *Anna Karenina* for being superior to any European novel.[13] In the Russian literary tradition, the very act of reading was fraught with the anxiety of reading a nonnative, "other" *(chuzhoi)* literature, and the act of reading a novel made the issue even more worrisome, since there was no novelistic tradition in Russia until the mid-nineteenth century and, most emphatically, no genuine novel of manners in the Russian tradition at all.

When, therefore, in what is arguably the first Russian novel (Alexander Pushkin's novel in verse, *Eugene Onegin* [1825]), Tatiana Larina opens her book and becomes the primordial Russian reading heroine, it is the French or English romance she peruses; without such diversion, cast back upon her native literature, she must seek refuge either in chapbooks, popular Church literature, or folklore: casting spells to conjure the name or image of her future spouse, interpreting dreams with Zadeck's dream book.[14]

Tatiana, whose name Tolstoy used for his heroine in the early drafts of *Anna Karenina*,[15] is described as a pale, dreaming consumer of epistolary novels, so immersed in foreign literary conventions that she writes her love letter to Eugene in French, a fact the narrator laments:

> I can foresee a complication:
> My country's honor to defend,
> I'll have to furnish a translation
> Of Tanya's letter in the end.
> She knew our language only barely,
> Read Russian magazines but rarely;
> In her own language she was slow
> To make her meaning clear, and so
> She wrote in French, be it admitted . . .
> I cannot help it, it is true:
> To speak milady's love, but few
> Have thought our native language fitted,
> Our haughty Russian hardly knows
> How to adjust to postal prose.
>   (3.26)[16]

Tatiana is only liberated from her romantic, literary dreams of Eugene when she invades her beloved's library in his absence and reads not just his books but, taking his library as a larger text, also his choice of books and marginalia. Thus she reads in the margins to read his reading and is disillusioned simultaneously with her beloved, with literature, and with the reading of literature as a reading of life ("life's novel"):

> And step by step my Tanya, learning
> His mind, at last begins to see
> The man for whom she has been yearning
> By willful destiny's decree
> More clearly than by face and feature:
> A strangely bleak and reckless creature,
> Issue of Heaven or of Hell,
> Proud demon, angel—who can tell?
> Perhaps he is all imitation,
> An idle phantom or, poor joke,
> A Muscovite in Harold's cloak,
> An alien whim's interpretation,
> Compound of every faddish pose . . .?
> A parody, perhaps . . . who knows?
>   (7.24)[17]

By opening a novel, Anna evokes Tatiana, but she is not a romantic escapist; instead, Victorian "realist" literature even more perniciously seduces Anna with scenes of domestic life and high estate rather than with scenes of romantic passion.

Ruined by Realism

As a reader, Anna succumbs to the novel as directive and stimulant. The power of the text is thus revealed immediately as a generator of mimetic initiation: Anna no sooner reads of an event than she longs to inscribe it in her own life. In describing this process, Tolstoy subtly interrogates Kant's designation of the aesthetic response as "disinterested" and illustrates his own theory of art as infectious. Anna's response is greater than a simple identification: the book becomes a microcosm of the society in which Anna seeks to read herself, a frame for the scene, a proscenium for the stage on which she will take up her role. Yet in her own moment of reading by candlelight, Anna is both a Russian reading a novel that is essentially alien and a woman, blocked by the phallogocentricity of the novel she reads. In order to allow the *mise en abîme* to occur, Anna's reading must project her into a marginalized and silent role in the text.

As one feminist critic notes, the consensus demanded by realist narrative "is the reader's only means for gaining access to the story; the very act of reading thus entails acceptance of the view that the world is a common world, a 'human world,' a world that is the 'same' for everyone."[18] Tolstoy's quarrel with the Victorian novel is based on his polemic with a literary realism that precludes the reality of certain other viewpoints in terms of culture, class, or gender. As early as 1851 Tolstoy wrote in his diary about the problem of writing "for the people" from the perspective of an aristocrat, invoking the analogy of the problem of gender identification in reading: "A sixteen-year-old boy, when he reads a scene in a novel about the seduction of the heroine, isn't roused to a feeling of indignation by it and doesn't put himself in the unfortunate woman's position, but involuntarily transfers himself to the role of the seducer and delights in a feeling of sensuality."[19]

Tolstoy's exploration of Anna's reading processes develops this early observation further. As Anna reads the realist English novel, she passionately accepts its realism as offering roles she could adopt; the narratives she reads are so many windows onto so many worlds; yet none of them offers a genuine outlet for her desires that thus become repressed and frustrated. Indeed, sublimated desire and repression color the language and imagery of this passage, as Gustafson has recently shown.[20]

Anna's reading takes place by candlelight in semidarkness, in a setting of flickering shadows and flame. This atmosphere recalls Plato's cave analogy from Book VII of *The Republic*, where deluded spectators in a gloomy cave watch (as Anna does in the train) "flicker-

ing figures in the twilight."[21] The Russian *litso* (literally face, here figure) in this passage recalls theatrical nomenclature and emphasizes
Anna's spectatorial role. Anna initially finds herself unable to concentrate on her book, but as she succumbs to the monotony of the same
flickering figures, her resistance to the text is overcome; she loses the
sense of the barrier between the fictive and the real world, which
now becomes a shadow-puppet theater, a world of Platonic shadow
knowledge.

Anna thus passes from being reluctant to read (*"Pervoe vremia ei
ne chitalos"*) to beginning to "read and to understand what she read."
As Anna disappears into the text, her alter ego, Annushka, falls into a
doze, symbolizing Anna's "sleeping" conscious mind. Anna feels discomfort as she reads (*ei nepriiatno bylo chitat*) because, "to follow
the reflection of other people's lives" arouses desires in her that cannot be fulfilled:

> [I]t was unpleasant for her to read, that is, to follow the reflection of
> other people's lives. She had too great a desire to live herself. If she
> read that the heroine of the novel was nursing an invalid, she longed
> to move with noiseless steps about the room of an invalid; if she read
> of a member of Parliament making a speech, she longed to be deliv-
> ering that speech; if she read of how Lady Mary had ridden after
> hounds and had provoked her sister-in-law, and had surprised every-
> one by her boldness, she wished to be doing the same thing herself.
> (106–107)

The three narratives Anna reads pose the problem of her blocked
identification with a text or vision of male-determined heroinism.
Her first identification is with a woman nursing a (male) invalid; a role
of service and one of the few socially acceptable careers for an unmarried woman, apart from that of governess.[22] It is this role that is
adopted by Varenka, the only spinster in the novel, and it is into this
role that Kitty, seeking her own heroinic resolution at the spa in Ger-
many, will project herself in emulation of her romanticized vision of
Varenka. Kitty considers Varenka a model or icon (*obrazets*) of "a dig-
nity in life—apart from the worldly relations of girls with men, which

so revolted [Kitty], and appeared to her now as a shameful hawking about of goods in search of a purchaser" (228).

But the role of attendant nurse is too oppressive for Anna. As Anna reads her part, she is forced to desire *(ei khotelos)* to walk *silently,* with "silent footsteps" *(neslyshnymi shagami),* to minimize her presence, effacing herself in the very process of taking action. It is interesting that one of Anna's most memorable features is precisely her unusually light and graceful step, out of proportion to her full figure: "She went out with the rapid step that bore her rather fully developed figure with such *strange lightness*" (69) (emphasis added). It is also "her swift, firm and light step which distinguishe[s] her from all other society women."

The text moves from silent action to enforced silence and censorship as Anna attempts to identify with a member of Parliament giving a speech, a desire that can only be totally blocked and frustrated: women have no voice, no representation in Parliament, no possibility for making themselves heard. Such is the recurrent lament of the women in Trollope's novels: for example, Lady Laura complains, "'A woman's life is only half a life, as she cannot have a seat in Parliament,'"[23] while Madame Max laments, "'What would I not give to be a member of the British Parliament. . . . The one great drawback to the life of a woman is that they cannot act in politics.'"[24] So strong is the enticement to politics that women in Trollope's novels are tempted to marry for politics: they (Alice Vavasour, Lady Laura Kennedy) hope to participate in Parliament vicariously, with their husbands acting as proxy, while Lady Glencora views her husband's appointment as Prime Minister as the opportunity to have "a cabinet of her own," a role at which she is so successful that her husband begins to entertain the "awful suspicion" that it was she who was Prime Minister, not he.

Frustrated in her attempts to identify with an oppressed woman or with a man with whom she cannot identify, Anna identifies a third time, with a woman rebelling against her oppression, riding to hounds and flouting social conventions. Anna's desire for this role is more strongly expressed than in the previous two identifications: "she felt like" *(ei khotelos)* becomes "she felt like doing that herself" *(ei khotelos èto delat' samoi)*. Anna's desires are checked, however: "But there was no possibility of doing anything" *(No delat' nechego bylo)*. There is no possibility of action within the world or within the novel she reads; she is as confined by the text as she is by the carriage or by the social sphere she occupies. Her only escape may be through the imagination. Anna therefore renews her reading with the desire to escape: "She intensified her reading" *(usilivalas' chitat')*. The novel has reached its climax and as she reads, her desire increases from "she felt like" *(ei khotelos)* to "she desired" *(ona zhelala)*: "The hero of the novel had almost attained his English happiness, a baronetcy and an estate, and Anna was feeling a desire to accompany him to his estate" *(s nim vmeste ekhat')* (107). Anna's position in the text she reads has become marginalized; she cannot "do it herself" *(delat' èto samoi)* but must "accompany" the protagonist. Thus she projects herself into the text as an ancillary viewpoint through a cross-identification. Blocked by gender difference from a full identification with the hero, she desires instead to accompany him. Anna's repressed identification with the hero as the embodiment of her own desire causes a vacillation between passive-aggressive modes. The oscillation in identification produced by the enforced passivity of her role as a woman results in what feminist critics term a "transvestite" or "hermaphroditic" identification with the male protagonist.[25]

The novel thus leads Anna into adultery through the evocation of desire for action, its frustration, and the displacement of desire onto a liaison with the male protagonist. The pursuit of English happiness brings about Anna's fall; she is seduced by visions of estate, not by that romantic "chorus" of voices of adulterous heroines that corrupts Emma Bovary.

Tolstoy's shift from the romantic presentation of adulterous heroines in the continental novel to Victorian realist representations that block any heroinic action or voice thus transforms the committing of adultery into a form of social transgression rather than the romantic pursuit of passion. The shame that Anna suddenly feels (and feels that the English hero ought to feel), is thus compounded of the sense of coarse materialism and exclusionary sexism underlying the narrative of "English happiness" as well as her recognition of the nature of the desire the novel has seduced her into feeling.

Pushkin makes explicit the fantasy text of Tatiana:

> He who adored Julie Wolmar,
> Malek-Adhel, and de Linar,
> Young Werther, by his passion rended,
> And Grandison, the demigod
> Who causes you and me to nod—
> Our tender dreamer saw them blended
> Into a single essence warm,
> Embodied in Onegin's form.
>   (3.9)[26]

However, Tolstoy does not need to tell us that the English hero has become Vronsky.

Anna's transformation from an active to a passive participant in the text is figured in her play with the paper knife (in Russian, a cutting knife: *razreznoi nozhek*) that accompanies her reading. As Gustafson observes, in the course of this passage the knife expands from a *"nozhichek"* (tiny little knife) to a *"nozhek"* (little knife) to a *"nozh"* (knife) as Anna's desire increases. The knife becomes a fetish, an enlarging, substitute phallus that Anna must wield or woo to gain entry into the world she decodes. The knife that cuts the pages operates as the cursor that indicates the breach between fiction and reality; thus, Anna places the knife against the window glass—the membrane that separates the world from the vision of the world, the frame that imprisons experience. The knife directed against the text purchases Anna's only possible entry into the pictured world: as she realizes there is no possibility of doing anything, "she twists the smooth little paper knife [*nozhichek*] in her little hands"; as she experiences increased desire and shame, she puts down the book, "tightly gripping the little knife [*nozhek*] in both hands." As she yields to her state of arousal and desire for Vronsky, she caresses her cheek with "the cool, smooth surface" of the knife *(nozh)* and then laughs "at the feeling of delight" that overwhelms her.[27]

In the course of the novel Anna becomes an obsessive reader, driven to books and morphine by her need to quiet and structure her libidinal impulses. Her habit of reading to organize her perceptions according to the mode of realism shapes the vision she has during her final carriage and train ride. Anna's hermeneutic decoding of street signs and passersby, shop fronts and crowd scenes, transforms these cinematic images into emblems that represent answers to the questions she poses to herself. The reflections associated with the image of the cinematic magic-lantern illusion recall similar reflections that Prince Andrei has on the eve of the battle of Borodino:

> [F]or the first time in his life the possibility of death presented itself to him. . . . And from the height of this perception all that had previously tormented and preoccupied him suddenly became illumined by a cold white light. . . . All life appeared to him like magic-lantern pictures at which he had long been gazing by artificial light through a glass.[28]

Prince Andrei's vision is illumined by a "cold white light," which, unlike Anna's, "casts no shadows." In icon painting no shadows are represented since the source of light is assumed to be divine and permeates what is represented rather than shining on it from an external light source. This evocation of iconic illumination suggests a transcendent quality in Prince Andrei's vision that is lacking in Anna's vision.

During Anna's journey to her suicide, she suddenly sees through human hypocrisy to the truth about human relations, now lit by a "glaring light" (792), a "piercing light which now revealed to her the meaning of life" (793). Each passerby that Anna sees becomes an illustration of the sordid side of human nature, so that the theater she constructs in a series of tableaux vivants through her carriage window becomes an almost allegorical parade of the Vices. A "red-cheeked clerk riding on a hired horse . . . wants everyone to admire him and is very pleased with himself" (793) (Vanity). Two boys buying dirty ice cream reflect human greed: "we all want what is sweet and nice. If not sweets, then dirty ice cream" (790) (Gluttony). A merchant crossing himself is really only interested in material gain: "He wants to

strip me of my shirt, and I him of his. Yes, that's the truth!" (791)
(Envy and Greed).

The act of reading and the interpretation of pictures or words
thus constitute the formalization of life's meaning for Anna, just as the
act of viewing pictures or icons crystallizes significance for Lyovin.
But where Lyovin's icon of Anna is imbued with emblematic transcendence and creates in him a feeling of compassionate humanity,
Anna's visions are retold in language, narrativized, and alienate her
from people. Tolstoy's privileging of sublime nonverbal vision over
the consciously narrated observation differentiates Lyovin's acceptance of faith that cannot be explicated fully: "to my heart has been
revealed a knowledge beyond all doubt and unattainable by reason"
(850). By contrast, Anna remains caught in a hyperrationalized state:
a chance remark overheard, "What else is reason given to man for than
to escape that which distresses him" strikes Anna as being in harmony
with her own thoughts as she glorifies an untempered rationalism.
Anna's grim "observations" of sordid reality, in their dispassionate cyn-
icism and ruthless induction, recall the attitude of the realist and naturalist novelists who believed they had achieved a scientific neutrality
in their representations. But these hyperrealist, naturalist scenes, illu-
minated by a light that inexorably exposes to Anna "the entire history
and all the crannies of the souls" (797) of the people she observes, do
not evoke pity or compassion in her. Instead, "[the people] were all
hateful to her" (794) and she moves "apart from them as if they were
lepers" (797). When she turns "that glaring light in which she was
seeing everything" on her own relations, her recollections of her love
for Karenin and for Vronsky fill her with "loathing"; she even questions the sincerity of her love for Seryozha.

The Lady with the Lamp

The vision inspired by a realist world view in Anna's final reading of
life from her carriage window culminates in her last suicidal vision,
which Tolstoy expresses in the metaphor of reading by candlelight,

thus making the tableau of Anna reading the controlling image for the entire novel. The candlelight (reading lamp) that illuminates Anna's text participates in the interplay of light and shadow imagery in the novel.[29] Reading this image cluster as a purely allegorical or emblematic symbolic system would invest light with positive attributes and functions, and darkness with the obverse. But to the extent that Tolstoy's use of shadow and light imagery reflects back to Plato, the imagery is more complicated than that. Initially, a discrimination is made between natural and man-made light. It is the natural light of sun, stars, and lightning that illuminates Lyovin's transcendent visions as the blinding light of insight, preceding his final enlightenment: "At the peasant's words that Fokanych lived for his soul, in truth, in God's way, undefined but significant ideas seemed to burst out as though they had been locked up, and all striving toward one goal, they thronged whirling through his head, *blinding him with their light*" (827). By contrast, Anna's light is the light of a candle, an artificial luster that, lifted to decode an inscription, suggests high priestly functions, the Promethean quest for technology, the Faustian bargain for knowledge. The hieratic candle, or taper, functions in a similar metaphor in *Middlemarch*, where Dorothea dreams of being the lamp holder for Casaubon, who himself is described as lifting his taper in the labyrinth of knowledge and becoming indifferent to sunlight. His puerile superannuated scholarship is thus ridiculed in Lowick, the name of his estate.

The image of a woman holding a lamp and armed with a knife evokes another myth more readily than that of the Promethean: the myth of Amor and Psyche. The latter myth reverses the valuation of light (inspired by doubt) and darkness (perpetuated by faith), as discussed further in chapter 7. In Anna's final readings through the frames of the carriage and train windows, the controlling metaphor of light and shadow takes on two different, opposing functions, making for a complexity of the closing passage that has often intrigued readers; indeed, John Bayley diagnoses Tolstoy as suffering from "metaphor trouble" in this particular sequence.[30] Tolstoy's use of candle and light and shadow imagery may seem trite and hackneyed, as Leontiev complained,[31] until, on closer reading the metaphor is shown to deconstruct itself, if we read against the originary mythic treatment of light and shadow in Plato's cave analogy.

The ambivalence of lighting is well established throughout the novel, as for example in the early scene where Lyovin's desire to begin a new life is countered by the illumination and reflection of his habitual self: "The study was gradually lit up as the candle was brought in. The familiar details came out: the stag's horns, the book shelves, the mirror . . . an open book. . . . As he saw all this, there came over him for an instant a doubt of the possibility of starting a new life" (99). The emblems index Lyovin's life: the stag horns establish his status both as a country gentleman and as a stag (bachelor); the bookshelves signify his intellectual pursuits; the mirror underscores the moment of self-recognition. Finally, the open book reiterates the image of reading by candlelight and Lyovin's struggle to transcribe from the rational works of philosophy a meaning for his life and to write his own book. Although light should have lit up Lyovin's new, supposedly enlightened, view of himself and his future, illumination instead brings him back into the cave of everyday appearances. He saw better in the dark.

A consideration of textual illumination must acknowledge that the lights within the text and in the reading metaphor have different sources. There is Anna's own reading light, which is amplified throughout her final passage into a searching, piercing beam, and then there is the light of the "bright evening sun" that illuminates her train window. Standing before the train, she plans to leap into the "shadow" between the cars and (in an early variant) thinks: "There the light will go out." She is caught in the automatic habit of crossing herself and then "suddenly the darkness that had covered everything for her was torn apart" (798). Light is darkness, darkness light, so that the final passage of Anna's suicide reiterates the problematics of the metaphor: "And the light of the candle by which she had read the book filled with troubles, falsehoods, sorrow and evil flared up more brightly than ever before, lighted up for her all that had been shrouded in darkness, flickered, grew dim, and was quenched forever."

The Woman with a Shadow:
Fables of Demon and Psyche

> Taking it in its deepest sense, the shadow is the invisible
> saurian tail that man still drags behind him.
>
> Jung

> "We've discovered that it's a monstrous, twining,
> twisted, coiling, venomous, swollen-throated,
> ravenously gaping-jawed Serpent that reposes
> with you secretly in the night."
>
> Psyche's sisters in *The Golden Ass*

> And the Lord God said unto the Serpent: Upon your
> belly you shall go . . . And I will put enmity between thee
> and the woman, and between thy seed and her seed; they
> shall bruise thy head and thou shalt bruise their heels.
>
> Genesis 3:15

Tolstoy's Quest for Mythopoesis

As we saw in the previous chapter, Anna's light illumined her reading
and despair; in the current chapter, we will find that Anna's shadow
and darkness symbolize her liberation. The shadow Anna casts is a
mythological one, drawn from folklore. The discussion of the shadow
thus returns us to a consideration of the issues of heroes and heroines
broached earlier. While a folkloric or mythic hero is an amalgam of
the hero and his shadow double, the heroine's acquisition of a shadow

calls more disturbing forces into play. Already constituted as other, a woman with a shadow is a doubled marker of gender and otherness. Tolstoy's use of a folkloric motif to develop the mythological potential of Anna's heroinism makes her singular among the heroines of nineteenth-century realist prose, and it renders his artistic achievement unique.

In *Anna Karenina* Tolstoy's use of shadow imagery and reference to a subtext (the folk tale of the "man without a shadow"), like the light imagery discussed in chapter 6, suggests the implementation of a mythological archetype and a sustained symbolic system that challenges our perception of the novel as an exemplary realist work and moves it closer to a symbolist mode. The presence of the subliminally evoked motif of the shadow figure of folklore and mythology reveals the extent to which random textual detail, seemingly motivated by the demands of verisimilitude, may be enlisted to illustrate a subtextual narrative. Tolstoy's subtext, the folk legend of a man without shadow, recalls at least three myths of transgression in pursuit of knowledge: the Faust legend, the myth of Amor and Psyche, and the biblical narrative of the fall in Genesis. As shown in chapter 6, light and shadow considered as symbols of *gnōsis* evoke the shadow figures and light of truth of Plato's cave analogy. *Anna Karenina* thus acquires a mythopoetic resonance while the eponymous heroine achieves mythological status and her actions are made meaningful because they are seen as a quest.

In his recent article, "On the Spatiality of Plots in the 19th-Century Novel," Iurii Lotman observes that the invariant plot structure of most folktales, as outlined by Vladimir Propp, consists of the hero's quest to improve his position in the world by winning necessary magic items, overcoming obstacles, performing tasks, exposing usurpers, and so on. Within such a paradigm, the hero is little more than a constituted plot function while the enactment of his triumph represents a Napoleonic victory over the chronotope of the narrative.[1] Lotman contrasts this folkloric heroic course to the trajectory of the mythic hero, where the emphasis is on restructuration and the questioning of the conditions of character and environment. The hero pursues a quest where the goal is genesis or rebirth of the self and the cosmos and the return from chaos to order. The European novel more closely resembles the fairy tale in its bourgeois obsession with material benefit and social victories; by contrast, Lotman proposes, the Russian novel is mythological: it responds to social crisis and its heroes must either assume or reject Messianic status. Tolstoy's combination of mythic and folkloric paradigms in *Anna Karenina* results in an adaptation of the narrative structure of the European novel of adultery to the Russian social novel's formula of the failure of the superfluous man; the effete, disengaged anti-activist overcome by inertia. Bending the novel of adultery to this purpose required a gender inversion that cast a woman in the (anti)heroic role rather than in her traditional part as the "strong woman," the superfluous man's foil.[2]

Novelistic rewritings of invariant plots automatically acquire variant nuances in meaning through the encoding of the semiotics of the culture and ideology within which the text is generated. Tolstoy's rejection of realism involved the denigration of the verisimilitudinous application of detail in favor of an exploitation of universally comprehensible metaphors and symbols. The use of mythic and folkloric elements in *Anna Karenina* thus constitutes the opening moves in Tolstoy's polemic with the European realist novel. In *What Is Art?* his views are stated as an unrestrained antirealist, antimimetic program:

> The essence of [mimesis] consists in supplying details accompanying the thing described or depicted. In literary art this method consists in describing, in the minutest details, the external appearance, the faces, the clothes, the gestures, the tones, and the habituations of the characters represented, with all the occurrences met with in life. . . . this abundance of detail makes the stories difficult of comprehension to all people not living within reach of the conditions described by the author . . . Strip the best novels of our times of their details and what will remain?[3]

In Tolstoy's view, "to compose a fairy tale . . . which will delight dozens of generations or millions of children and adults, is incomparably more important and more fruitful than to compose a novel or symphony."[4]

Tolstoy's valorization of folk literature, particularly the popular genres of the folk tale *(skazka)*, fable *(basnia)*, and proverb *(poslovitsa)*, antedates his conversion: he had adopted a new aesthetic in the 1860s and 1870s as a result of his work with the peasant children on his Yasnaya Polyana estate ("Who Should Teach Whom How to Write?" [1865]). His interest in folk literature led him to compose almost exclusively within these genres, beginning with his *Primer* (1875) and continuing with his postconversion "Stories for the People." This preoccupation dominated his artistic practice as he began *Anna Karenina*; his inspiration for the novel seems to have been the result of his resolution that the only hope for Russian literature was a union of popular art with belles lettres.[5] The intention was not for belles lettres to masquerade in folkloric costume or for authors to rewrite mythology in a schematic, Wagnerian manner; rather, Tolstoy desired to infuse developed literary models with mythic tonality. In its most subtle application, the mythological modality could be elicited by what Lotman has termed a "cliché" or what Jungian critics consider an archetypal figure or motif: a detail, fragment, or block of text that activates in the reader's consciousness the entire meaning and resonance of myth. Tolstoy's famous attack on the "superfluity of detail" as the characterizing feature of mimetic realism must, therefore, be juxtaposed with his other view of textual detail, the "labyrinth of linkages" *(labirint stseplenii)*, the explication of which, in Tolstoy's opinion, constitutes the most essential task of literary criticism.[6] Inside Tolstoy's labyrinth, "realistic" details are subverted into a symbolic system.

Despite the dark coloration and foreshadowing role of the imagery in *Anna Karenina,* most critics have minimized Tolstoy's patterns of imagery, seeing them as unmotivated textures, and have failed to acknowledge their semiotic potential. For example, William Rowe notes: "In *Anna Karenina* more than any other work of his, Tolstoy established ominous connections between apparently insignificant details."[7] Yet Rowe's own discussion of the novel's imagery is limited to a catalog without commentary.

The perfusion of shadow imagery throughout the novel creates a series of penumbral duplications of the same shape. The shadow figure cannot be devalued as an "insignificant detail" once the noticeable citation of the literary subtext of the shadow story causes the reader to recall a narrative tradition that explicates the otherwise enigmatic motif. We are even more inclined to ascribe significance to the shadow subtext when we note that its citation in the novel occurs in the first scene Tolstoy composed:[8]

> "Anna has changed a great deal since her trip to Moscow. There is something strange about her," her acquaintance said.
> "The main change is that she brought back with her the shadow of Aleksei Vronsky," said the ambassador's wife.
> "Well, what of it? Grimm has a fable: the man without a shadow, a man deprived of a shadow. And this was his punishment for something. I never could understand how it was a punishment [*v chem nakazanie*]. Although it should be unpleasant for a woman without a shadow."
> "Yes, but women with shadows usually come to a bad end," said Anna's acquaintance. (144)

Little critical attention has been paid to the implications this passage has for the novel, perhaps because there is no known fable or folktale about a man without a shadow by Grimm. Other possible subtexts that have been proposed are two *Kunstmärchen*, both pseudofolkloric versions of the Faust legend: Chamisso's *Peter Schlemihl* and Andersen's "The Shadow."

The numerous revisions Tolstoy made of this first scene suggest that considerable reflection accompanied the placement of the shadow subtext here in the final version of the novel. In the earlier redactions of this scene, the guests take an almost satanic pleasure in anticipating Anna's fall: "the conversation crackles merrily like a bonfire" (143). In the final version, the diabolical tone of the conversation is muted but still audible in the reference to an outfit of *diable rose* and in the demonic nuances of the shadow tale. The discussion of a story of transgression and punishment emphasizes these intimations of descent.

The reference to a fable suggests to the reader the inevitability of outcome and the didactic, even simplistic, presentation of a morally divided universe that characterizes literary reworkings of Aesopian genres. These are the same features that readers often resent in Tolstoy's authorial voice. Perhaps no critic has stated the case against Tolstoy the moralist as well as D. H. Lawrence in his famous indictment: "When the novelist puts his thumb in the scale to pull down the balance to his predilections, that is immorality."[9] Indeed, Tolstoy, in directing the course of his heroine's life, often seems every bit as heartless and relentless as the aspen leaves Anna gazes upon: "Standing still and looking at the tops of the aspen trees waving in the wind, with their freshly washed, brightly shining leaves in the cold sunshine, she knew that they would not forgive her, that everyone and everything would be as merciless to her now as was that sky, that green" (307). Reading *Anna Karenina* as a fable lends the novel the tone of a fictive universe where ends are ineluctably determined by beginnings and where, as in tragedy, the character's *hamartia* brings about a fall, inspiring the audience with fear and pity. Yet the discussion of the shadow story in debate dialogizes what would otherwise be perceived, in Bakhtin's terms, as a monologic resolution of the novel's problematic theme.[10]

The fable, like the proverb or parable, is a genre composed in what Mikhail Bakhtin terms "absolute language": the language that "does not say, but is itself a saying."[11] The clear tone of distanced authority in which Tolstoy wrote fables, parables, and science lessons for his *Primer* is an inimitable example of that pure, laconic, and commanding type of discourse advocated by his beloved Schopenhauer, who wrote in *The Art of Literature*: "There is no style of writing but should have a certain trace of kinship with the *epigraphic* or *monumental* style, which is, indeed, the ancestor of all styles."[12] It has become a commonplace among Tolstoy critics to observe that Tolstoy's implied narrative voice resonates with authority precisely because of the impression that it is authorless. This sense of a dispassionate, Olympian creator made Tolstoy's readers "feel that an eye watches from above,"[13] or that Tolstoy "watches life from on high and only rarely makes a remark similar to a scientific generalization."[14] This sense of height or distance, achieved by what D. S. Mirsky calls Tolstoy's "puritanical prose . . . purged to chemical purity"[15] impelled Bakhtin to hypostatize Tolstoy as an exemplar of a "monolithically monologic" author, whose characters' voices are ultimately silenced by the "last word" of their creator.[16]

In his analysis of Tolstoy's absolute language, Morson observes that Tolstoy often employs absolute language in the margins of discourse: in chapter titles, epigraphs, appendices, and digressions.[17] In *Anna Karenina* Tolstoy all but avoids this use of absolute language by scrupulously removing all chapter titles and epigraphs that appeared in the earlier variants, except for the chapter title "Death," and he places all quotations, allusions, parables, and disquisitions in the mouths of his characters. The notable exceptions are the novel's epigraph and opening proverbial sentence. By giving his characters proverbs and biblical quotations to recite, Tolstoy dialogizes all recognized authority while purifying the authorial discourse of any identifiable opinion or ideology. As a result, the authorial voice remains insistently neutral and dispassionate, unrelated to any specific personality, milieu, or linguistic style. Instead of relying on the literary or topical allusions so commonly found in the nineteenth-century European novel, the implied narrator illustrates with unadorned descriptions of common physical sensations or experiences. Tolstoy's authorial voice in *Anna Karenina* thus sounds sourceless and traditionless, disembodied and dispassionate. It has the resonance and authority of biblical and philosophical diction while all other "authorities," from Plato to Scripture itself, are contaminated by their association with the character who recites and often distorts the quotation.

The citation of the shadow story is no exception: despite its status as a monologic genre, the fable is quoted in dialogue, not in the voice of absolute authority, and thus the moral of the fable is dialogized as well. As in Socratic dialogue, the reader is summoned to play the role of an interlocutor who is wiser than the one instructed by Socrates. The unnamed speaker who refers to the fable has missed the point ("I never could understand . . .") and has given the wrong author's name. Her perplexity anticipates the critical debate over *Anna Karenina*, particularly over the novel's epigraph, "Vengeance is mine. I will repay." The reader thus attempts, if only momentarily, to resolve the novel's problematic of guilt and punishment through reference to the mysterious and ambiguous folktale.

The reader must begin by solving the riddle of which shadow tale the unnamed speaker had in mind. The misattribution of the story to the Brothers Grimm is puzzling, unless the evocation of the English denotation of the name Grimm was intentional, and this is a valid conjecture in the case of a novel that is replete with descriptions of English manners and contains many English phrases, puns, names, and expressions. Alternately, the citation of Grimm may have been intended to legitimize a literary work by attributing it to a genuine folk source.

The speaker calls the story not a folk tale (*skazka* or *märchen*, the genre in which it belongs) but a fable (*basnia*). While working on *Anna Karenina*, Tolstoy read and translated numerous *märchen* and fables for his previously mentioned anthology, the *Primer*. Among them is his version of Aesop's (or possibly Ovid's) fable of a dog and her reflection, which Tolstoy retitled, significantly enough, "A Dog and her Shadow."[18] The aforementioned two stories usually proposed by commentators—Chamisso's *Peter Schlemihl* and Andersen's "The Shadow"—both exhibit significant intertextual connections with *Anna Karenina*. Of the two authors, Andersen seems to be the more likely choice since Tolstoy's admiration for him is well documented: he translated Andersen's "The Emperor's New Clothes" (*Novoe tsarskoe plat'e*) for his *Primer*, and his diaries mention other translations of Andersen tales.[19] The reference to Grimm, a collector of *märchen*, further implicates the writer of *Kunstmärchen*, Andersen rather than Chamisso. Although Andersen thus seems to be the most likely source, both shadow stories will be considered here as an intertextual unit, especially since Andersen's tale opens with a reference to Chamisso's tale as the protagonist recalls his homeland, "the cold climates [where] everyone knows the story of the man without a shadow." The intertextual dependence of Andersen's story on Chamisso's tale affords another reason for assuming that the unnamed speaker read and did not understand Andersen (rather than Chamisso), since she is confused about the reason for and mode of the punishment. In *Peter Schlemihl*, the crime and punishment are clearly described and motivated while Andersen's more subtle, psychologized version requires the reader to interpret the story within a literary tradition.

Both stories typify nineteenth-century European literary treatments of the Faust legend and other tales of demonic possession or haunting by doubles, shadows, and men in black, in the tradition of Hoffmann and Poe and culminating in Nietzsche's *Zarathustra* and other fin-de-siècle explorations of the divided self. The modern exploration of the psychological nuances of the Faust legend has resulted in an interpretive introjection of (external) demonic figures into the psyche of the protagonist.[20] Reading stories of demonic shadows as psychic projections places these narratives in the tradition of tales of split personalities, alter egos, doppelgängers, autoscopy, lost reflections, and the like, especially since the shadow is obviously a duplicate, dark self. In Russian literature the tradition initiated by Mozart's "man in black" in Pushkin's *Mozart and Salieri* would culminate in the shadow-populated world of Bely's *Petersburg*, where each protagonist is haunted by his enantiomorphic, mirror-image shadow self.

The ubiquitous occurrence of the shadow figure in world literature and in dreams caused Jung to identify it as one of the primary archetypes in his theory of the collective unconscious: in Jungian theory the "loss of the shadow" is a metaphor for intrapsychic conflict, repression, and projection; the stories about the man without a shadow relate in mythologic terms the struggle for psychic integration, and the resolution of the philosophical and ethical problem of good and evil in the world and in the psyche.

The evil nature of the Mephistophelean figure in Chamisso's *Peter Schlemihl* renders the tale an obvious adaptation of the Faust legend.[21] Peter Schlemihl is pursued by a mysterious man in gray who is capable of granting his most extravagant wishes. The man in gray offers Peter a purse containing an inexhaustible supply of gold pieces in exchange for the loan of Peter's shadow. Peter assents to the exchange; yet he finds that as a shadowless man he must avoid daylight or any light that would reveal his lack of a shadow and expose him to social ostracism and persecution. He has several social and romantic misfortunes when his lack of a shadow, which he cleverly conceals, is nonetheless revealed by moonlight or by informers. He is continuously pursued by the man in gray, who now proffers a new contract:

return of the shadow to Peter in exchange for his soul. Peter resists this temptation, even when it is the only opportunity to save his beloved from a terrible fate. He ends by roaming the world, forever isolated from human contact.

In Andersen's "The Shadow," a scholar traveling in the south confines himself to the indoors during the day to avoid the heat. In the evenings, music, shadowy images, and a single glimpse of a woman from a neighboring balcony attract his attention, but he fears to leave his study. Impulsively acting at his shadow's urging, the scholar allows his shadow to separate from him and cross to the neighboring balcony to gain entrance to the house where the scholar hesitates to enter. The shadow disappears and does not return. The scholar soon grows another shadow, albeit a thin and sickly one, and returns to his native land. Sometime later he is accosted by a well-dressed man in black who is in fact his former shadow in disguise and who now convinces him to accept him as a companion. Eventually, the shadow succeeds in claiming that it is the real man and the scholar is his shadow. Under these terms, the shadow usurps the scholar's position in the world, steals his beloved's affections, and arranges for the scholar to be executed.

Andersen's scholar, seduced by the influence of music and beauty but enervated by his agoraphobia, willingly yields control of his vital darker self, as Dr. Jekyll, exhilarated by the Promethean quest for scientific knowledge, legitimizes and enables Mr. Hyde's emergence and autonomy. The Andersen story also retains the role reversal of Mephisto-servant to scholar-master; yet in this treatment the demonic shadow is clearly recognizable as an extension of the scholar's personality, an embodiment of that anarchic spirit of initiative and passion that breaks free of its enforced confinement indoors. That is why Andersen's story is more psychological in tone than Chamisso's tale; the crime is repression and the punishment is the loss of one's position in the world. In Andersen's story of psychic conflict, symbolized by the separation of a man and his shadow, no diabolical intermediary is required. Instead, we see the introjection of the diabolical into a personality ruptured by an intrapsychic fissure. Tolstoy's depiction of Anna's cognitive dissonance rests tensely between these two

meta-narratives; that is, between the superstitious folk notion of demonic possession and the psychological reading of demons as projections or archetypes of the collective unconscious.

The Shadow of *Anna Karenina*

Anna enters the novel as a Victorian stereotype of the Angel in the
House, making peace in the Oblonsky household and surrounded by
a bevy of children. She is almost immediately transformed into the
demonic siren or femme fatale possessed by passion in the tradition of
the mid-Victorian sensation novel of adultery such as *Wuthering
Heights* or *Lady Audley's Secret*. Nina Auerbach suggests that this
fusion of angelic and demonic characteristics in nineteenth-century
representations of women reflects social ambivalence toward and patriarchal distrust of feminine sexuality.[22] Since angels are asexual, the
expression of sexuality in the Angel in the House is perceived as a fall
to the demonic and anarchic. In von Hofmannsthal's libretto, *The
Woman without a Shadow* (*Die Frau ohne Schatten* [1915]), the an-
drogyny of the peri (the bisexual angel of Persian mythology) is expressed as the lack of a shadow that prevents the peri from becoming
a human woman who will conceive and bear children.[23] The shadow
in this case becomes the signifier of fecundity and thus reaffirms the
demonic or dark qualities attributed to feminine sexuality.

The story of the temptation of a woman and the exchange of her
shadow for eternal beauty is told in a work with which Tolstoy may
have been familiar, a poem by the Austrian poet Nikolaus Lenau
(1802–1850) entitled, significantly enough, "Anna." At the beginning
Anna of the poem is admiring her reflected beauty in a pond when a
supernatural figure appears to offer her eternal beauty in exchange
for her shadow and the promise that she will renounce childbearing.
The narcissism of this Anna recurs in Anna Karenina, who practices
birth control to remain sexually attractive to Vronsky. Thus, the transformation of gender in *Anna Karenina* from a "man without a
shadow" to a "woman without a shadow" abrogates any straightfor-
ward, psychological reading of Tolstoy's use of the "man without a

shadow" as a metaphor for the struggle between the rational and the irrational self. When this psychic struggle is enacted by a female protagonist, the motif evokes male anxiety about female sexuality and the desirability of the female body. The shadow (feminine in gender in Russian) is a penumbral, feminine Other, a demonic seductress, an archetypal Eve. If we return to the primary text of original sin we find the shadow in its originary shape as the serpent in Eden. When God condemns it to slide along the ground worrying the heel of woman and her offspring, forever crushed beneath her heel, the early conflation of serpent, shadow, and woman is revealed.

Early variants of the novel emphasized the demonic nature of Anna's vitality: the title of the chapter describing Anna's passion for Vronsky was "The Devil" in an early draft, and Anna and Vronsky refer to her jealousy as "the demon." Anna has "something uncanny, demonic and fascinating in her" (89); her face glows "with a bright light, but this glow was not one of joyfulness, but suggested the terrible glow of a conflagration in the middle of a dark night" (154).

Vronsky's role as shadow demon is implied by imagery that associates Vronsky both with shadow and with Faust: in the early stages of his pursuit of Anna, he is cast as Mephistopheles in the form in which he first appeared to Faust, a dog. Vronsky is repeatedly described as expressing "humble submission" (87), "reverential ecstasy" (109), the look of an "abject setter-dog" who wishes to please. It is this "utter subjection, that slavish devotion, which [does] so much to win her" (199). At the scene of their first meeting, the whining of a dog in the luggage compartment is audible as Anna's train arrives from Petersburg. In an episode subsequently removed from the novel, Lyovin is terrorized by a mad dog that exacerbates his obsessive dread of death and is somehow linked in his mind with the fearful image of a peasant. The emblem of Lyovin's panic thus connects the demonic Mephistopheles in his incarnation as a dog with Lyovin's vision of a peasant with a matted beard, undoubtedly the same disheveled peasant who haunts Anna and Vronsky and plays the role in the novel of the "shadow of death." The hierophantic nature of this peasant with matted beard and sack recalls the Tiresias figure of the blind, leprous peasant who fulfilled a similar function in *Madame Bovary*.[24] An

enigmatic statement of Anna's may be explained as an obscure reference to Mephistopheles in his canine incarnation and as her recognition of demonic figures as projections from a troubled psyche: on her
final journey to the train station, Anna silently addresses a family em-
barking on an outing, "The dog you're taking with you will be of no
help to you—you can't get away from yourselves" (792). Her observation is immediately followed by recollections of the early days of
Vronsky's courtship and her memories of him as an "abject setter-
dog" (792).

In addition to his trait of doglike servility, Vronsky is repeatedly
accompanied by shadows throughout the novel. In the fateful meeting at Bologoe station, as Anna steps onto the platform, "the bent
shadow of a man glided by *at her feet*" (109) (emphasis added). Vronsky then interposes himself between Anna and the light of the lamp-
post and stands in the shadow. Anna must "gaze into the shadow" to
read his expression. Whenever Vronsky contemplates nature, his vision includes shadows, as when he admires the cloud of midges and
the shadow over his carriage "in the already lengthening shadow of a
lush lime tree" (307) or the slanting shadows over the fields as he
rides to a rendezvous with Anna: "Everything he saw from the carriage window . . . was as fresh, and gay, and strong as he was himself:
. . . the slanting shadows that fell from the houses, and trees, and
bushes, and even from the rows of potatos" (332). Later, at his estate,
his face will be shadowed by leaves as he discusses his relationship to
Anna with Dolly: "Daria Aleksandrovna looked with timid inquiry
into his energetic face, which under the lime trees was continually
being lighted up in patches by the sunshine, and then passing into
complete shadow again" (653). After Anna's death, as he waits at the
train station to depart for the Balkans: "In the slanting shadows cast
by sacks piled up on the platform, Vronsky . . . strode up and down
like a wild beast in a cage" (812).[25]

The definitive association of Vronsky with the shadow figure
occurs in the conversation quoted above. In the various redactions of
the dialogue, an interesting evolution in grammatical structure suggests a shift in emphasis that resulted from the introduction of the
shadow subtext. In the earlier versions of the passage, before the

shadow story was mentioned, the acquaintance states that Vronsky has become Anna's shadow *(sdelalsia eia teniu)*. In the final version of the passage, when the reference to the shadow story is introduced, Anna is said to have brought back with her the "shadow of Aleksei Vronsky" *(ten Alekseia Vronskogo)*: Vronsky no longer exists; his shadow has been snared by Anna. His diabolical nature is expressed in his exultant acquiescence in the "terror" of their passion: "Our love, if it *could* be stronger, will be strengthened because there is something terrible in it" (456). This demonic statement was even more villainous in the earlier version, where their love was to be strengthened "by the crime, the evil that we have done to [Karenin]." Tolstoy's revisions minimize Vronsky's role: no longer the primary actor ("he became her shadow"/*sdelalsia eia teniu*), he becomes the passive agent of Anna, who "brings back with her" the shadow of Vronsky.

Tolstoy used shadow imagery with precisely the same nuances in his dramatic work *A Living Corpse,* a curious reprise of *Anna Karenina.* In the play, the characters of Karenin and Anna are rearranged, although the basic plot of an adulterous love affair remains the same; it concludes, however, with a fictitious suicide derived from Chernyshevsky's *What Is to Be Done?* Karenin, stuffy and old-fashioned as ever, now plays the adulterous lover while the husband, Fedya, is a rake and spendthrift who simulates his suicide in order to permit his wife to remarry without being subjected to the stigma of divorce. In recounting the experience of his loveless marriage to Liza, Fedya credits his wife with being consciously faithful to him; yet he recognizes the force of her unconscious passion for Karenin. As was the case with Chernyshevsky's Olga, the heroine's unconscious, repressed sexuality is first recognized by her husband. In Fedya's account, Liza's repressed desire casts a shadow over his family life, although the dialogue that follows questions the source of the shadow: Is it Liza's passion for Karenin? Or Fedya's animosity and suspicion toward his wife?

> *Fedya:* The very best love is unconscious love. I believe she always did love him; but as an honest woman, she did not confess it even to herself. But . . . a shadow of some kind always lay across our family life . . . but why am I confessing to you?

Prince Abrezkov: Please do! . . . I understand you, I understand you, I understand that the shadow, as you so well express it, may have been . . .

Fedya: Yes, it was; and that perhaps is why I could not find satisfaction in the family life she gave me, but was always seeking something and being carried away.   (Act 3)[26]

If we view Vronsky as a shadow and the power relationship of Anna and Vronsky as that of owner and shadow, or a lady and a dog (in Chekhov's retelling), Anna would appear to be the passive victim who succumbs to, rather than the one offering temptation, as Princess Miagkaia subsequently argues: "How can she help it if they're all in love with her and follow her about like shadows?" (145). When we pursue this interpretation, it is Vronsky who, having become possessed and having yielded to his shadow, now seduces and compromises Anna to gain authority over her soul. In the course of the novel Vronsky assumes the powerful position, just as the shadow usurps the scholar's position or the man in gray (Mephistopheles) gains power over Peter Schlemihl. Vronsky's power over Anna gives him the responsibility and culpability for the problematic aspect of their "position." The description of Vronsky as a murderer bending over Anna's body after the consummation of their love affair suggests that he is morally responsible for her fall, just as he is to blame for the death of his horse, Frou-Frou. This view has been argued convincingly by many critics; the most convincing textual support for this interpretation is the scene at the races where Vronsky makes a "clumsy" movement in the saddle and breaks Frou-Frou's back.

In discussing this scene, Barbara Hardy rejects as too schematic any facile comparison of Anna to Frou-Frou or a reading of Vronsky's horsemanship as an allegory of the course of his relationship to Anna: "[the events] exist in themselves, as characteristic and particular demonstrations."[27] Yet the comparison of a woman to a horse and man's command over woman to his horsemanship is a commonplace in literature. For example, in *Can You Forgive Her?*, a novel that is a significant intertext for *Anna Karenina*, Trollope related the attempts of a handsome rake, Burgo Fitzgerald, to seduce into adultery the spirited Lady Glencora, who is married to a passionless bureaucrat. Burgo enters the novel on horseback and recklessly rides a horse to death, destroying a creature "much nobler than himself": "He rode at the bank as though it had been the first fence of the day, striking his poor beast with his spurs. . . . The animal rose at the bank, and in some way got upon it, scrambling as he struck it with his chest, and then fell headlong into the ditch at the other side, a confused mass of head, limbs, and body. . . . Poor noble beast, noble in vain! . . . His master's ignorance had killed him."[28] In a subsequent ballroom scene, when Burgo waltzes Lady Glencora to exhaustion until she is on the verge of eloping with him, she is compared to a winded horse: "The waltzers went on till they were stopped by want of breath. . . . Then she put up her face, and slightly opened her mouth, and stretched her nostrils—as ladies as well as horses do when the running has been severe and they want air."[29]

In Russian literature, brutalizing horses has traditionally been used as a metaphor for the abuse of women, from the exchange of a woman for a horse in Lermontov's "Bela" to the implicit connection between Raskolnikov's dream vision of a horse flogged to death and his murder of Lizaveta and the pawnbroker.[30]

Alternately, Gustafson has recently argued for Anna's culpability; he suggests that she falls because of her rejection of psychic growth; her repression forces her inner demons to "escape" as projections that control her and propel her into adultery. Possessed by the chthonic forces of her own unconscious, she succumbs to despair and ends her life. According to this interpretation, Vronsky has no autonomous existence and serves merely as the pretext for Anna's projection of her inner demons and as the chosen catalyst for the irrepressible irruption of her inner conflict. In this sense, Anna conjures Vronsky's appearance at Bologoe station.

Achieving psychic integration, or what Gustafson terms "at-one-ment," may be translated into Jungian terms as "assimilating the shadow." Such a process in folk or mythological narratives may be represented in the figure Campbell describes as the liminal threshold guardian, who blocks the path prescribed for the hero/ine, and who withholds the essential aid (information or magic items) without which the quest will fail. The true hero/ine is known by his or her ability to conciliate the threshold guardian. Thus, it is the task of the archetypal hero/ine to master and assimilate the shadow in order to fulfill his or her quest. The quest internalized becomes a fable of psychomachy; such a narrative achieves mythic status and signals the return of the novel to mythology. As Freud suggested, "The psychological novel in general probably owes its peculiarities to the tendency of modern writers to split up their egos by self-observation into many component egos, and in this way to personify the conflicting trends in their own mental life in many heros."[31] Jung's description of the shadow figure as a psychic projection matches Freud's view of novelistic personae as component egos. According to Jung, the shadow is a symptom of repression, a form of psychic disturbance resulting from the repression of taboo libidinal impulses: "Where [vital forces] are repressed or neglected, their specific energy disappears into the unconscious with unaccountable consequences. . . . Such tendencies form an ever-present and potentially destructive 'shadow' to our conscious mind. Even tendencies that might in some circumstances be able to exert a beneficial influence are transformed into demons when they are repressed."[32] It is the total suppression of vital forces (or the "animus") that we recognize as one of Anna's most characteristic traits. In her first appearance at the train station, "her nature was so brimming over with something that against her will it showed itself now in the flash of her eyes, and now in her smile. Deliberately, she shrouded the light in her eyes, but it shone against her will in the faintly perceptible smile" (67). The same light will be entirely repressed when she returns to Karenin: "Undressing, she went into the bedroom, but her face had none of that eagerness which, during her stay in Moscow, had fairly flashed from her eyes and her smile; on the contrary, now the fire seemed quenched in her, hidden somewhere far away" (119).

Anna's repression and internal conflict are easily described as a classic case study of psychic dissociation: "everything was beginning to be doubled in her soul" (305) and "her soul was beginning to split in two" (311). Her very name, being palindromic, suggests a doubled self, a reflecting center. By the time she gives birth, she describes

herself as two separate beings. Her sense of emotional dualism is mirrored in her dream of having two husbands (both named Aleksei);[33]
her conflict is literalized when she finds herself pulling her hair on
both sides of her head (306). Her sense of dissonance increases to the
extent that she feels alienated from her own identity—a sensation
that initially allows her to indulge in an uncensored manner in the
fantastic images produced by her unconscious on the train ride from
Moscow to Petersburg: "And what am I myself? Myself or some other
woman?" (107). Her estrangement from herself, which Jung would
define as possession by an alien psychic element, the animus, becomes uncanny when, just prior to her suicide, she fails to recognize
herself in the mirror and indulges in a narcissistic, autoerotic moment:
"'Who's that?' she thought, looking in the mirror at the swollen face
with strangely glittering eyes that looked at her in a frightened way.
'Why, it's me!' she suddenly understood. . . . Then she lifted her hand
to her lips and kissed it" (784–85). The novel promotes a schizoid vision of multiple Annas as she is surrounded by doubles of herself: her
servant, Annushka, her daughter, Annie, and her adopted daughter,
Hannah. Anna expresses her sense of self-alienation when, close to
death, she pleads with Karenin for forgiveness: "There is another
woman in me, I'm afraid of her: she loved that man, and I tried to hate
you, and could not forget about her that used to be. I'm not that
woman. Now I'm my real self, all myself" (434).[34]

Anna's failure to achieve psychic integration, or to assimilate the
shadow, has often been juxtaposed to Lyovin's achievement of a tenu-
ous balance in his striving toward good. In keeping with the novel's
structure of consistent parallels between the two protagonists, Lyovin
must master his own shadow, the "shadow of temper" *(ten' ogor-
cheniia)* (581). In learning tolerance, relaxing his demands for perfection, Lyovin acknowledges his own imperfections and accepts the
checkered pattern of daily life, the flaws and inadequacies of human
nature. Emblematic of Lyovin's transformation is his attitude toward
fallen women, whom he initially classifies as "all disgusting" and beyond pity: "in such love there can be no tragedy" (46). His rejection of
Christ's chastisement, "Let he who is without sin cast the first stone,"
is criticized by Stiva: "'You want the reality to be invariably corre-

sponding all the while with the aim—and that's not how it is. You want a man's work, too, always to have a definite aim, and love and family life always to be undivided—and that's not how it is. All the variety, all the beauty of life is made up of light and shadow'" (47).

Lyovin's acceptance of darkness as a necessary component of light accompanies his growing acceptance of imperfection in himself and others, as discussed in chapter 5. Lyovin's achievement of grace involves the recognition that faith must be preserved under the imperfect circumstances of life: "Real life had only for a time overcast the spiritual peace he had found, but it was still untouched within him" (837). At the height of his ecstatic conversion, Lyovin contemplates the alternation of light and dark in the sky as lightning flashes: "At each flash of lightning the Milky Way, and even the bright stars vanished, but as soon as the lightning died away, they reappeared in their places" (849). His ultimate realization is of the inseparability of light and shadow: "I shall go on in the same way, losing my temper . . . falling into angry discussions. . . . But my life has an unquestionable meaning of goodness which I have the power to put into it" (957).

Contrasting Anna's failure to Lyovin's (relative) success, as so many critics have done, is too facile a construct that ignores the all-important significance of gender difference. In a system that oppresses women and morbidizes their sexuality, what other choice is there but repression for a woman who experiences all of her psycho-sexual drives? It is hard to suppose what kind of movement toward a sustained inner life and toward psychic autonomy a woman can accomplish when her husband denies her any separate existence at all: "[Karenin] began to think of [Anna], about what she was thinking and feeling. *For the first time,* he vividly imagined her private life, her thoughts, her desires, and the thought that she could and should have her own autonomous life seemed to him so dreadful *(strashno)* that he hastened to drive it away" (153) (emphasis added). Within the confines of a life that denies her spiritual growth and autonomy, Anna's only avenue for the pursuit of complete psychic awareness is through adulterous passion. Thus, Anna's captivation by a shadowy demon lover may be read as a version of the originary myth of the ecstatic lover, who engages in the passionate, erotic pursuit of endless desire ultimately subtended by the death drive.[35] Jung would consider that the attraction of this type of shadow figure is that it reflects animus possession, domination by a demonic lover who, like Eros in the Psyche myth, "lures women away from all human relationships and . . . cut[s] a woman off from the reality of life."[36]

Amor and Psyche

Casting Vronsky as an animus or Eros, the erotic death demon, is textually supported by the echoes of Apuleius's "Amor and Psyche" in the novel: Vronsky's role as the dutiful son of a mother renowned for her beauty and promiscuity reflects the relations of Amor and Venus. Like Venus, Mme. Vronskaia is responsible for introducing her son to the woman he will fall in love with and whom she will later persecute. Like Amor and Psyche, Vronsky and Anna have a daughter. The seclusion enforced on Anna by her separation from society encloses her in Amor's dwelling and provokes in her the types of doubt that drove Psyche to violate Amor's edict and examine the sleeping God by candlelight. In a tableau reminiscent of the myth, Anna illuminates the sleeping Vronsky: "He was asleep there, and sleeping soundly. She went up to him, and holding the candle above his face, she gazed a long while at him. Now when he was asleep, she loved him so much that at the sight of him, she could not keep back tears of tenderness. But she knew that if he awakened he would look at her with cold eyes" (781). Anna's illumination of Vronsky follows a scene where, reading by candlelight, she senses the inevitability of suicide as the only escape from her situation. Her candle gutters and shadows descend upon her from every direction and plunge her in darkness. Anna's reading by candlelight becomes the controlling metaphor for the entire novel when Tolstoy repeats the metaphor to describe her last hours and death. Thus, lifting her lamp to see and casting shadows and light in order to read and know love—this image interconnects every illumination in the novel and suggests the ultimate meaning of the shadow imagery. Anna's candlelight reading of the novel, of love, of life, repeats Psyche's transgression in pursuit of knowledge and her own weakness in needing to affirm with the light of reason the intuitive life of passion associated mythologically with darkness and shadow. Yet it is a light of knowledge that is suppressed by the patriarchy; the transgression consists of lighting a lamp to see the truth, but the light will drive the beloved away.[37]

In the final sequence of the novel's penultimate part, Anna, like Psyche, is cast out of Amor's paradise of love and embarks on a journey as a result of Mme. Vronskaia's machinations, which recall Venus's scourge on Psyche. In Anna's final views of life framed by the windows of her carriage and train, the controlling metaphor of light and shadow takes on two different and opposing meanings, reversing the standard valuation. The ambivalence of light and shadow in the final passages of Anna's life plays upon the salvific potential of each and allows them their essential integration. As in Plato's cave analogy, any interior illumination becomes an artificial construct, brightening a dark perception with the false assurance of vision. Amor's palace thus repeats Plato's cave, a region of confinement in which illumination may either reveal the artifice or display and varnish it. The cave is also a symbol of the womb, as Luce Irigaray notes in her commentary on Plato's "Hystera."[38] Men may remain in Plato's cave out of ignorance or pleasure; women must remain there by the demands of Love. Thus, Lee Edwards writes of Psyche's lamp of truth: "Once lit in the novel, Psyche's lamp reveals the stark harshness of the system that has so long confined her."[39] As long as Anna is confined to reading by candlelight, she can never escape her confinement, the imprisonment of the scholar without a shadow. Trapped indoors, she can never see the light of genuine enlightenment that will blind Lyovin, the wanderer in nature, at the close of the novel.

The death or departure of revolutionary or deviant heroes and heroines in Russian literature—from Chatsky in *Woe from Wit* (1825) or Bazarov in *Fathers and Sons* (1862) to *Anna Karenina*—evokes another archetypal paradigm, that of *askesis* or transcendence, the martyrdom and agonistic self-immolation of the avant-garde on the barricade or cross, which redeems and inspires those who remain bound to the mundane. While it has been suggested that the death and transfiguration of such a character may reflect the author's ambivalence in affirming deviance,[40] the fall may reenact Satanic splendor; the martyrdom may be an *imitatio Christi*. Thus, the pursuit of a tragic end ultimately challenges the system that predicts and enforces such a doom. For Anna Karenina, a victim of the oppression and dependent status of women in the nineteenth century, the pursuit of passionate love is the only action available that will liberate her from social constraints and place the life of the individual spirit above the life of the social body. The quest is that of Psyche, who transgressed in her desire to know love and thus is cast out of paradise. Psyche's reward and apotheosis, like Ulysses's return, affirm the reader's positive view of Olympus. The death of the hero/ine may seem a punishment in this tradition of the folktale or romance, where physical and material benefit (beauty rather than ugliness, wealth rather than poverty) reflect the evaluative dimension of good and evil. But mythic figures transcend this dichotomy by constituting an amalgam of oppositions and a restructuration of the material plane according to spiritual imperatives. Such a process characterizes the action of myth, where heroes and heroines die in order to be transfigured for a cosmic benefit.

Within the tragic and mythic tradition, Anna's death does not constitute a punishment but instead a liberation from her confinement in a social arena where the quest for the development of an autonomous self, emblematized as the acquisition of a shadow, represented an unforgivable transgression.

Picking a Mushroom and Escaping the Marriage Plot

> [*Anna Karenina*] is all sour, it reeks of . . . old maids.
>
> Turgenev

> The highest type of old maid has made no sacrifice, nor is she in any sense a victim, for marriage as a state is not necessary to her idea of happiness.
>
> *Blackwood's Edinburgh Magazine* (1866)

> And thus it was . . . that the learned gentleman came upon the subject of botany, that is to say, upon the subject of mushrooms. These creatures of the shade, luxuriant and anomalous forms of organic life, are fleshy by nature, and closely related to the animal kingdom. Dr. Krokowski went on to speak of a mushroom . . . which in its form was suggestive of love, in its odor of death. For it was a striking fact that the odor of the Impudicus was that of animal decay. . . . Yet even today among the ignorant, the mushroom passed for an aphrodisiac.
>
> Thomas Mann, *The Magic Mountain*

Labyrinths and Linkages

Discussing the types of linkages Tolstoy felt were so essential to his novelistic artistry in *Anna Karenina*, Elizabeth Stenbock-Fermor institutes a captivating image that is consistent with her deployment of the architectural metaphor: "Some links are barely noticeable; they

Mushroom (*syroezhka*)

are like the ornaments in medieval cathedrals: plants and animals, related to parables and tradition, constantly reappearing around columns, along arches, or as fill-ins in corners, and all connected structurally and symbolically to the fundamental essence of the building."[1] It is easy to imagine the edifice budding out in mushrooms, bears, plants with insects, lacy patterns, all of the images that intertwine in *Anna Karenina* to imbricate the major thematic concerns of

"Jam-making" by N. I. Piskariov, 1932

the novel on what can only be considered the subliminal level. Such a profusion of forms, especially when pictured in a visual, architectural sense, belongs to the mode of the grotesque, which Bakhtin defines as the use of images and motifs to establish the reproductivity and cyclicity of the physical plane.[2]

It may seem anomolous to consider Tolstoy an artist of the grotesque, especially if he is seen as a realist, since Bakhtin considers that realism severs the grotesque from its cyclicity: "The last thing one can say of the real grotesque is that it is static; on the contrary it seeks to grasp in its imagery the very act of becoming and growth, the eternal incomplete unfinished nature of being."[3] In the modern period, what Bakhtin calls "degenerate petty realism" depicts only "the process of degeneration and disintegration[.] The positive pole of grotesque realism . . . drops out and is replaced by moral sententiousness and abstract concepts. What remains is nothing but a corpse . . . alienated and torn away from the whole in which it had been linked to that other, younger link in the chain of growth and development."[4]

What we consider standard realism thus represents only the decaying side of the grotesque body—in satirical types such as bureaucrats, old crones, and the like.

Characterizing Tolstoy as an artist of the grotesque is not inconsistent with earlier critical evaluations of Tolstoy, most particularly Merezhkovsky's concept of Tolstoy as a "seer of the flesh." Tolstoyan depictions of festive occasions and mass spectacles (mummers, hunts, balls, races, elections) may be compared to Brueghel's paintings of folk celebrations. While Tolstoy's mass spectacles are as different as can be imagined from the group scenes in Dostoevsky that Bakhtin associates with carnivals, Tolstoy's arena is no less populous, no less popular, no less festive. And to give just one example, the young Rostovs' cross-dressing to join the mummers at Christmas reflects the reversal of values and hierarchies associated with carnivals. Tolstoy is also not deaf to the use of the grotesque for satiric purposes, to wit his descriptions of Lidia Ivanovna, the séance sequence, Grinev's fingernails, and the fly-catching lawyer; Karenin himself, with his large ears and cracking knuckles, occasionally verges on the grotesque. In his use of small ornamental motifs, such as the mushroom and other flora in Varenka's proposal scene, which is the subject of this chapter, Tolstoy borrows the botanical imagery of folklore and folk poetry. Moreover, in his figuring of the lower strata of the human body, his imagery verges on the grotesque in its brightest, most natural form. Tolstoy's artistry thus belongs at "the summit of grotesque and folklore realism."[5]

Despite appreciations of Tolstoy's use of interconnected images and events, those representing the dominant trend in the criticism resist seeing the symbolic imagination in Tolstoy, arguing that such a view would render his art too allegorical.[6] Thus, John Bayley criticizes Tolstoy's uses of foreshadowing devices in *Anna Karenina* as "obtrusive" and schematic, "too symbolically decisive, . . . Tolstoy's symbolic touch is far from delicate, . . . [and] the linkages by means of metaphor are almost a substitute for the symbolic imagination, as if Tolstoy felt that a novel ("the first I have attempted") required something of the sort."[7] Instead, Bayley praises what he perceives to be the random details of verisimilar realism: "These facts seem more meaningful as well as more vital than the metaphoric pattern, the omens,

and the . . . parallels."[8] As an example of these "facts" or "random details," Bayley mentions "Kitty struggling with a pickled mushroom as
she asks Lyovin if there are bears on his estate."[9] Bayley ascribes to
this detail an innocence it does not sustain under closer scrutiny.

In the scene in question, where gestures, looks, and ciphers rather
than words and actions accomplish Kitty and Lyovin's betrothal, Kitty
states: "You've killed a bear, I've been told!" (405). Lyovin's successful
bear hunt is onomastically significant: Kitty *is* "Tiny Bear," a nickname that in turn is meant to be a pun on Behrs, the maiden name of
Tolstoy's wife. Lyovin has caught his bear/Behrs, just as Kitty now attempts to capture her mushroom—a symbol, as I will try to show in
this chapter, of an available male. Furthermore, Kitty's pursuit of the
mushroom on her plate sets "the lace quivering over her white arm"
(405) in a seductive, flirtatious action. In an earlier scene, the lace
on Anna's sleeve is caught, as she is caught by Vronsky's attentions:
"Anna Arkadevna, with her quick little hand, was unfastening the lace
of her sleeve, caught in the hook of her fur cloak, and with bent head,
listening with rapture to the words Vronsky murmured as he escorted
her down" (150). She only extricates herself "suddenly, at the very
moment she unhooked the lace." Thus, Lyovin's successful bear hunt
and Kitty's mushroom chase figure their romantic pursuit of each
other in their betrothal scene.

The Courtship Plot

In his scenes of courtship and seduction—even as early as the silent
dialogue between a man and a woman in his first prose experiment,
"The History of Yesterday"—Tolstoy relies on the semiotics of gesture
and sexual attraction, and the discourse of details. The problem of
courtship is discussed at the beginning of *Anna Karenina* within the
triangular cultural contrast of English, French, and Russian traditions: "How marriages are to be arranged now the Princess could not
find out from anyone. The French way, of parents deciding a daughter's fate, was not accepted, and was even condemned. The English
way, of giving a girl perfect freedom, was also rejected, and would

have been impossible in Russian Society. The Russian way, of employing a professional match-maker, was considered monstrous, and was laughed at by everybody" (41). The problem of how marriages are made and the literary and social conventions of the courtship plot are causally linked in Tolstoy's treatment of the problem of adultery. The debate over the woman question that occupies the guests at the Oblonskys' dinner party proceeds from a recognition of the economic necessity for a woman to marry or to face the limited choices for self-sufficiency as a nurse, companion, governess, or prostitute. The discussion emphasizes the inevitable link between the socioeconomic forces propelling women into loveless marriages and the adultery that frequently results when a woman discovers love after she has been sold in marriage to an incompatible husband. Tolstoy thus reiterates the basic arguments of the woman question as it was formulated in Victorian society as the problem of redundant or superfluous women. Yet when Dolly offers the Victorian answer, that unmarried women can always find a place as an "aunt" caring for relatives' children, Lyovin is convinced of the fallacy of this argument (with which he had initially agreed) as he observes Kitty's reaction:

> "No," said Kitty, blushing, but looking at him all the more boldly with her truthful eyes; "a girl may be in such a situation that she cannot live in the family without humiliation, while she herself. . . ."
>
> At the hint he understood her.
>
> "Oh, yes," he said, "Yes, yes, yes—you're right; you're right!"
>
> And he saw all that Pestsov had been maintaining at dinner about the freedom of woman, simply from getting a glimpse of the terror of an old maid's existence and its humiliation in Kitty's heart, and loving her, he felt that terror and humiliation, and at once gave up his arguments. (418)

Tolstoy thus questions the traditional Victorian confinement of women to the domestic sphere in this recognition of woman's need to find meaningful, independent occupation, and by describing Lyovin's change of heart, he perhaps intends to effect the same change in his reader. He further explodes the conventions of the English novel of courtship and marriage, replacing Lyovin's proposal speech with a game of ciphers. In his literary exploration of what he called "the most important event in a girl's life," Tolstoy rejects the premise of Victorian literary and social conventions, which requires marriageable girls to be totally innocent and restrains them from indicating their feelings until they have received a proposal. Such a state of enforced passivity, combined with the false picture of romance presented by literature, disables young women in their sole chance to determine their destiny, as Dolly complains to Lyovin: "'To you men, free and able to choose, it's always clear who you love. But a maiden is in a position of expectation, with that feminine, maidenly modesty, a maiden who sees you, a man, from afar, takes everything at face value. A maiden might often have such feelings that she doesn't know who she loves or what to say'" (285).

Varenka's Choice

Tolstoy counters Victorian victimizing conventions, both literary and social, with a native Russian version of the courtship plot, an "antiproposal" scene: the mushroom-picking episode where Varenka does not receive Koznyshev's marriage proposal. The isolated scene that involves two minor characters and has no repercussions for subsequent plot actions or other characters is nonetheless embroidered with a delicacy of ornament and detail and an almost baroque overlay of pastoral imagery. In its placement in the novel, the scene is heavily framed and demarcated by the other characters' discussion of marriage proposals that accompanies the action, much like the commentary of a Greek chorus. The striking setting of this scene as a solitary gem of nonaction in the midst of a rushing plot and Tolstoy's rich, textured shading and painting of the nonevent focus our attention on this episode as a moment of vital importance; it is not, as other critics have characterized it, a "disposable" scene, or "one of the moments of waste in the novel."[10]

That Varenka has an important function in the novel connected primarily with the theme of the old maid and the wedding proposal is supported by the consistent application of imagery as her emblematic tag: the leitmotif of the umbrella and the mushroom. The continuous association of Varenka with umbrellas and mushrooms foreshadows the fatal scene of her nonproposal and thus alerts us to the feminocentric theme of the courtship plot, and to Varenka's moment of choice and exalted status as a single woman resisting a loveless marriage.

Varenka is metonymically connected with mushrooms from her first appearance, when she opens an umbrella, and later she is described as "the one in the mushroom hat." In the scene where Kitty and Varenka argue over Varenka's sincerity in pursuing a life that does not involve love or marriage, Kitty snatches Varenka's umbrella away from her and breaks it. Finally, in the nonproposal scene, mushrooms not only form the pretext for the outing, but the substance of the conversation; in fact, Tolstoy imitates the use of flowers and plants in oral literature to emblematize the protagonists' emotions. Thus, mushrooms, like the birch trees and other flora in this passage, constitute a folkloric version of the pathetic fallacy and also provide the protagonists with a folkloric discourse predicated on the collective wisdom of Russian popular literature.

The full significance of Varenka's mushroom picking and its meaning as a motif and pretext in the proposal scene, especially in the context of mycophiliac Russian culture, has never been elaborated. In folklore and mythology the mushroom is a universal image of sexuality, combining both phallic and vaginal characteristics; it is furthermore a sacred food item that is connected with a variety of popular (usually) sexual taboos and a complex folklore of mycology.[11] The umbrella, or parasol, is popularly considered to be closely related to the mushroom, as names of mushrooms, riddles, and folklore demonstrate. For example, mushrooms are often named umbrellas—as with the Russian name "speckled umbrella" *(zont pyostry)*—and there are such riddles as "it has a stem, it has a hat, but it's not a mushroom" (umbrella) *(est i koreshok, est i shliapka, a ne grib [zont])* or "What is a white umbrella standing in the field?" (mushroom).[12]

Mushrooms are privileged motifs in Russian folk culture, both as sacral objects in the mushroom cult and as semiotic objects in a rich folkloric tradition. In his *Semiotics of the Mythological Conceptions about Mushrooms,* Toporov comments about mushrooms in Russian folklore:

[I] had occasion to observe the atmosphere of mystery and taboo which surrounded the topic of mushrooms even in the villages around Moscow in the pre-war period. In answer to innocent questions about mushrooms one had to endure the rebukes of old women (sometimes even of relatively young women) who viewed this interest in mushrooms as a display of depravity or shamelessness. One would hear again and again such remarks as "you're still little, when you grow up you'll find out" or "only girls know this; boys have no reason to." One also encountered more particular interdictions (for example, there are certain types of mushrooms for pregnant women or for maidens), as well as certain identifications of mushrooms or proscriptions relating to them (at least among juvenile boys), sayings, superstitions, etc. One could not help but have the impression that behind these deeply differentiated taboos, that were relaxed only when one was in the woods or in the company of other boys, there lay something possessing an extremely rich semantics and having a direct relation to the sphere of the "indecent."[13]

This semantic field is easily organized around the distinctions that are basic to culture as elaborated by Lévi-Strauss in *The Raw and the Cooked*: raw-cooked, inedible-edible, masculine-feminine, adult-child, married-unmarried. Furthermore, in many cultures there is an implicit and explicit isomorphism between culinary proscriptions and rules for marital relations; for example, the French *consommer* applies to both marriage and meals. A Russian reader would automatically recall the idiomatic expression, "you'll eat a mushroom *(sesh grib)*: you'll have nothing—you'll be unsuccessful." In Russian culture, the picking of mushrooms was viewed as a courtship ritual and is described as such in Melnikov-Pechersky.[14] In some cases, the courtship is ritualized in games, such as one game that has been documented in Lithuania, Belorussia, and Russia in which men and women pair off in rows, reciting: "To pick mushrooms / To pick mushrooms / But not boletus . . . / Each finds his own / Takes it by the hand."[15] Folk sayings refer to the mushroom as a marrying phallus: "What's for me, an old mushroom, to do with a young wife?" *(Kuda mne, staromu gribu, s molodoi zhenoi vozitsia?)* Against the background of this folklore, for Varenka and Koznyshev to pick mushrooms is to set the stage for courtship; for them to discuss mushrooms is to invoke that rich semantic field of double entendres and "indecent" subjects that the topic and the setting invite.

When we have read with this aspect of mushrooms in mind, Sergei Ivanovich's proposal to accompany the mushroom picking expedition takes on additional color. His banal comment, "I love looking for mushrooms; I find it a nice occupation *(khoroshee zaniatie),*" elicits a blush from Varenka. As the expedition sets off, both Varenka and Sergei Ivanovich are given mushroomlike attributes: Tanya puts on Sergei Ivanovich's hat (the wearing of a hat [*shliapa*] is always used in descriptions or identifications of mushrooms), while Varenka wears a white kerchief and a yellow spotted (stippled) dress. It takes only a little work of the imagination to connect Varenka's appearance (white top, spotted yellow "stem") with the mushroom she and Sergei Ivanovich will later try to describe (its underside looks like the chin of an unshaven man). Similarly, with her white kerchief over her black hair, black and white attire, and her "light, rapid step" (579), Varenka recalls Anna, whose own choice in marriage proved fatal. With choices in love symbolized in the choices in mushroom picking between food and poison, Anna's description of Vronsky's love as food for a starving man takes on added poignancy.

We may recall that in the passage under consideration, Koznyshev fully intends to propose to Varenka. The traditional reading of the episode, which is that *both* characters lack sufficient passion, is controverted by the botanical imagery. What we know of Sergei Ivanovich's thoughts indicates that he is seriously in love: "The feeling he had for her was something special that he had felt long, long ago, and only once, in his early youth" (588). Whatever love may mean to Sergei Ivanovich, he has now experienced it for the second time. His feeling of "happiness in being near [Varenka] continually grew and grew, and at last reached such a point that . . . he put a huge birch mushroom . . . into her basket" (588). The mushroom is described in unusual detail and initiates the use in this scene of botanical imagery as a folkloric symbology. Sexual attraction and desire are thus revealed, as in a folk song, through the natural imagery that ornaments the action. The mushroom Sergei Ivanovich gives to Varenka is a birch mushroom on a slender stalk with an upcurling rim. The birch is a folk symbol of maidenhood, and the inverted cap of the mushroom reveals its androgynous structure and the ambivalent concave/convex characteristics that make it a symbol of both masculine and feminine sexuality. Sergei Ivanovich next walks further into the forest, penetrating into the depths of a primeval, secluded natural sphere and thus finding a region or zone where taboos are lifted and where constraints of behavior may be abandoned.[16] The birch trees again suggest the attribute of the young maiden and recall the Russian proverb, "the heart of a young girl is like a dark forest."

Walking into the heart of the wood, Sergei Ivanovich comes to a standstill by a "bushy spindle tree" (*berezkleta*) whose etymological root recalls the birch, and he contemplates the erect rosy-red catkins, whose name in Russian, "seryozhki," may be read as a diminutive of Sergei, Koznyshev's name, thus evoking the erect phallus as a homunculus or diminutive self. In a series of gestures that may be read as sexual metaphors, Sergei Ivanovich tries to light his cigar but has difficulty getting his match to ignite on the damp trunk of the birch.

That Koznyshev's attraction to Varenka is genuine is affirmed by the Shcherbatsky women's discussion of the couple. The gathering of the Shcherbatsky women on the porch in a "woman's kingdom" (Lyovin's observation) evokes the women's world of folk wisdom. Their needlework and their commentary seems purely classical; like the Greek chorus they discuss the significance of the events about to be enacted; like the Fates conspiring to bring Dido her beloved, their cooking of the jam is reminiscent of the witches' brew. The preparation of jam becomes an onomastic echo of the event: in Russian, the word for jam, "*varen'e*," is related to the diminutive Varenka (although no etymological connection is being suggested here—merely a recognition that linguistic play provides emphasis). The issue of when the jam will be ready, of waiting until precisely the right moment, is isomorphic to Varenka's readiness to receive a proposal and to the importance of the sense of timing, while the description of oozing pink scum in the jam suggests vaginal arousal.

The discussion of Varenka opens with a comment on her dress: "precisely the kind of thing one should give one's servants," which acknowledges Varenka's dependent status and economic reliance on marriage. Then Dolly affirms Koznyshev's attraction to Varenka. However, Kitty's summation of the relationship as she enumerates Varenka's positive qualities reveals her doubts that Koznyshev's feelings are reciprocated: "Thirdly, that she should love him. And that is . . . That is, it would be so good!" (581). Varenka's own thoughts reflect the same ambivalence: "To be the wife of a man like Koznyshev after her position with Mme Stahl, was to her imagination, the height of happiness. Besides, she was almost certain that she was in love with him" (591).

As Koznyshev approaches Varenka with the intention of proposing, she is protecting the mushrooms from the little boy Grisha, who wants to pick them. Instead, Varenka calls to the little girl Masha to pick a mushroom. (The name of the mushroom is *syroezhka*, another onomastic echo of Sergei/Seryozhka?) This vignette places the power of selection with the female, in spite of social and literary conventions that give the voice and initiative to the male, who is to "propose." The mushroom Varenka shows to little Masha is pierced through by a blade of grass: "split in half across its rosy cap by a dry blade of grass." Masha picks the mushroom and finishes splitting it in half, revealing its feminine interior.

Tolstoy's treatment of this scene emphasizes imagery and gesture, while denying the primacy of language and proposal texts altogether. Composed entirely according to the rhetoric of novelistic declarations of love, Koznyshev's prepared speech ("Varvara Andreevna, when I was very young, I set before myself the ideal of the woman I loved that I would be happy to call my wife. I have lived through a long life, and now for the first time I have met what I sought in you. I love you, and offer you my hand" [590]) is never delivered.

The novelistic rhetoric of declarations and proposals is ridiculed quite explicitly in *Family Happiness*:

> "A man may say that he is in love, and a woman can't," she said.
> "I disagree," said he . . . "What sort of a revelation is that, that a man is in love? A man seems to think that whenever he says the

word, something will go pop!—that some miracle will be worked, signs and wonders, with all the big guns firing at once! . . . "

"Then how is a woman to know that a man is in love with her, unless he tells her?" asked Katya.

"That I don't know," he answered; "every man has his own way of telling things. If the feeling exists, it will out somehow. But when I recall novels, I always fancy the crestfallen look of Lieutenant Strelsky or Alfred when he says, 'I love you Eleanora,' and expects something wonderful to happen at once, and no change at all takes place in either of them—their eyes, their noses and their whole selves remain exactly as they were."[17]

The point seems to be that the verbal declaration of love is fallacious—either love has already been declared and an understanding reached or the man is deluding himself.

For example, the "proposal" scene between Lyovin and Kitty takes place with minimal linguistic contact; even the ciphers they sketch in chalk on the table are ignored after they begin to escape "confused, verbose discussion" and instead share a "laconic, clear, almost wordless communication" (417). The nonsemantic aspect of this scene seems even clearer when we note that in the biographical incident on which it is based, Tolstoy's fiancée, Sonya, was completely unable to decipher the code, but understood Tolstoy's intentions well enough. Similarly, when Lyovin arrives the next morning at the Shcherbatsky house to formalize his suit, no speeches are made, parental consent is given, and Kitty accepts him, all without the Victorian convention of "asking Father." Instead, Kitty's parents immediately embrace Lyovin with the words "So, it is settled."

Anna and Vronsky's future is also determined without words or rather without meaningful words, as Kitty observes them with horror at the ball: "They were speaking of common acquaintances, keeping up the most trivial conversation, but to Kitty it seemed that every word they said was determining their fate and hers. And strange it was that they were actually talking of how absurd Ivan Ivanovich was with his French, and how the Eletsky girl might have made a better match, yet these words were important for them, and they felt just as Kitty did" (87). Or, in *Resurrection*: "They spoke of the injustice of power, of the sufferings of the unfortunate, of the poverty of people, but the reality was that their eyes, gazing at each other as they talked, kept asking, 'Could you love me?' and answering, 'I could.'"[18]

The Shcherbatsky women's discussion of Varenka's proposal acknowledges that courtship is a nonverbal phenomenon:

> "Mama, how did Papa propose?" Kitty suddenly asked. . . .
> "You imagine, I suppose, that you invented something new? It's always just the same: it was settled by the eyes, by smiles. . . ."
> "How nicely you said that, Mama! It's just by the eyes, by smiles that it's done," Dolly assented. (582)

In the realm of nonverbal communication, the gendered restrictions of courtship discourse are diminished, and it becomes possible for the woman to declare her love and thus compromise herself, as Kitty acknowledges to Varenka. She recalls her last dance with Vronsky when the look "full of love she had given him, to which he made no response, cut her to the heart with an agony of shame" (86):

> "The humiliation," said Kitty, "the humiliation one can never forget, can never forget," she said, remembering her expression at the last ball during the pause in the music.
> "Where is the humiliation? Why, you did nothing wrong?"
> "Worse than wrong—shameful." . . .
> "Why, what is there shameful?" she said. "You didn't tell a man who didn't care for you that you loved him, did you?"
> "Of course not; I never said a word, but he knew it. No, no, there are looks, there are ways." (235)

And there are also ways of telling a man he is not loved and his suit is not welcome. At the moment when Koznyshev is about to deliver his proposal speech, Varenka blocks his intended pass by allowing commonplace language to divert him from his intention:

> Varenka saw that he wanted to speak; she guessed of what, and felt faint with joy and panic. They had walked so far away that no one

could hear them now, but still he did not begin to speak. It would have been better for Varenka to be silent. After a silence it would have been easier for them. . . . But against her will, as it were accidentally, Varenka said,

"So, you found nothing?" (591)

Her disruptive words, which are an annoyance to Koznyshev, are also a statement of negation, a rejection of what Koznyshev had indeed found, the genuine desire to propose to her. Taking the hint, Koznyshev "reads" Varenka's demeanor, which reveals anguished expectation but no desire. The smiles and looks, which are so impossible to counterfeit, are not there. We might recall Princess Maria, whose anxiety in meeting Anatole Kuragin worsened her appearance but who, in front of Nikolai Rostov, is filled with grace and beauty. Taking the cue from Varenka, Koznyshev, "as if it were against his will," begins to speak about mushrooms, asking a taboo-violating question that elicits an "indecent" reply from Varenka:

"What's the difference between a white and a birch mushroom?"
"There's no difference in the cap, it's in the stalk."

Koznyshev's use of folk humor to conclude the exchange also exposes his duplicity, since his subsequent sketch of the mushroom ("a birch mushroom looks like a dark man who hasn't shaved for two days" [591]) reveals that he knows its appearance quite well.

Both Varenka and Koznyshev act in this sequence "as if it were against their will," an expression of the involuntary or autonomic behavior that reflects their irrepressible unconscious impulses. The question of freedom of will, which preoccupied Tolstoy throughout his writing of *War and Peace* and which he rediscovered in Schopenhauer during his writing of *Anna Karenina,* is explored in *Anna* in specifically psychological terms as the interaction between conscious intent and unconscious desire. In dissuading Koznyshev, Varenka thus acts according to a natural honesty against what appear to be her own best interests. In fact, she resists entering into a loveless marriage, despite her understandable desire for the status and security of marriage.

Although Koznyshev later concocts a salve for his ego by rationalizing his failure to propose as loyalty to the memory of his childhood sweetheart, the subverbal communication of the nonproposal scene indicates that Varenka rejected his suit.

Varenka's single state, her conviction that there are "so many more important things" than love and marriage, and her continual attention to others' needs prefigure the idealized single women of Tolstoy's postconversion writings. For example, in *Resurrection* Maria Pavlovna, who is "wholly absorbed in finding opportunities to serve others,"[19] "knew and was even pleased to know that she was beautiful, but far from enjoying the impression she made . . . she was frightened of it and was disgusted and horrified by all love affairs. The men among her comrades who were aware of this, even those who might have been drawn toward her, no longer dared to show their admiration, but treated her as they would have treated a man."[20] The character of Varenka and her escape from the life path of love and marriage point the way to Tolstoy's ultimate view, that equality between the sexes can only occur when there is an absence of the sexual power relations and possession that are the inevitable accompaniments of the nineteenth-century bourgeois marriage.

CONCLUSION

After *Anna Karenina*

In *Resurrection* Katiusha Maslova's tendrils of black, curly hair, willfully escaping from beneath her white kerchief, her black, squinting eyes, and her contemplation of suicide at a railway station suggest a reprise of Anna Karenina, or perhaps her resurrection in a character who is more explicitly a victim. Her position as a household dependent from the lower classes, her narrative of ruin through seduction, childbirth, and abandonment, and her subsequent life as a prostitute are more closely associated with the traditional story of the fallen woman than is Anna's story. Similarly, the intention Nekhliudov has of rescuing Katiusha through a fictitious marriage echoes the novelistic clichés of the nineteenth-century social novel. But Tolstoy refutes this plot line every bit as emphatically as Dostoevsky does when he ironically quotes Nekrasov's lines: "Enter now, both bold and free / Be mistress of my house and me" in the scene where his Underground Man fails to rescue the prostitute Liza. The difference is that Tolstoy allows a woman's voice to speak: "'Go away! I'm a convict and you are a prince—you have no business to be here!' she said, her face distorted with rage, pulling away her hand. 'You want to save yourself through me,' she went on rapidly, as though in haste to pour out every feeling in her heart. 'You had your pleasure from me, and now you want to get your salvation through me. I loathe you!'"[1]

Maslova refuses to be the tool for Nekhliudov's redemption, as she had earlier been the tool for satisfying his sexual desire. She works her own spiritual resurrection without Nekhliudov's help, through her

own experiences and especially through her relationship with the
saintly, asexual Maria Pavlovna:

> [U]nconsciously, [Katiusha] accepted Maria Pavlovna's views and
> came to imitate her in everything.
>
> Maria Pavlovna was in her turn touched by Katusha's devotion
> and began to love her. They were also drawn together by the repul-
> sion they both felt to sexual love. One hated it because she knew all
> its horrors, while the other, having never experienced it, regarded it
> as something incomprehensible and repugnant, and offensive to
> human dignity.[2]

Nekhliudov ultimately realizes that he must overcome his own prej-
udices against women and conflicts about married life when the
possibility of a real marriage—rather than a fictitious marriage to
Maslova—fills him with horror and when he is momentarily seduced
by his close encounter with aristocratic family life.

Fictitious or real, marriage does not and cannot provide the solution for the social oppression Nekhliudov now sees enacted upon the
poor by the wealthy and upon women by men. Like Pozdnyshev in
The Kreutzer Sonata, he draws the conclusion that ways of thought
must change, not merely institutions. Substituting fictitious marriage
for a consummated marriage merely substitutes one form of using
women for another. While Pozdnyshev is only capable of viewing his
wife as a sister when she is dying—hence ultimately framed and iconi-
cized—and while Lyovin only achieves this vision of Anna with the
assistance of a great work of art, Nekhliudov is able to achieve it without framing Katiusha:[3]

> Now [Nekhliudov] felt toward [Katiusha] as he had never felt before,
> and this feeling had nothing in common with either that early sense
> of romantic exaltation or the sensual love which he had afterward felt
> for her. Nor was it at all like the self-satisfaction, rooted in the sense
> of doing his duty, which had after the trial led him to make his offer
> of marriage. It was, quite simply, the same pity and tenderness that
> he experienced on first seeing her in the prison. . . . It was the same
> feeling, but with this difference: once it had been fleeting, now it

was settled. Whatever he happened to be doing or thinking, his mood was always tender and pitiful, not toward Maslova alone, but towards the whole world.[4]

In arriving at this position, Tolstoy acknowledged the necessity for freeing a woman's beauty from its economic and sexual entrapment and for pursuing instead a sublime involvement with humanity. Yet, despite the fact that Tolstoy's views were more explicitly developed and conscious at the time he was writing *Resurrection,* his readers may find his ideas more powerfully expressed in *Anna Karenina,* unarguably the greater work of art.

The great art witnessed in *Anna Karenina* generates awe, vision, transcendence, and awareness of the sublime in its viewers. Art that merely infects with the desire for mimesis, whether of a good or bad model, fails, just as imitating Varenka does not work for Kitty. By his own criterion, Tolstoy would probably have to acknowledge that *Resurrection* was an artistic failure.

I have attempted in this study to renegotiate some of the more familiar critical terrain of Tolstoy's biography that has shaped our understanding of Tolstoy's views on the issues discussed in the previous chapters, and I have sought to provide the backdrop for our reading of Tolstoy's novel. In so doing, I hope to have challenged standard views of authorial misogyny and standard critical practice that attribute sexism to a text. By choosing to focus in my readings on clusters of imagery related to the field of vision, light and shadow, representation, corporality and sexuality, I have sometimes offered readings of passages that have been well traversed in the criticism and have taken for granted these established critical interpretations in order to concentrate on the wealth of available meanings and interconnections that may not have been remarked upon before. Alternately, I have considered scenes and passages that cannot be considered significant in themselves but that, through the accretion of the novel's symbolic system, acquire the status of a linkage in the labyrinth.

The labyrinth of *Anna Karenina* is an enclosure that by its very artifice reminds us we are enclosed and thus points our vision to what is not or cannot be contained, and to the means of entrance and exit traversing the frame. Lyrical moments in the novel that generate this type of aesthetic response supersede the twists and turns of narrative and instead produce awe at the dizzying effect of creation.

In *Anna Karenina* Tolstoy creates a series of lyrical moments that exceed the exigencies of narrative and the bounds of verisimilitude. It is my contention that while engaged with a lyrically motivated moment, the reader is catapulted beyond the desire for another reality into pure gnosis; Tolstoy pictures this sense of awe or transcendence in the reader or viewer in his own description of Lyovin before Anna's portrait. Furthermore, he explores the parameters of human vision and insight, enlightenment and blindness, and the formation of imaged realities and framed compositions as strategies motivated by the human need to establish meaning, context, and coherence in life. His characters are thus given a quest beyond the usual one of pursuit of marriage and estate for the hero or heroine of the realist novel. Tolstoy's execution of a portrait of his heroine is meant to transfigure her and transfix his readers. Within the frame of his canvas every detail is significant, and each play of light and shadow reminds us that we are earthbound, gazing at art, at another reality altogether.

NOTES

Introduction

1. As reported by the curatorial staff at Yasnaya Polyana. Philip Rogers, personal communication, 1988.

2. Although Tolstoy rejected *Anna Karenina* along with his entire "preconversion" oeuvre, the fact remains that Tolstoy, the artist in pursuit of a new art, did write novels, and *Anna Karenina* was written at the critical juncture in the development of his aesthetic theory. His views on art and his pursuit of mythopoesis are readily apparent in the novel, as many critics have noted, most recently Silbajoris.

3. John Bayley, *Tolstoy and the Novel.* New York: Viking, 1966, p. 235.

4. Not solely the practice of male authors. George Eliot's Dorothea, for example, is elaborately carved, painted, and framed throughout *Middlemarch*.

5. Although this spelling is not consistent either with the Library of Congress transliteration system or with common usage, I utilize it here, first, to emphasize the connection between this surname and the first name of the author, pronounced Lyoff. Second, the spelling "Levin" suggests a Jewish background that is inappropriate.

6. In developing this terminology, I am deeply indebted to the work of Richard Gustafson and to his inspired notion of emblematic realism. Rimvydas Silbajoris's important work on Tolstoy's aesthetics and his art has also impressed me profoundly, although his book appeared after this manuscript was largely completed.

7. It could be argued that Tolstoy belongs to the tradition of Romantic Realism outlined by Donald Fanger. Because Tolstoy is not usually seen as sharing affinities with Gogol and Dostoevsky, Fanger's representative Romantic Realists, I find this notion more problematic than the solution I propose, of establishing a sui generis category for Tolstoy on the cusp of symbolism.

Chapter 1

1. Jacques Derrida, *The Truth in Painting*. Trans. Geoff Bennington and Ian McLeod. Chicago: University of Chicago Press, 1987. A brief version of this chapter was delivered as a paper at the annual meeting of the American Association for the Advancement of Slavic Studies, November 1989.

2. Henry James, preface to *The Awkward Age*. New York: Penguin Classics, 1966, p. 10.

3. Boris Uspensky, *A Poetics of Composition: The Structure of the Artistic Text and Typology of a Compositional Form*. Trans. Valentina Zavarin and Susan Wittig. Berkeley: University of California Press, 1973, p. 137.

4. Uspensky, 146.

5. Iuri Lotman, *The Structure of the Artistic Text*. Trans. Ronald Vroon. Ann Arbor: Michigan Slavic Publications, 1977, p. 209.

6. Derrida, 11–12.

7. Boris Tomashevsky, "Literature and Biography" [Literatura i biografiia, *Kniga i revoliutsiia* 4 (1923):6–9]. Trans. Herbert Eagle. In Vassilis Lambropoulos and David Neal Miller, eds., *Twentieth Century Literary Theory: An Introductory Anthology*. Albany: SUNY Press, 1987, p. 117.

8. See, for example, W. K. Wimsatt, Jr., and Monroe C. Beardsley, "The Intentional Fallacy." In Lambropoulos and Miller, 103–115.

9. Gary Saul Morson, "Dostoevskij's Anti-Semitism and the Critics: A Review Article." *Slavic and East European Journal* 27 (1983):302–317.

10. I refer the interested reader to Ruth Crego Benson's study, where a complete overview of Tolstoy's misogynist remarks is available.

11. Consider, for example, Andrea Dworkin's reading of *The Kreutzer Sonata* where any feminist qualities of the text are negated by the fact that Tolstoy continued to have sexual relations with his wife.

12. I refer primarily to the following three monographs: Judith Armstrong, *The Unsaid Anna Karenina*. New York: St. Martin's Press, 1988; Ruth Crego Benson, *Women in Tolstoy: The Ideal and the Erotic*. Urbana: University of Illinois Press, 1973; and Mary Evans, *Reflecting on Anna Karenina*. London: Routledge, 1989. Numerous works could be cited that perpetuate this reading of Tolstoy. In addition, I am responding to uncountable conversations with students and colleagues who share a perception of Tolstoy as misogynist and who regard my thesis with profound skepticism. An important exception is Barbara Heldt's chapter "Tolstoy's Path to Feminism," in *Terrible Perfection: Women in Russian Literature*. Bloomington: Indiana University Press, 1987. See chapter 2 of this book for a more thorough evaluation of feminist criticism of Tolstoy.

13. The views I have sketched have their most thorough expression in Ruth Crego Benson's study of women in Tolstoy. Typical of prevailing opinion is this statement, taken from the entry on "Women and Russian Literature," in *Hand-*

book of Russian Literature. Ed. Victor Terras. New Haven: Yale University Press, 1985, p. 520:

> For Lev Tolstoi the woman question did not exist except, as in his opinion expressed in 1905 in an afterword to Chekhov's "The Darling," . . . [as] "a vulgar, fashionable movement confusing both men and women." He considered a woman's calling (and her superiority to man) to be her sublime capacity for love and sacrifice. . . . Tolstoy's good women, as in *War and Peace,* are innocent as girls and become chaste wives and dedicated mothers, like Natasha and Princess Marie, or useful, selfless spinsters, like Sonya; adulteresses, like Hélène Bezukhov, wreak evil and perish by it—even the lovely heroine of *Anna Karenina.* Hence, there is no need to develop a woman's mind, still less her imagination. A worldly, frivolous education makes even blameless girls into traps for masculine lust and leads to tragedies, such as in *The Kreutzer Sonata,* while carnal passion breeds crime, as in *The Power of Darkness.*

14. The problems in finding Tolstoy's biography in the maze of engineered events and self-directed performances is discussed by Gary Saul Morson, *Hidden in Plain View: Narrative and Creative Potentials in "War and Peace."* Stanford, Calif.: Stanford University Press, 1987.

15. Some early reviews of Tolstoy's philosophy were L. Obolenskii, "L. N. Tolstoi o zhenskom voprose, iskusstve, i nauke." *Russkoe bogatstvo* 4 (1886): 167–176, and V. G. Chertkov, *O polovom voprose: Mysli L. N. Tolstogo.* Izd. Christchurch: Svobodnogo slova, 1901.

16. Four translated editions had appeared in Russia within two years of its publication in England in 1869. Strakhov's review of Mill's book provoked Tolstoy into writing a letter to Strakhov that expressed antipathy toward the women's liberation movement and endorsed Strakhov's opinion that prostitution was a valuable profession, necessary for the existence of the family. Although Tolstoy probably thought better of this position almost immediately since the letter remained unsent, these early outrageous statements have been cited ad nauseam to indict him as a misogynist. It should also be noted that part of Strakhov's rejection of the woman question was motivated by his sense that it was a European import, not an issue native to Russian culture. Tolstoy undoubtedly concurred with this assessment.

17. "Early Essays on Marriage and Divorce." In John Stuart Mill and Harriet Taylor Mill, *Essays on Sex Equality.* Chicago: University of Chicago Press, 1970, p. 73.

18. John Stuart Mill, "Early Essays," 71.

19. Ibid., 75.

20. Ibid., 76.

21. Ibid., 77.

22. Harriet Taylor Mill, *The Enfranchisement of Women.* In Mill and Mill, 100.

23. John Stuart Mill, *The Subjection of Women.* In Mill and Mill, 179.

24. For a succinct history of the woman question as imported to Russia from Europe, see Jane McDermid, "The Influence of Western Ideas on the Development of the Woman Question in Nineteenth-Century Russian Thought." *Irish Slavonic Studies* 9 (1988):21–36. For a general historical treatment of the women's liberation movement in Russia, see Richard Stites, *The Women's Liberation Movement in Russia: Feminism, Nihilism, and Bolshevism, 1860–1930.* Princeton: Princeton University Press, 1978.

25. In fact, many feminist thinkers of the nineteenth century considered that Russian women were better off than their European counterparts.

26. Stites, 174.

27. Figures are cited in Stites, 57 and 60.

28. Anthony Trollope, *Can You Forgive Her?* Oxford: Oxford University Press, 1973, p. 286.

29. Liubov Andreevna Vorontsova, *Sofia Kovalevskaia.* Moscow, 1957.

30. Cited in Stites, 74.

31. Leo Tolstoy, *What Then Must We Do?* Trans. Aylmer Maude. Bideford, Devon: Green Books, Ford House, Hartland, 1991, p. 233.

32. Tolstoy's views on the woman question as expressed in *What Then Must We Do?* occasioned some journalistic discussion in 1886. Tolstoy was attacked by Skabichevsky and defended by Obolensky. Their polemic prompted Tolstoy to clarify his views in the essay "Men's and Women's Work," which he published that same year in Obolensky's journal.

33. For a discussion of the "new" sexual morality at the turn of the century as it related to Tolstoy's views on the "sex question" and the "marriage question," see Peter Ulf Møller, *Postlude to The Kreutzer Sonata: Tolstoy and the Debate on Sexual Morality in Russian Literature in the 1890s.* Leiden: E. J. Brill, 1988.

34. Leonid Obolensky, "Voprosy v noveishei belletristike." *Russkoe bogatstvo* 3 (1890):188–200.

35. Paigel's *Adam, Eve, and the Serpent* demonstrates quite clearly that early Christianity was an antifamily force.

36. I use this term to refer to the current trend in French feminism represented by such thinkers as Cixous, Irigaray, and Kristeva, who suspect the masculinist formation of earlier feminist thought.

37. Leo Nikolaevich Tolstoy, *Brak i polovaia liubov' s predisloviem V. Chertkova.* Rabochee knigoizdatel'stvo, 1919, p. 30.

38. Kathleen Blake, *Love and the Woman Question in Victorian Literature: The Art of Self-Postponement.* Totowa, N. J.: Barnes & Noble, 1983, p. xiv.

39. Cited in the translation by Louise and Aylmer Maude of *Great Short Works of Leo Tolstoy.* New York: Harper & Row, 1969, p. 386.

40. Chodorow even denies women any special capacity for nurturance and thus minimizes biological differences between the sexes. Despite the fact that

with this view there is the attempt to disregard the extremely powerful experiences of pregnancy, childbirth, and breast-feeding, the view is widely adhered to.

41. Tolstoy, *Brak,* 51.

42. Nancy Miller, *The Heroine's Text.* New York: Columbia University Press, 1986.

Chapter 2

1. Letter to Strakhov, 23–26 April 1876. In *Tolstoy's Letters,* 2 vols. Trans. and ed. R. F. Christian. London: Athlone, 1978, vol. 1, pp. 296–297.

2. Lionel Trilling, from *The Opposing Self* (1955). In Edward Wasiolek, ed., *Critical Essays on Tolstoy.* Boston: G. K. Hall, 1986, p. 148.

3. Matthew Arnold, "Count Leo Tolstoy" (1887). In Henry Gifford, ed., *Leo Tolstoy: A Critical Anthology.* Harmondsworth, Middlesex: Penguin, 1971, p. 63.

4. Philip Rahv, "Tolstoy: The Green Twig and the Black Trunk," (1946). In Gifford, 22.

5. Vladimir Nabokov, "Tolstoy." Translated by Dmitri Nabokov. *New York Review of Books* 35, 3 (March 3, 1988): p. 6.

6. Gary Saul Morson, chap. 1 in *Hidden in Plain View: Narrative and Creative Potentials in "War and Peace."* Stanford, Calif.: Stanford University Press, 1987.

7. Quoted by S. Shchukin in *Russkaia mysl',* no. 10, p. 45. Cited in Sydney Schultze, *The Structure of "Anna Karenina."* Ann Arbor: Ardis Press, 1982, p. 57.

8. E. M. Forster, from *Aspects of the Novel* (1927). In Gifford, 193.

9. Richard Gustafson, *Leo Tolstoy: Resident and Stranger.* Princeton: Princeton University Press, 1986, p. xiii.

10. Paul de Man, *Blindness and Insight: Essays in the Rhetoric of Contemporary Criticism* (1971), 2d ed. *Theory and History of Literature,* vol. 7. Minneapolis: University of Minnesota Press, 1983, p. 9.

11. J. Hillis Miller, *The Ethics of Reading: Kant, de Man, Eliot, Trollope, James, and Benjamin.* New York: Columbia University Press, 1986, p. 1.

12. Wayne C. Booth, *The Company We Keep: An Ethics of Fiction.* Berkeley: University of California Press, 1988.

13. *Tolstoy's Letters,* vol. 1, pp. 296–297.

14. This viewpoint was essential to the earliest formulations of Russian formalist poetics and to a program that became increasingly important as the formalist critics developed their theories. Formalist critical practice, therefore, does not quite deserve the reputation it has acquired in recent years for operating within a vacuum or for absence of contextualization.

15. This schematization overlooks a third critical path taken by Nancy Miller in *The Heroine's Text,* in which she posits that the so-called dysphoric plot of fall, ruin, and death may actually be redemptive or represent the enactment of free will (e.g., *La Princesse de Clèves, La Dame aux Camillas*); by contrast, the euphoric plot of marriage and material prosperity signals the spiritual death of the heroine.

16. Margaret R. Higonnet, introduction to *The Representation of Women in Fiction.* Ed. Carolyn Heilbrun and Margaret R. Higonnet. Baltimore: Johns Hopkins University Press, 1981, pp. xviii–xix.

17. Iurii Lotman, *The Structure of the Artistic Text.* Trans. Ronald Vroon. Ann Arbor: Michigan Slavic Contributions, no. 7, 1977, p. 211. The shift from referring to Anna as "woman" to referring to her as "person" is indicative of the recasting of Anna's tragedy from local to universal interest.

18. Mary Evans, *Reflecting on Anna Karenina.* London: Routledge, 1989, p. 22.

19. Evans, 84.

20. Judith Armstrong, *The Unsaid Anna Karenina.* New York: St. Martin's Press, 1988, p. 184.

21. Armstrong, 124.

22. John Bayley even places Flaubert's words in Tolstoy's mouth: "In such a relation it does not matter how apparently dissimilar is the creator from his creation: it is not a kinship of externals and ideas but of a deeper psychological identification. . . . like Flaubert with his heroine, Tolstoy—had he been given to such comments—could have said: "Madame Karenine, c'est moi." *Tolstoy and the Novel.* Chicago: University of Chicago Press, 1966, p. 201.

23. "What [Tolstoy] loves in Anna is his own sexuality," comments Armstrong in her most succinct summation of Tolstoy's unconscious drives as embodied in the novel. See Armstrong, 94.

24. "Tolstoy, ty dokazal s terpen'em i talantom, / Chto zhenshchine ne sleduet 'guliat'' / Ni s kamer-iunkerom, ni s fligel'-ad"iutantom, / Kogda ona zhena i mat'." The translation in chapter 2 is mine. Cited in A. V. Knowles, ed., *Tolstoy: The Critical Heritage.* London: Routledge & Kegan Paul, 1978, p. 292.

25. Barbara Heldt forms an important exception. See "Tolstoy's Path to Feminism" in her book *Terrible Perfection: Women and Russian Literature.* Bloomington: Indiana University Press, 1987.

26. As Dworkin does, for example, in the first chapter of her book *Intercourse.* New York: Macmillan, 1987. Tolstoy himself argued in the afterword to *The Kreutzer Sonata* that chastity, like other ideals, is difficult to achieve and that what is important is continued effort.

27. R. F. Christian, *Tolstoy: A Critical Introduction.* Cambridge: Cambridge University Press, 1969, p. 181.

28. René Wellek, "The Nineteenth-Century Russian Novel in English and American Criticism." In *The Russian Novel from Pushkin to Pasternak*. Ed. John Garrard. New Haven: Yale University Press, 1983, p. 250.

29. David H. Stewart, "*Anna Karenina*: The Dialectic of Prophecy." *PMLA* 79 (1964):266–274.

30. Gustafson, 131–132.

31. Evans, 35.

32. Richard Freeborn, *The Rise of the Russian Novel*. Cambridge: Cambridge University Press, 1973, p. 121, n. 2.

33. Emphasis added. V. Markov, review in *Nedelia*, no. 1 (1878). Translated in Knowles, 308.

34. Emphasis added. A. V. Stankevich, "Anna Karenina and Lyovin." *The European Courier*, nos. 4–5 (1878). Translated in Knowles, 296, 304.

35. Stewart, 274.

36. "From Homer on, there have been those who contend that fatherhood, unlike motherhood, is a learned role, not a natural one. If that's true, it could explain why so many absent fathers feel awkward in their relationships with their children, and avoid them rather than learn to cope." Nina J. Easton, "Life without Father," *Los Angeles Times Sunday Magazine*, 19 June (Father's Day) 1992, p. 18.

37. Evans, 40.

38. Gifford, 301.

39. For a discussion of this theme in Russian literature, see Ellen Chances, *Conformity's Children: An Approach to the Superfluous Man in Russian Literature*. Columbus, Ohio: Slavica, 1978.

40. Evans, 3–4.

41. Armstrong, 24.

42. Boris Eikhenbaum, *Tolstoy in the Seventies*. Trans. Albert Kaspin. Ann Arbor: Ardis Press, 1982, p. 138.

43. Christian, 175.

44. Viktor Shklovsky, *Lev Tolstoy*. Moscow: Progress, 1978, p. 436.

45. The best, most recent discussion of this problem that I was able to read only after my manuscript was completed appears in Robert Louis Jackson, "On the Ambivalent Beginning of *Anna Karenina*." In E. de Haard, T. Langerak, and W. G. Weststeijn, eds., *The Semantic Analysis of Literary Texts*. Amsterdam: Elsevier, 1990, pp. 345–352. Jackson concludes that "for Tolstoj the *ethical* injunction—'do not judge'—is also an *esthetic* injunction—one that must govern the authorial stance of the artist, that is, his relationship to his heroes. . . . Tolstoj does not judge Anna. He understands her" (p. 346).

46. Fyodor Dostoevsky, "*Anna Karenina* kak fakt osobogo znacheniia," *Dnevnik pisatelia*, 1877. Polnoe sobranie Sochinenii in 23 vols. Petrograd: Prosveshchenie, vol. 21:238–239.

47. Cited in Eikhenbaum, 145. Eikhenbaum shows quite convincingly that Tolstoy originally simply translated Schopenhauer's *"Mein ist die Rache"* into an inaccurate Russian version, *"Otmshchenie moe"* (which persisted through several drafts of the early variants), and only later corrected his Russian text against the church Slavic.

48. It is more than likely that Tolstoy had read these novels by the time he was composing *Anna Karenina*. He mentions Ellen Wood in his correspondence with admiration and refers to her as *"bol'shoe vliianie"* in his list of literary influences. *East Lynne* offers many intertextual resonances with *Anna Karenina*. There are eight novels by Mrs. Henry Wood and eleven novels by Trollope in the library at Yasnaya Polyana. The significance of Trollope for Tolstoy has been well documented. Tolstoy is known to have read the entire Palliser series as it appeared in print, and *Phineas Redux* was published just one year before *Anna Karenina*. (See chapter 3 for a more extensive discussion of the Victorian literary influences on *Anna Karenina*.)

49. For a comprehensive study of all the references to the biblical passage in the novel, see Rebecca S. Hogan, *The Wisdom of Many, the Wit of One: The Narrative Function of the Proverb in Tolstoy's "Anna Karenina" and Trollope's "Orley Farm."* Unpublished doctoral dissertation, University of Colorado, 1985.

50. Tony Tanner, *Adultery in the Novel: Contract and Transgression*. Baltimore: Johns Hopkins University Press, 1979, p. 14.

51. E. Depuy, *Les Grands Maîtres de la littérature russe au dix-neuvième siècle* (1885); cited in Knowles, 326.

52. D. H. Lawrence, from his introduction to *Cavalleria Rusticana*. In Gifford, 197.

53. Depuy, cited in Knowles, 329.

54. Harold Bloom, introduction to *Leo Tolstoy's "Anna Karenina."* Ed. Harold Bloom. New York: Chelsea House, 1987, p. 6.

55. Robert Louis Jackson, "Chance and Design in *Anna Karenina*." In Bloom, 34.

56. Martin Price, "Tolstoy and the Forms of Life: 'Inexorable Law,'" In Harold Bloom, ed. *Leo Tolstoy's "Anna Karenina*," New York: Chelsea House, 1987:111–123.

57. E. B. Greenwood, *Tolstoy: The Comprehensive Vision*. New York: St. Martin's Press, 1975, pp. 117–118.

58. D. H. Lawrence, from *Study of Thomas Hardy*. In Gifford, 150.

59. Barbara Hardy, chap. 4 in *The Appropriate Form*. London: Athlone, 1964.

60. Jackson, "Chance and Design in *Anna Karenina*." In Bloom, 34.

61. The terms *heroine-ism* and *heroinism* were apparently introduced into the criticism by Diana Trilling in "The Liberated Heroine." *Partisan Review* 45

(1978):501–522 and by Ellen Moers in her *Literary Women: The Great Writers*. New York: Doubleday, 1976.

62. Armstrong, 120.

63. Rachel M. Brownstein, *Becoming a Heroine: Reading about Women in Novels*. Harmondsworth, Middlesex: Penguin, 1982, p. 82.

64. Iuri Lotman, "The Origin of Plot in the Light of Typology." *Poetics Today* 1 (1979):161–184. Teresa de Lauretis, "Desire in Narrative." In *Alice Doesn't*. Bloomington: Indiana University Press, 1984.

65. Olga Freidenberg, "Three Plots or the Semantics of One: Shakespeare's *The Taming of the Shrew*." In *Formalism: History, Comparison, Genre. Russian Poetics in Translation* 5 (1978):30–51.

66. These issues are elaborated in chapter 7.

67. Lee Edwards, *Psyche as Hero: Female Heroism and Fictional Form*. Middletown, Conn.: Wesleyan University Press, 1984, p. 4.

68. Edwards, 9.

69. Evans, 83.

70. Joan Templeton, "The *Doll House* Backlash: Criticism, Feminism, and Ibsen." *PMLA* 104 (1989):33.

71. Cited in Elaine Showalter, "The Unmanning of the Mayor of Caster-bridge." In Dale Kramer, ed., *Critical Approaches to the Fiction of Thomas Hardy*. London: Macmillan, 1979, pp. 99–115.

72. Tanner, 12–13.

73. Much has been made of the fact that Anna apparently has little maternal love for her daughter, Ani. This, together with her rejection of future childbearing through contraception, is taken as a sign of her depravity and loss of maternal instinct. We ought to remember that Anna almost died in her last childbed and therefore medical counsel probably advised her to avoid future pregnancies. Other critics have suggested that Anna felt an unconscious rivalry with a child of her own sex and could only be gratified by the adulation of a male child (see Armstrong). However, while there is no question that Anna does not love Ani as she loved Seryozha, this does not necessarily imply an absence of maternal feeling. Just as an infertile woman who desperately longs for children of her own may find the presence of other people's children intolerable, so Ani is a continual, painful reminder to Anna that she has lost Seryozha: "[She] went to the nursery. 'Why, this is wrong—this isn't he! Where are his blue eyes, his sweet shy smile?' was her first thought when she saw her chubby, rosy-cheeked little girl with her black, curly hair." From *Anna Karenina*. Trans. C. Garnett, ed. and introd. L. J. Kent and N. Berberova. New York: Random House, Modern Library, 1965, p. 794. Unless otherwise stated, this is the edition used for the subsequent quotations in the text.

74. See Nancy Chodorow, *The Reproduction of Mothering: Psychoanalysis and the Sociology of Gender*. Berkeley: University of California Press, 1978.

75. Mary Belenky, Blythe Clichy, Nancy Goldberger, and Jill Tarule, *Women's Ways of Knowing*. New York: Basic Books, 1987.

76. Other feminist critics attack the "idealization of motherhood" in both its feminist and antifeminist forms as being an attempt to romanticize traditional female spheres of influence as idyllic realms of desexualized and powerless femininity. See, for example, Jessica Benjamin, *The Bonds of Love: Psychoanalysis, Feminism, and the Problem of Domination*. New York: Pantheon Books, 1988.

77. Gary Saul Morson, "Prosaics: An Approach to the Humanities." *The American Scholar* 57 (Autumn 1988):523.

78. Gary Saul Morson, "Prosaics in *Anna Karenina*." *Tolstoy Studies Journal* 1 (1988):4.

79. Morson's theory of prosaics and its applications to Tolstoy's aesthetics and oeuvre will be discussed in chapter 3.

80. I stress the primacy of Victorian literary models for the creation of a Russian myth of childhood. As Andrew Wachtel recently demonstrated (*The Battle for Childhood: Creation of a Russian Myth*. Stanford: Stanford University Press, 1990), Tolstoy's own autobiographical novel, *Childhood*, served as the basis for the subsequent development of an idealized vision of family life in Russian literature. Wachtel minimizes the importance of European, and especially Victorian, literary models for the subsequent development of that myth in Russian literature since "almost every account of childhood published in Russia after 1852 turned to Tolstoy (and not to Rousseau, Dickens, Töpffer, or others) for inspiration" (44). However, Tolstoy's own myth of childhood was clearly constructed or, as A. N. Wilson puts it, "Copperfielded" on the Western model (*Tolstoy*, pp. 88–95).

81. "Èkaia milochka nevesta-to, kak ovechka ubrannaia! A kak ni govorite, zhalko nashu sestru." *Anna Karenina, PSS* vol. 19: p. 23.

82. Sara Ruddick, "Maternal Thinking." In Barrie Thorne and Marilyn Yalom, eds., *Rethinking the Family*. London: Longman, 1982, pp. 84–85. See also her later work, *Maternal Thinking: Towards a Politics of Peace*. Boston: Beacon Press, 1989.

83. It is interesting to note that the cultural icon of the Lady with the Lamp echoes the mythological figure of Psyche mentioned in this chapter and discussed in greater detail in chapter 7. Elizabeth Helsinger, Robin Lauterbach Sheets, and William Veeder (*The Woman Question: Society and Literature in Britain and America 1837–1883*, vol. 3: *Literary Issues*. Chicago: University of Chicago Press, 1983) point to three stereotypes of women in Victorian literature: the angel in the house, the fallen woman (demon), and the angel out of the house. The latter category would apply to Varenka, who, we may remember, is frequently referred to as an angel in the course of the novel.

84. Maria Torgovnick, *Closure in the Novel*. Princeton: Princeton University Press, 1981, p. 73.

Chapter 3

1. Diary entry, 2 October 1865. In *Tolstoy's Diaries,* 2 vols. Trans. and ed. R. F. Christian. New York: Charles Scribner's Sons, 1985, vol. 1.

2. *Lady Audley's Secret* is in the library at Yasnaya Polyana.

3. Diary entry, 31 October 1853, *Tolstoy's Diaries,* 76.

4. Charles Dickens, *Dombey and Son.* Harmondsworth, Middlesex: Penguin, 1970, pp. 692–693.

5. Matthew Arnold, "Count Leo Tolstoy." In Henry Gifford, ed., *Leo Tolstoy: A Critical Anthology.* Harmondsworth, Middlesex: Penguin, 1971, p. 69.

6. Mrs. Henry Wood (Ellen Price), *East Lynne* (1861). New Brunswick, N. J.: Rutgers University Press, 1984, p. 237.

7. Gary Saul Morson, *Hidden in Plain View: Narrative and Creative Potentials in "War and Peace."* Stanford: Stanford University Press, 1987, p. 78.

8. Introduction by Leonard J. Kent and Nina Berberova to their revised version of the Constance Garnett translation of *Anna Karenina.* New York: Random House, Modern Library, 1965, p. xix.

9. For specific work on Tolstoy and English literature, see Edwina J. Blumberg, "Tolstoy and the English Novel: A Note on *Middlemarch* and *Anna Karenina.*" *Slavic Review* 30 (1971):561–569; M. H. Futtrell, *Dickens and Three Russian Novelists: Gogol, Dostoevsky, and Tolstoy.* London: 1955; Rebecca S. Hogan, *The Wisdom of Many, the Wit of One: The Narrative Function of the Proverb in Tolstoy's "Anna Karenina" and Trollope's "Orley Farm."* Unpublished doctoral dissertation, University of Colorado, 1985; W. Gareth Jones, "George Eliot's *Adam Bede* and Tolstoy's Conception of *Anna Karenina,*" *Modern Language Review* 61 (1966):473–481; Shoshona Knapp, "Tolstoj's Reading of George Eliot: Visions and Revisions," *Slavic and East European Journal* 27 (1983):318–326. See also the work of Philip Rogers.

10. The term is applied in the sense used by Sandra M. Gilbert and Susan Gubar, *The Madwoman in the Attic: The Woman Writer and the Nineteenth-Century Literary Imagination.* New Haven: Yale University Press, 1979. They define palimpsestic texts as "works whose surface designs conceal or obscure deeper, less accessible (and less socially acceptable) levels of meaning," p. 73.

11. Richard Barickman, Susan MacDonald, and Myra Stark, *Corrupt Relations: Dickens, Thackeray, Trollope, Collins, and the Victorian Sexual System.* New York: Columbia University Press, 1982, p. 3.

12. See Boris Eikhenbaum, *The Young Tolstoy.* Trans. Gary Kern. Ann Arbor: Ardis Press, 1972, for a discussion of Tolstoy's diaries as tools for self-analysis and as laboratories for exploring human psychology.

13. Leo Tolstoy, "The First Step" (1881). *PSS* vol. 24:280–284.

14. Diary entry, 3 October 1865, *Tolstoy's Diaries,* 185.

15. Diary entry, 31 October 1853, *Tolstoy's Diaries,* 76.

16. Second draft for an introduction to *War and Peace*. Norton Critical Edition, the Maude translation. Ed. George Gibian. New York: Norton, 1966, p. 1363.

17. Henry Gifford, "Introduction." In Henry Gifford, ed., *Leo Tolstoy: A Critical Anthology.* Harmondsworth, Middlesex: Penguin, 1971, p. 209.

18. Georg Lukacs, *Studies in European Realism.* New York: Grosset & Dunlap, 1964, p. 203.

19. The recent work of Richard Gustafson, *Leo Tolstoy: Resident and Stranger.* Princeton: Princeton University Press, 1986, and Gary Saul Morson, *Hidden in Plain View: Narrative and Creative Potentials in "War and Peace."* Stanford: Stanford University Press, 1987, has attenuated this view. Gustafson creates a new category of emblematic realism to describe the difference between Tolstoy's work and European literary practices, while Morson reaffirms the view of Tolstoy as innovator that was first developed by the Russian formalists. Even within the native Russian realist tradition, which was established as a naturalist, even Gogolian school, Tolstoy necessarily occupies a sui generis position.

20. Dmitry S. Mirsky, *A History of Russian Literature from its Beginnings to 1900.* New York: Vintage, 1958, pp. 262–263.

21. In so doing, he overlooked the great appeal this type of detail may have, for the reader from the margins of society, who may feel that she is thus initiated into a world otherwise closed to her. In his essay "Prosaics: An Approach to the Humanities" (*The American Scholar* 57 [Autumn 1988]:515–528), Gary Saul Morson indicates the pleasure we derive from gazing at the exotic paraphernalia of everyday life in photos of cabinets from earlier periods. However, the meaning of trivial items and a knowledge of their use are elusive for the uninitiated. This loss of meaning was Tolstoy's concern.

22. Leo Tolstoy, *What Is Art?* Trans. Almyer Maude. New York: Macmillan, 1960, p. 154.

23. *What Is Art?*, 101–102, 154.

24. Roman Jakobson, "What Is Realism in Art?" Trans. Karol Magassy. In *Readings in Russian Poetics: Formalist and Structuralist Views.* Ed. Ladislav Matejka and Krystyna Pomorska. Ann Arbor: Michigan Slavic Publications, pp. 38–46.

25. Roland Barthes, *"L'effet du réel."* *Communications* 11 (1968): 85–90.

26. My list is partially based on the discussion of motivation in Catherine Theimer Nepomnyashchy, "Introduction: The Poetics of Motivation," *The Poetics of Motivation: Time, Narrative, and History in the Works of Solzenicyn, Sinjavskij, and Pasternak.* Unpublished doctoral dissertation, Columbia University, 1987. Somewhat like Genette (Gerard Genette, *"Vraisemblance et motivation,"* *Figures II.* Paris: Editions du Seuil, 1969) Nepomnyashchy argues that the separate categories of realistic and artistic motivation may be combined. Genette, for example, sees the function of all motivation as primarily a concession to *"l'illusion*

réaliste." However, it could be argued that this conflation relies on a historiciza-
tion of realism as the raison d'être for every new avant-garde. While this aspect of
realistic motivation is certainly a feature of artistic motivation, both Tomashevsky
and Shklovsky also create a definition of realistic motivation that should, perhaps,
be renamed "verisimilar motivation": "We demand an elementary 'illusion' from
every work, i.e., no matter how conventional and artificial a work, its perception
must be accompanied by a sense of the reality of what is taking place." (See Boris
Tomashevsky, *Teoriia literatury.* Moscow: Gosudarstvennoe izdatel'stvo, 1928;
Ann Arbor: University Microfilms, 1963, pp. 144–145. Trans. Nepomnyashchy.)
The latter motivation is conceived of as being in opposition to artistic motivation.
The conventions for realizing verisimilitude obviously vary generationally, according to artistic movements. Thus, realistic motivation and artistic motivation
are two opposed aspects of textual dynamics, as Shklovsky asserts: "The forms of
art are explained by their conformity to the laws of art [and, nota bene, would be
understood to be artistically motivated] and not by 'realistic' motivation." (See
Viktor Shklovsky, "Parodiinyi roman: 'Tristram Shendi' Sterna," *Texte der rus-
sichen Formalisten,* 2 vols. Ed. Jurij Streidter and trans. Nepomnyashchy. Munich: W. Fink, 1969–1972, vol. 1, p. 298.) This statement represents Shklovsky's
extremist view that most textual motivations are superficial devices concealing
the more vital motivation of the form of the artistic work itself. Or, as Tomashevsky explains later in a more reasoned fashion, "Since the laws of composition
of the *siuzhet* [Story, A. M.] have nothing in common with verisimilitude, every
introduction of motifs is a compromise between this objective verisimilitude and
literary tradition. . . . between realistic illusion and the demands of artistic con-
struction" (Tomashevsky, 147, 150, translated by Nepomnyashchy).

27. The term was apparently coined by Shklovsky in "Parodiinyi roman"
and refined by Tomashevsky.

28. Shklovsky, "Parodiinyi roman," 258.

29. Tomashevsky, 145–146.

30. Tomashevsky, 149–150.

31. Morson, "Prosaics," p. 8.

32. Such a view may be particularly attractive to the literary critic, especially in this poststructuralist moment since it liberates the critic from the urgent
need to weave every loose end into a complete, unified artistic design. It has the
additional advantage that any textual elements that contravene the critic's reading
can be proclaimed random and insignificant, and any critical reading based on
such details can be indicted for overinvesting detail with meaning.

33. Morson, *Hidden in Plain View,* 173.

34. Ibid., 173–189.

35. Ibid., 94.

36. Indeed, the character of Protogenes could have served Tolstoy as a
model for Mikhailov since he is "extremely poor, and extremely devoted to his art

and consequently not very productive." Pliny the Elder, *Natural History* bk. 35, sec. 36. H. Rackham, ed. Cambridge: Loeb Library, vol. 9, 1961:98–101.

37. Pliny the Elder, *Natural History,* 98–105.

38. For a complete discussion and experimental examination of the concept of linguistic iconicity, or phonetic symbolism, as a functional feature of poetic discourse, see Amy Mandelker, *New Research in Phonetic Symbolism: The Poetic Context.* Unpublished doctoral dissertation, Brown University, 1982.

39. Elizabeth Deeds Ermarth, *Realism and Consensus in the English Novel.* Princeton: Princeton University Press, 1983, pp. xii, x.

40. J. Hillis Miller, *The Form of Victorian Fiction.* Notre Dame, Ind.: University of Notre Dame Press, 1968, p. 137.

41. Of course, the terms realism and Romanticism were used interchangeably in the early years of criticism to refer to works we now identify as realist. See Donald Fanger, *Dostoevsky and Romantic Realism: A Study of Dostoevsky in Relation to Balzac, Dickens, and Gogol.* Chicago: University of Chicago Press, 1965.

42. Mikhail Bakhtin, "Discourse in the Novel," In Michael Holquist, ed., *The Dialogic Imagination.* Trans. Caryl Emerson and Michael Holquist. Austin: University of Texas Press, 1981, pp. 327–328.

43. Paul de Man, "Dialogue and Dialogism." In *The Resistance to Theory.* Theory and History of Literature, vol. 33. Minneapolis: University of Minnesota Press, 1986, p. 111.

44. The formalists themselves, especially Eikhenbaum, characterized Tolstoy in this way.

45. Gustafson, xiv.

46. I deliberately employ this term in two different senses: I conflate the Peircean semiotic definition with a theological, Augustinian view of semiosis as divine inscription.

47. Gustafson, 202.

48. Ibid., 212.

49. Paul de Man, *The Rhetoric of Romanticism.* New York: Columbia University Press, 1984, pp. 6–7.

50. Gustafson, 204.

51. Ludwig Wittgenstein, *Tractatus Logico-Philosophicus.* Trans. D. G. Pears and B. F. McGuinness. London: Routledge & Kegan Paul, 1961.

52. Tolstoy, *What Is Art?,* 44–45.

53. Ibid., 29. Tolstoy's omission may be due to the fact that in his discussion of German aesthetics he relies on one secondary source, Schasler's *Kritische Geschichte der ästhetik* (1872).

54. Immanuel Kant, *Critique of Judgement,* bk. 2. Trans. J. H. Bernard. New York: Hafner, 1931, p. 391.

55. Kant, 392.

56. Ibid., 393–394.

Chapter 4

1. James Joyce, "The Dead," from *Dubliners*. In *The Portable James Joyce*. New York: Viking Press, 1946, p. 227.

2. Mary Ann Caws discusses this phenomenon in her chapters on James and Woolf in *Reading Frames in Modern Fiction*. Princeton: Princeton University Press, 1985.

3. Luce Irigaray, *Speculum of the Other Woman*. Trans. Gillian C. Gill. Ithaca, N.Y.: Cornell University Press, 1985.

4. Edith Wharton, *The House of Mirth*. New York: New American Library, 1980, p. 7.

5. Marcel Proust, *Swann's Way*, from *A Rembrance of Things Past*, vol. 1. Trans. C. K. Scott Moncrieff and Terence Kilmartin. New York: Random House, 1981, pp. 87–88.

6. *Swann's Way*, 88.

7. Ibid., 88.

8. "The Dead," 227.

9. See Leslie A. Johnson, "The Face of the Other in *Idiot*," *Slavic Review* 50 (4) (1991): 867–878.

10. Judith Fetterley, "The Temptation to Be a Beautiful Object: Double Standard and Double Bind in *The House of Mirth*." *Studies in American Fiction* 5 (1977): 199–212, 205.

11. Wendy Steiner, "The Causes of Effect: Edith Wharton and the Economics of Ekphrasis." *Poetics Today* 10:2 (Summer 1989): 279–297.

12. Charles Dickens, *Dombey and Son*. New York: Penguin, 1970, p. 367.

13. *Dombey and Son*, 470.

14. *Dombey and Son*, 473.

15. Mary E. Braddon, *Lady Audley's Secret*. New York: Penguin, 1985, pp. 60–61.

16. Men's portraits are treated differently in literature as the source of demonic alterity, as for example in *The Portrait of Dorian Gray*, the portrait in *The House of the Seven Gables*, or Gogol's *The Portrait*.

17. Mikhail Bakhtin, "The Problem of the Text in Linguistics, Philology, and the Human Sciences: An Experiment in Philosophical Analysis." In *Speech Genres and Other Late Essays*. Trans. Vern W. McGee and ed. Caryl Emerson and Michael Holquist. Austin: University of Texas Press, 1986, p. 115.

18. See Bakhtin's essay on the bildungsroman in *Speech Genres*. This account is somewhat oversimplified and would eliminate from consideration the narrative practices in iconic and medieval painting where characters appear simultaneously on different portions of the canvas.

19. Nicole Loraux, *Tragic Ways of Killing a Woman*. Cambridge: Harvard University Press, 1987.

20. In Nastasya Filipovna's case, the stabbing leaves only the tiniest mark and scarcely any blood is spilled. Myshkin suggests this is because the blade went directly into the heart, but the result also permits Dostoevsky to paint a final portrait of absolute immobility unperturbed by evidence of violence.

21. The terms proposed here are primarily my own, but they are informed by discussions of real and fictitious suicides in Barbara T. Gates, *Victorian Suicide: Mad Crimes and Sad Histories*. Princeton: Princeton University Press, 1988.

22. The term *ideological suicide* was suggested to me by Deborah Martinsen's work on suicide in Dostoevsky, *Dostoevsky and the Temptation of Rhetoric*. Unpublished doctoral dissertation, Columbia University, 1990.

23. Margaret R. Higonnet, "Speaking Silences: Women's Suicide," *The Female Body in Western Culture: Contemporary Perspectives,* Susan Rubin Suleiman, ed. Cambridge: Harvard University Press, 1985, 1986: p. 70.

24. See Gates.

25. Gates, 98.

26. See Elaine Showalter, *The Female Malady.* New York: Pantheon Books, 1985.

27. Higonnet, 81.

28. Florence Nightingale herself was anorectic and often close to death until she was able to liberate herself from her family and take up nursing. The citation is from volume 2 of her *Suggestions for Thought to Searchers after Religious Truth.* Cited in Gates, 36.

29. Higonnet, 77.

30. David H. Stewart, "*Anna Karenina*: The Dialectic of Prophecy." *PMLA* 79 (1964):266–282.

31. Henry Gifford, "Introduction." In Henry Gifford, ed., *Leo Tolstoy: A Critical Anthology.* Harmondsworth, Middlesex: Penguin, 1971, p. 85.

32. See Gates, chap. 7.

33. Roland Barthes, *S/Z, An Essay.* Translated by Richard Miller. New York: Farrar, Straus and Giroux, Hill and Wang, 1974, p. 262.

Chapter 5

1. Leo Tolstoy, *What Is Art?* Trans. Almyer Maude. New York: Macmillan, 1960, p. 105. Brief versions of this chapter were delivered as lectures at the Tolstoy Society Symposium, the annual meeting of the American Association of Teachers of Slavic and East European Languages, December 1987, and at the Slavic Seminar, Columbia University, March 1988.

2. For a standard summation of the topos, see Murray Krieger, "Ekphrasis and the Still Movement of Poetry, or Laokoon Revisited." In Frederick McDow-

ell, ed., *The Poet as Critic*. Evanston, Ill.: Northwestern University Press, 1967, pp. 3–26.

3. Roland Barthes, "L'effect du réel." *Communications* 11 (1968):88.

4. Gotthold Ephraim Lessing, *Lacoön: An Essay upon the Limits of Painting and Poetry*. Trans. Ellen Frothingham. Boston: Little, Brown, 1910, p. 117.

5. Recent studies and bibliographies on the topic of *ut pictura poesis* may be found in Arno Dolders, "*Ut Pictura Poesis:* A Selective Annotated Bibliography," *Yearbook of Comparative and General Literature* 32 (1983):105–124; Judith Dundas, "Style and the Mind's Eye," *The Journal of Aesthetics and Art Criticism* 37 (1979):325–335; Alexander Gelley, "The Represented World: Toward a Phenomenological Theory of Description in the Novel," *The Journal of Aesthetics and Art Criticism* 37 (1979):415–422; John Graham, "*Ut Pictura Poesis:* A Bibliography," *Bulletin of Bibliography* 29 (1972):13–15; Henry Markiewicz, "*Ut Pictura Poesis* . . . A History of the Topos and the Problem," *New Literary History* 18 (1987):535–558; Roy Park, "*Ut Pictura Poesis:* The 19th Century Aftermath," *The Journal of Aesthetics and Art Criticism* 28 (1969):155–164.

6. Barthes, 87.

7. Mary Ann Caws, *Reading Frames in Modern Fiction*. Princeton: Princeton University Press, 1985, p. 30.

8. Jean-Paul Sartre, *Les Mots*. Paris: Gallimard, 1968, p. 171.

9. Both Anna and Lyovin are also authors, whose books remain unfinished.

10. Margaret R. Higonnet, "Speaking Silences," in *The Female Body in Western Culture: Contemporary Perspectives*. Susan Rubin Suleiman, ed. Cambridge: Harvard University Press, 1985, 1986, p. 69.

11. The problem of the description of the personality and the failures of portraiture preoccupied Tolstoy in his earliest writings, as evidenced in a diary entry from 1851: "It seems to me that actually to *describe* a man is impossible . . . words give no understanding of a man but make a pretense of delineating him while more often than not only misleading [the reader]" (*PSS* 46:67). Tolstoy then proceeds to describe a man in a manner that is reminiscent of the salon game "portrait moral": first he relates what he has heard of the man's reputation from others, then he describes his appearance, and finally he describes the impression the actual man made upon him. Tolstoy employs the same procedure in relating Lyovin's visit to Anna: first he hears Stiva's account of her, then he views her portrait, and finally he is affected by her actual presence.

12. John Bayley, *Tolstoy and the Novel*. New York: Viking, 1966, p. 235.

13. An example of a Tolstoy misquotation. M. A. Balakirev's piece is known simply as *King Lear* (1860). *King Lear of the Steppes* is a novella by Turgenev (*Stepnoi Lir*). Tolstoy's own title, *King Lear in the Steppe* (*Korol' Lir v stepi*), differs from both.

14. Tolstoy was probably referring to the projected sculpture of Pushkin

submitted in competition for the centennial by M. M. Antokol'skii (1843–1902). A sketch of the planned sculpture was exhibited in 1875.

15. Lessing, 39.

16. Lessing casts the issue of invisibility in neoplatonic terms as the separation of upper and lower spheres: "with the loss of all distinction to the eye between the visible and the invisible beings, all the characteristic traits must likewise disappear, which serve to elevate the higher order of beings above the lower." See Lessing, 77.

17. Lessing, 80–81.

18. For a more thorough discussion of these issues in relation to *What Is Art?*, see Bayley, chap. 6.

19. Mack Smith, Jr., *Figures in the Carpet: The Ekphrastic Tradition in the Realistic Novel*. Unpublished doctoral dissertation, Rice University, 1981, p. 725.

20. Victor Terras, *Belinskij and Russian Literary Criticism: The Heritage of Organic Aesthetics*. Madison: University of Wisconsin Press, 1974, p. 282.

21. Boris Eikhenbaum, *Tolstoy in the Seventies*. Trans. Albert Kaspin. Ann Arbor: Ardis Press, 1972, p. 127.

22. It is interesting to note that in Russian the word for education (*obrazovanie*), like the German word *Bildung*, is based on a root meaning "to shape, form, build." However, in Russian the root *obraz* is also used to refer to icons. Thus, in popular etymology, to acquire learning implied "becoming like the images (icons)," that is, becoming like the saints. For Russians, therefore, the concept of education has a marked spiritual component as well as a visual realization.

23. In response to a letter criticizing Tolstoy for lack of structure in *Anna Karenina*, Tolstoy replied: "I pride myself on the architecture—the arches are so joined that it is impossible even to notice the keystone." Letter to S. A. Rachinsky, 27 January 1878, *PSS* 62:377. Criticism on *Anna Karenina* has taken up the metaphor; the most successful work along these lines is that of Elisabeth Stenbock-Fermor, *The Architecture of Anna Karenina: A History of Its Structure, Writing, and Message*. Lisse, Belgium: Peter de Ridder Press, 1975. Stenbock-Fermor argues quite convincingly that the keystone scene is the Oblonskys' dinner party, which contains the central, symposiac debate on the woman question. In "Tolstoy's Portrait of Anna: Keystone in the Arch," *Criticism* 18 (1976):1–14, Joan Grossman argues that Lyovin's viewing of Anna's portrait is the keystone scene.

24. Stenbock-Fermor notes a symmetrical, architectural structure in the novel, built around the opening and closing scenes at railroad stations and the symposial debates on love. According to her diagram, the keystone scene is the Oblonskys' dinner party at which Dolly pleads with Karenin to forgive Anna, Lyovin and Kitty become betrothed, and the company discuss the woman question.

25. After this manuscript was completed, Ronald LeBlanc's article, "Levin Visits Anna: The Iconography of Harlotry," appeared in *Tolstoy Studies Journal* 3

(1990):1–21. LeBlanc makes several of the same points I make here but draws a different conclusion, that "the visit to Anna's—metaphorized as a trip to a brothel—can be seen as the culmination of a process at work throughout the novel whereby the hero gradually loses his innocence and compromises his values as he becomes less a 'savage' and more a 'civilized' nobleman" (15). LeBlanc thus adheres to the critical view of Tolstoy as holding negative opinions on women and sexuality.

26. We are reminded of David Copperfield, who, on the occasion of his first debauchery, studies his face in the mirror and concludes that only his hair looks drunk. I am indebted to Elizabeth Beaujour for drawing my attention to another intertext for this passage, Dostoevsky's *Notes from the Underground,* where the Underground Man pauses prior to consummating his purchase at the brothel and glances in the mirror. It is in keeping with his perverse, reverse logic that the recognition of his drunken, disheveled state gives way to an overcompensating narcissism: "I caught sight of myself in a mirror. My agitated face seemed to me repulsive in the extreme: pale, vicious, mean, with tangled hair. 'All right, I'm glad of it,' I thought; 'I'm glad to seem repulsive to her; I like that.'"

Looking into a mirror suggests self-examination and the awakening of the conscience, as well as psychic dissociation or projection, the emergence of the uncanny twin, or double. Other characters in the novel also look into mirrors or refuse to do so, as is the case with Dolly when she visits Anna at Vronsky's estate. In a critical scene before her suicide, Anna looks into the mirror and does not recognize herself.

27. Freud's theories on the scopic drives, voyeurism, and exhibitionism, as developed in his 1915 essay "Instincts and Their Vicissitudes" (see Sigmund Freud, *Complete Psychological Works of Sigmund Freud,* 24 vols. Revised and ed. James Strachey. London: Hogarth Press, 1953–1974) were later reworked by Jacques Lacan in his concepts of the "mirror phase" and the "Gaze." The Lacanian theory of the unconscious discourse of the "Gaze" is based on a system of shifts or alternations between voyeurism and exhibitionism. The voyeur refuses to be seen as an object and attempts to assume power through visual dominance while the exhibitionist refuses to be shown or to see and is similarly dogmatic in determining the rejection of the visual field. Lyovin's role as a voyeur and Anna's exhibitionism in the public arena and with Vronsky are echoed in Lyovin's "screwing up his eyes" while trying to see more clearly and Anna's habit of "screwing up her eyes" while refusing to see.

28. Feminist critics of the representation of women in art argue that "women cannot be represented as themselves, since we cannot know their identities. They are simply present as a consciousness of being perceived and represented as objects. Hence the duplicitous mystery of women in portraits whose gaze outward is really turned inward on themselves." Margaret R. Higonnet's in-

troduction in Carolyn Heilbrun and Margaret R. Higonnet, eds., *The Representation of Women in Fiction.* Baltimore: Johns Hopkins University Press, 1983, p. xx.

29. The Eugubine Tables were written in an undeciphered Northumbrian
dialect and were discovered in 1444 in Eugubium, Italy. It is interesting to note
that the treatise on the tables that Karenin is reading is in French. Like Vronsky's
portrait in French style of Anna in Italian costume, Karenin's portrait of Anna is
coded in Italian and framed by the French language.

30. *What Is Art?*, 227.

Chapter 6

1. Percy Lubbock, *The Craft of Fiction* (1921). Partially reprinted in
Henry Gifford, ed., *Leo Tolstoy: A Critical Anthology.* Harmondsworth, Middlesex: Penguin, 1971, p. 175.

2. One early reviewer of *War and Peace* considered Dolokhov and Anatole
Kuragin to be the heroes of the novel. For a fascinating discussion of early critical
responses to the formal peculiarities of *War and Peace,* see Gary Saul Morson,
Hidden in Plain View: Narrative and Creative Potentials in "War and Peace."
Stanford, Calif.: Stanford University Press, 1987. Morson comments: "Had Tolstoy continued the work through 1825 or 1856 as he once intended, what would
have been the eventual status of Prince Andrei?" (59).

3. Vladimir Nabokov, "Anna Karenin." In *Lectures on Russian Literature.*
New York: Harvest, 1981, pp. 137–243.

4. The preoccupation with and consciousness of "position" *(polozhenie)*, a
motif that Tolstoy borrowed from Trollope, afflicts the main characters of *Anna
Karenina.* This problem is discussed by Michael Holquist in "The Supernatural
as Social Force in *Anna Karenina.*" In Amy Mandelker and Roberta Reeder, eds.
*The Supernatural in Russian and Baltic Literature: Essays in Honor of Victor
Terras.* Columbus, Ohio: Slavica, 1988, pp. 176–190.

5. J. Hillis Miller, "Self and Community." In *The Form of Victorian Fiction.* South Bend, Ind.: University of Notre Dame Press, 1968, p. 135.

6. Anthony Trollope, *Barchester Towers.* London: Penguin, 1982, p. 495.

7. Nancy Miller, *The Heroine's Text: Readings in the French and English
Novel.* New York: Columbia University Press, 1986, p. x.

8. As many critics have noted, carriages and trains provide settings for insight, debate, and meditation throughout the novel. The inside of the carriage is a
stage for confined action; the window offers a composed vision of "external reality." Trains of thought are set in motion by locomotion, usually with a deleterious
effect. Tolstoy's personal antipathy to trains is well known and Anna's semipsy-
chotic states on the train anticipate those of Pozdnyshev in *The Kreutzer Sonata.*
On the image of the railroad in *Anna Karenina,* see M. S. Al'tman, "'Zheleznaia

doroga' v tvorchestve L. N. Tolstogo," *Slavia* (Prague), Rocnik 34 Sesit 2 (1965), and Gary R. Jahn, "The Image of the Railroad in *Anna Karenina.*" *Slavic and East European Journal* 25 (1981):8–12.

9. Roland Barthes, *S/Z: An Essay.* Trans. Richard Miller. New York: Hill and Wang, 1974, p. 33. See also Rachel M. Brownstein, *Becoming a Heroine: Reading about Women in Novels.* Harmondsworth, Middlesex: Penguin, 1984.

10. Judith Fetterley, *The Resisting Reader: A Feminist Approach to American Fiction.* Bloomington: Indiana University Press, 1978, p. xii.

11. The situation is well characterized by William Mills Todd, *Fiction and Society in the Age of Pushkin.* Cambridge: Harvard University Press, 1986.

12. *The Letters of Henry James,* dated early 1872. Cited in George Steiner, *Tolstoy or Dostoevsky: An Essay in the Old Criticism.* New York: Alfred A. Knopf, 1956, p. 31.

13. Fyodor Dostoevsky, "*Anna Karenina* kak fakt osobogo znacheniia," *Dnevnik pisatelia,* 1877, Petrograd: Prosveshchenie, vol. 21: 238.

14. On p. 78 of his study *Fiction and Society in the Age of Pushkin,* William Todd summarizes the literary situation in early nineteenth-century Russia by placing it on the grid of Jakobson's communication schema:

Folklore, Popular Religion, Curiosities

Anonymous Scribe   Tales, Songs, Novels   Viewer, Reader

Chapbook, Broadsheet

Mixed style (ecclesiastical, bureaucratic, language of commerce)

15. Tolstoy's rereading of Pushkin inspired him to begin *Anna Karenina* after abandoning his project on Peter the Great. For an excellent study of Pushkin's influence on *Anna Karenina,* see David A. Sloane, "Pushkin's Legacy in *Anna Karenina,*" *Tolstoy Studies Journal* 4 (1991):1–20.

16. Alexander S. Pushkin, *Eugene Onegin: A Novel in Verse.* Trans. Walter Arndt. New York: Dutton, 1963, p. 73. Book and verse references are given in the text; page numbers referring to Arndt's translation are given in the notes.

17. Arndt, 175.

18. Elizabeth Ermarth, "Fictional Consensus and Female Casualties." In Carolyn Heilbrun and Margaret R. Higonnet, eds., *The Representation of Women in Fiction.* Baltimore: Johns Hopkins University Press, 1981, p. 5.

19. Diary entry, March-May 1851. In *Tolstoy's Diaries,* 2 vols. Trans. and ed. R. F. Christian. New York: Charles Scribner's Sons, 1985, vol. 1, p. 27.

20. Richard Gustafson, *Leo Tolstoy: Resident and Stranger.* Princeton: Princeton University Press, 1986.

21. The Platonic dialogue most often discussed in the criticism on *Anna*

Karenina is the *Symposium*. See Irina Gutkin, "The Dichotomy between Flesh and Spirit: Plato's *Symposium* in *Anna Karenina.*" In Hugh McLean, ed., *In the Shade of the Giant: Essays on Tolstoy.* Berkeley: University of California Press, 1989, pp. 84–99. For a more general treatment of Platonic philosophy in Tolstoy, see Donna Orwin, "Freedom, Responsibility, and the Soul: The Platonic Contribution to Tolstoi's Psychology." *Canadian Slavonic Papers* 25 (December 1983):501–517. Tolstoy himself considered Plato and Schopenhauer the only two genuine philosophers in the Western tradition: "Plato is sharply distinguished from all the others, in my opinion, by the correctness of his philosophical method." Letter to Strakhov, 30 November 1875. *Tolstoy's Letters 1880–1910*, 2 vols. Trans. R. F. Christian. London: Athlone, 1978, p. 285.

22. In fact, it was a delegation of Russian nurses to the Crimean front that inspired Florence Nightingale to pursue her career in nursing. However, initially these was skepticism that Russia's nurses would be able to withstand the horrors of the front, either physically or emotionally. It was even suggested that their actual role would be to act as prostitutes for the soldiers rather than as nurses.

23. Anthony Trollope, *Phineas Finn* (1869). Oxford: Oxford University Press, 1973, chap. 6, p. 58.

24. *Phineas Finn,* chap. 40, p. 26.

25. Sigmund Freud in "A Child Is Being Beaten" (in *Sexuality and the Psychology of Love.* Ed. Philip Rieff. New York: Collier Books, 1963) acknowledges this phenomenon: "She turns herself in fantasy into a man, without herself becoming active in a masculine way" (128). Mary Ann Doane comments, "The female spectator is . . . imaged by the text as having a mixed sexual body—she is, ultimately, a hermaphrodite." See *The Desire to Desire: The Woman's Film of the 1940s.* Bloomington: Indiana University Press, 1987, p. 19.

26. Arndt, 65.

27. That Vronsky, through conflation with the knife, becomes Anna's phallus is literalized in the episode where, "lacking a knife," Anna uses a photograph of Vronsky to remove her son's photograph from its frame.

28. Leo Tolstoy, *War and Peace.* Trans. Aylmer and Louis Maude. Ed. George Gibian. New York: Norton, 1968, p. 858.

29. A sustained discussion of the imagery of candlelight, light, and darkness in *Anna Karenina* may be found in Elisabeth Stenbock-Fermor, *The Architecture of Anna Karenina.* Lisse, Belgium: Peter de Ridder, 1975.

30. John Bayley, *Tolstoy and the Novel.* New York: Viking, 1966.

31. "What are these words? This candle, etc.? A beautiful allegory, and nothing more! A clever way of concealing our total ignorance and incomprehension of reality at such a moment. What candle? . . . Upon looking, even briefly, into this matter and removing the poetic veil of beautiful words, we find that it is impossible to imagine anything here at all." Konstantin Leontiev, *Analiz stil' i vedenie: o romanakh Gr. L. N. Tolstogo: Kriticheskii ètiud* (1890). Trans. in Henry

Gifford, ed., *Leo Tolstoy: A Critical Anthology.* Harmondsworth, Middlesex: Penguin, 1971, p. 86.

Chapter 7

1. Iurii Lotman, "On the Spatiality of Plots in the 19th Century Russian Novel" (O siuzhetnom prostranstve siuzhet russkogo romana XIX stoletiia). *Trudy po znakovym sistemam* 20 (1987):102–114; Vladimir Propp, *Morphology of the Folktale.* Trans. Laurence Scott. Austin: University of Texas Press, 1968. In his article on "The Origin of Plot in the Light of Typology" (*Poetics Today* 1 [1979]:161–184), Lotman formulates this heroic trajectory in a spatial configuration that is similar to that of the "monomyth" of Joseph Campbell's theories in *The Hero with a Thousand Faces.* Princeton: Princeton University Press, 1973. I delivered a brief version of this chapter as a paper, "The Shadow of *Anna Karenina,*" at the annual meeting of the Association for the Advancement of Slavic Studies, Boston, November, 1987.

2. For discussions of this tradition, see Vera S. Dunham, "The Strong Woman Motif." In Cyril Black, ed., *The Transformation of Russian Society.* Cambridge: Harvard University Press, 1960, and Barbara Heldt, *Terrible Perfection: Women in Russian Literature.* Bloomington: Indiana University Press, 1987. The absence of any developed tradition of the novel of adultery in Russian literature makes Tolstoy's adaptation even more striking.

3. Leo Tolstoy, *What Is Art?* Trans. Aylmer Maude. New York: Macmillan, 1960, p. 154.

4. Ibid., 178.

5. Letter to Strakhov, 3 March 1872. In *Tolstoy's Letters,* 2 vols. Trans. and ed. R. F. Christian. London: Athlone, 1978, vol. 1, pp. 242–243.

6. In April 1876 Tolstoy wrote to Strakhov: "People are needed in the criticism of art who will show the absurdity of searching for thoughts in a work of art, who will instead direct the reader through the endless labyrinth of linkages [*labirint stseplenii*] which is the essence of art." In *Tolstoy's Letters,* 2 vols. Trans. and ed. R. F. Christian. London: Athlone, 1978, vol. 1, pp. 296–297. See chaps. 2 and 3.

7. William W. Rowe, *Leo Tolstoy.* Boston: Twayne, 1986, p. 86.

8. According to a variety of accounts, Tolstoy was inspired to begin *Anna Karenina* after reading a fragment of Pushkin's prose that began, "The guests assembled at the dacha." For a full discussion of the compositional history, see N. K. Gudzii, "Istoriia pisaniia i pechataniia *Anny Kareninoi.* In *PSS* 29:577–643. In the Pushkin fragment, the guests discuss the adulterous behavior of a society lady and speculate on her future. The fragment concludes with the fallen woman abandoned by her lover and contemplating suicide. For an excellent study of Tol-

stoy's encounter with the Pushkin fragments, see David A. Sloane, "Pushkin's Legacy in *Anna Karenina.*" *Tolstoy Studies Journal* 4 (1991):1–20.

9. Cited in Henry Gifford, "Anna, Lawrence and 'the Law.'" In Henry Gifford, ed., *Leo Tolstoy: A Critical Anthology.* Harmondsworth, Middlesex: Penguin, 1971, p. 301.

10. This observation follows Caryl Emerson's excellent critique of Bakhtin's view of Tolstoy as an essentially monologic author. (See "The Tolstoy Connection in Bakhtin," *PMLA* [January 1985]:68–80.) Gary Saul Morson's *Hidden in Plain View: Narrative and Creative Potentials in "War and Peace"* (Stanford, Calif.: Stanford University Press, 1987) develops the perception that, in Emerson's words, "Tolstoy is . . . more thoroughly polyphonic than Dostoevsky." See Caryl Emerson, "Problems with Bakhtin's Poetics," *Slavic and East European Journal* 32 (1988):503–525.

11. I am paraphrasing Gary Saul Morson's succinct and elegant exposition of Bakhtin's theory of absolute language from chapter 1, "Tolstoy's Absolute Language" in *Hidden in Plain View.*

12. Artur Schopenhauer, *The Art of Literature.* Trans. T. Bailey Saunders. Ann Arbor: University of Michigan Press, 1960, p. 21.

13. A. A. Fet, letter to Tolstoy, 26 March 1876. In George Gibian, ed., "Backgrounds and Sources," *Anna Karenina.* Trans. Almyer Maude. New York: W. W. Norton, 1970, p. 750.

14. Boris Eikhenbaum, cited in Gibian, 815.

15. Dmitry S. Mirsky, *A History of Russian Literature.* New York: Alfred A. Knopf, 1926, p. 252.

16. Mikhail Bakhtin, *Problems of Dostoevsky's Poetics.* Trans. Caryl Emerson. Minneapolis: University of Minnesota Press, 1984, p. 56.

17. This statement is not intended as a generalization since Morson also illuminates the use of absolute language throughout Tolstoy's oeuvre. Morson's thesis is that the intrusion of absolute language into the narrative of *War and Peace* constitutes a violation of novelistic boundaries and an irruption of extranovelistic discourse into the novel.

18. In Tolstoy's version of the fable, a dog carrying food sees her shadow with what appears to be a larger portion of meat. She drops her portion in order to steal from her own shadow and ends up with nothing. The obvious moral, that any crime against another is actually a crime perpetrated against oneself, is repeated in "Karma," Tolstoy's adaptation of the story.

19. Andersen's story has had considerable influence on Russian literature. Together with the legend of Mozart's "man in black" in Pushkin's Little Tragedy, *Mozart and Salieri,* Andersen's story apparently serves as a subtext for Chekhov's "Black Monk" *(Chernyi monakh).* The black monk appears to the scholar Kovrin under circumstances that are similar to those under which Andersen's scholar releases his shadow: a balcony, music, and the presence of a beautiful woman. The

lithograph illustration for the story used in one Russian translation shows a scholar seated opposite a well-dressed but vulgar demonic figure in a frock coat—a visual representation that may have influenced Dostoevsky's description of Ivan Karamazov and his devil. The shadow, or man in black, appears on the Russian stage in Blok's *Fairground Booth (Balaganchik)* and in Olesha's unfinished play, *The Man in Black.* Shvartz adapted Andersen's story into an indictment of Stalinist society in his drama *The Shadow (Ten').* A brief discussion of this tradition in Russian literature and in Esenin's long lyric poem, *The Man in Black,* may be found in Amy Mandelker, "The Haunted Poet: Esenin's *Černyj čelovek* and Musset's 'La Nuit de décembre,'" in Amy Mandelker and Roberta Reeder, eds., *The Supernatural in Slavic and Baltic Literature.* Columbus, Ohio: Slavica, 1988, pp. 226–245.

20. For a discussion of the evolution of cultural perceptions of demonic possession and psychic disintegration in the genius figure from antiquity to modern literature, see Ken Frieden, *Genius and Monologue.* Ithaca, N.Y.: Cornell University Press, 1985.

21. Chamisso also dramatized the legend in his *Faust.*

22. Nina Auerbach, *Woman and the Demon: The Life of a Victorian Myth.* Cambridge: Harvard University Press, 1982.

23. *Die Frau ohne Schatten* is apparently based on a Swedish legend in which a young girl admiring her reflection in a pool is approached by a supernatural figure who offers her eternal beauty in exchange for her shadow and her fecundity.

24. Could this French connection be the solution to the mystery of why the peasant mutters in French?

25. The synecdochical use of a shadow to indicate abdication of moral responsibility appears in response to desire for a woman in both the case of Vronsky and that of Andersen's scholar. The appearance of a shadow self in another realist novel also occurs in response to sexual temptation. In Eliot's *Adam Bede,* which Tolstoy claimed made the greatest impression on him during the years he wrote *Anna Karenina,* the young squire Arthur Donnithorne rides to a forbidden rendezvous with Hetty Sorrel: "[his] shadow flitted rather faster among the sturdy oaks of the chase than might have been expected from the shadow of a tired man on a warm afternoon." The physical similarities between the fallen heroines of the two novels has been discussed by Gareth Jones, "George Eliot's *Adam Bede* and Tolstoy's Conception of *Anna Karenina,*" *Modern Language Review* 61 (1966):473–481. Eliot's influence on Tolstoy has been explored in articles by Edwina J. Blumberg, "Tolstoy and the English Novel: A Note on *Middlemarch* and *Anna Karenina.*" *Slavic Review* 3 (1971):561–569, and by Shoshona Knapp, "Tolstoy's Reading of George Eliot: Visions and Revisions." *Slavic and East European Journal* 27 (1983):318–326.

26. Leo Tolstoy, "The Living Corpse." Trans. by Louise and Aylmer Maude. In *Plays by Leo Tolstoy.* London: Oxford University Press, 1923, p. 260.

27. Barbara Hardy, "Tolstoy's *Anna Karenina*." In *The Appropriate Form: an Essay on the Novel*. London: Athlone, 1964, p. 315.

28. Anthony Trollope, *Can You Forgive Her?* Oxford: Oxford University Press, 1973, 1:186.

29. Ibid., Book 2. p. 102.

30. In addition to the similarities in spirit between Anna and Frou-Frou, there were onomastic links in the early variants where Anna was Tatiana and Frou-Frou was Tanya (the diminutive of Tatiana). The name Frou-Frou was apparently borrowed from the eponymous adulterous heroine of a popular bouffe on the European stage. Among critics who exonerate Anna and indict Vronsky on the basis of the race scene are Viktor Shklovsky, *Zametki o proze russkikh klassikov*, Moscow: Sovetskii pisatel', 1953; John Bayley, *Tolstoy and the Novel*, London: Chatto and Windus, 1966; Albert Cook, "The Moral Vision: Tolstoy." In Ralph Matlaw, ed., *Tolstoy: A Collection of Critical Essays*. Englewood Cliffs, N.J.: Prentice-Hall, 1967; R. F. Christian, *Tolstoy: A Critical Introduction*. Cambridge: Cambridge University Press, 1969; and Helen Muchnic, "The Steeplechase in *Anna Karenina*." In *Russian Writers: Notes and Essays*. New York: Random House, 1971. The most recent critics who adopt the opposite viewpoint include Gary Browning, "The Death of *Anna Karenina*: Anna's Share of the Blame," *Slavic and East European Journal* 30 (1986):327–339 and Richard Gustafson in *Leo Tolstoy: Resident and Stranger.* Princeton: Princeton University Press, 1986. In his article "Prosaics in *Anna Karenina*," Gary Saul Morson states that he will be taking the "anti-Anna line" in his forthcoming book.

31. Sigmund Freud, "The Relation of the Poet to Day-Dreaming." In *On Creativity and the Unconscious*. New York: Harper, 1958, p. 51.

32. Carl G. Jung, "Approaching the Unconscious." In Carl G. Jung, ed., *Man and His Symbols*. New York: Dell, 1968, p. 22. Some psychoanalytic feminist critics, such as Judith Armstrong (*The Unsaid Anna Karenina*, New York: St. Martin's Press, 1988) interpret Anna as representing a fragment of Tolstoy's own personality, specifically his anima, and regard Anna's death as implying that Tolstoy was unable to resolve his own psychic conflicts.

33. Irina Paperno has convincingly argued that this dream is a polemical response to the "rational" polyandry proposed by Chernyshevsky in *What Is to Be Done?* See her *Chernyshevsky and the Age of Realism: A Study in the Semiotics of Behavior.* Stanford, Calif.: Stanford University Press, 1988, pp. 154–155. Tolstoy thus exposes the absurdity of a male-developed radical feminism for the women who were expected to adopt it, and he renders uncanny the true meaning of such a resolution.

34. It is interesting that Tolstoy himself used a similar excuse in a plea for forgiveness that he wrote in his wife's diary: "Sonya, forgive me, I have only just realized that I am to blame. . . . There are days when one seems guided not by one's will but by some irresistible external law. . . . somewhere inside me there is

a fine person, but at times he seems to be asleep. Love him, Sonya, and do not reproach him too much." *The Diaries of Sophia Tolstoy.* Translated by Cathy Porter, O. A. Golinenko et al., eds. New York: Random House, 1985, p. 23.

35. I rely here on Denis de Rougemont's characterization of adulterous passion in *Love in the Western World.* Translated by M. Belgion. New York: Pantheon Books, 1956.

36. M.-L. von Franz, "The Process of Individuation." In C. G. Jung, ed., *Man and His Symbols,* 202.

37. Erich Neumann (*Amor and Psyche—The Psychic Development of the Feminine: A Commentary on the Tale by Apuleius.* Princeton: Princeton University Press, 1956) considers Psyche's action to represent a willingness to pursue love through separation. A Freudian-Lacanian reading would suggest that the love of darkness repeats the infantile attachment to a nonspecific, unnameable mother. Striking the light and envisioning and naming leads to the ultimate loss.

38. Luce Irigaray, *Speculum of the Other Woman.* Trans. Gillian C. Gill. Ithaca, N.Y.: Cornell University Press, 1985.

39. Lee Edwards, *Psyche as Hero: Female Heroism and Fictional Form.* Middletown, Conn.: Wesleyan University Press, 1984, p. 143.

40. For a discussion of Russian literature in these terms, see Ellen Chances, *Conformity's Children: An Approach to the Superfluous Man in Russian Literature.* Columbus, Ohio: Slavica, 1978.

Chapter 8

1. Elisabeth Stenbock-Fermor, *The Architecture of Anna Karenina: A History of Its Structure, Writing, and Message.* Lisse, Belgium: Peter de Ridder Press, 1975, p. 107.

2. Mikhail Bakhtin, *Rabelais and His World.* Trans. Hélène Iswolsky. Bloomington: Indiana University Press, 1984.

3. Bakhtin, *Rabelais,* 52.

4. Ibid., 53.

5. Ibid., 52.

6. See primarily Barbara Hardy, *The Appropriate Form: An Essay on the Novel.* London: Athlone, 1964. Most recently, Gary Saul Morson has argued for the recognition of textual details as unrealized prosaic potentials. (See the discussion in chapter 3.)

7. John Bayley, *Tolstoy and the Novel.* London: Chatto & Windus, 1966, pp. 216–217.

8. Bayley, 215.

9. Ibid., 215.

10. Hardy, 126.

11. See, for example, J. M. Allegro, *The Sacred Mushroom and the Cross*. Garden City, N.Y.: Doubleday, 1970, and R. G. Wasson and V. P. Wasson, *Mushrooms, Russia, and History*. New York: Pantheon, 1957.

12. V. V. Mitrofanova, *Zagadki* ("Riddles"). Leningrad: ANSSSR, 1968, p. 123.

13. V. N. Toporov, *The Semiotics of Mythological Conceptions about Mushrooms*. Trans. Stephen Rudy. *Semiotica* special issue 53–54 (1985):296.

14. Melnikov-Pechersky, *V lesakh*, bk. 1, pt. 2. Cited in Toporov, 330.

15. *Lietuviuu tautosaka*. Cited in Toporov, 344.

16. Even Old Testament law follows this precept: a woman is not dishonored by rape that occurs in the forest—only by rape occurring in the fields or in the city.

17. Leo Tolstoy, *Family Happiness* (1859). Trans. J. D. Duff. In *The Death of Ivan Ilyich and Other Stories*. New York: New American Library, Signet, 1960, pp. 28–29.

18. Leo Tolstoy, *Resurrection* (1898). Trans. Vera Traill. New York: Signet, 1961.

19. Tolstoy, *Resurrection*, 357.

20. Ibid., 356.

Conclusion

1. Leo Tolstoy, *Resurrection* (1898). Trans. Vera Traill. New York: Signet, 1961, p. 164.

2. Tolstoy, *Resurrection*, 357.

3. The fact that he is able to do so is partly a result of the fact that Nekhliudov's character is meant to serve as a moral standard. Nonetheless, as an ideal, he suggests Tolstoy's vision of equality between the sexes.

4. Tolstoy, *Resurrection*, 360–361.

BIBLIOGRAPHY

General

Allegro, J. M. *The Sacred Mushroom and the Cross*. Garden City, N.Y.: Doubleday, 1970.

Allen, Elizabeth Cheresh. *Beyond Realism: Turgenev's Poetics of Secular Salvation*. Stanford, Calif.: Stanford University Press, 1992.

Alter, Robert. "The Novel and the Sense of the Past." *Salmagundi* (Fall-Winter 1985–1986):68–69.

Anderson, Olive. *Suicide in Victorian and Edwardian England*. Oxford: Clarendon, 1987.

Auerbach, Nina. *Woman and the Demon: The Life of a Victorian Myth*. Cambridge: Harvard University Press, 1982.

Bakhtin, Mikhail. *The Dialogic Imagination*. Trans. Caryl Emerson and Michael Holquist. Ed. Michael Holquist. Austin: University of Texas Press, 1981.

———. *Problems of Dostoevsky's Poetics*. Trans. Caryl Emerson. Minneapolis: University of Minnesota Press, 1984.

———. *Rabelais and His World*. Trans. Hélène Iswolsky. Bloomington: Indiana University Press, 1984.

———. *Speech Genres and Other Late Essays*. Trans. Vern W. McGee. Ed. Caryl Emerson and Michael Holquist. Austin: University of Texas Press, 1986.

Barickman, Richard, Susan MacDonald, and Myra Stark. *Corrupt Relations: Dickens, Thackeray, Trollope, Collins, and the Victorian Sexual System*. New York: Columbia University Press, 1982.

Barthes, Roland. "L'effet du réel." *Communications* 11 (1968).

———. *S/Z: An Essay*. Trans. Richard Miller. New York: Hill and Wang, 1974.

Belenky, Mary, Blythe Clichy, Nancy Goldberger, and Jill Tarule. *Women's Ways of Knowing*. New York: Basic Books, 1987.

Benjamin, Jessica. *The Bonds of Love: Psychoanalysis, Feminism, and the Problem of Domination*. New York: Pantheon Books, 1988.

Black, Cyril E., ed. *The Transformation of Russian Society: Aspects of Social Change Since 1861*. Cambridge: Harvard University Press, 1960.

Brooks, Peter. *Reading for the Plot: Design and Intention in Narrative.* New York: Vintage, 1984.

Brownstein, Rachel M. *Becoming a Heroine: Reading about Women in Novels.* Harmondsworth, Middlesex: Penguin, 1982.

Burke, Edmund. *A Philosophical Inquiry into the Origins of Our Ideas of the Sublime and the Beautiful.* Ed. James T. Boulton. London: Routledge and Kegan Paul, 1958.

Campbell, Joseph. *The Hero with a Thousand Faces.* Princeton: Princeton University Press, 1973.

Caws, Mary Ann. *Reading Frames in Modern Fiction.* Princeton: Princeton University Press, 1985.

Chances, Ellen. *Conformity's Children: An Approach to the Superfluous Man in Russian Literature.* Columbus, Ohio: Slavica, 1978.

Chodorow, Nancy. *The Reproduction of Mothering: Psychoanalysis and the Sociology of Gender.* Berkeley: University of California Press, 1978.

Davidovich, M. G. *Zhenskii portret u russkikh romantikov pervoi poloviny XIX veka.* In A. I. Beletskii, ed. *Russkii romantizm.* Leningrad: 1927.

de Lauretis, Teresa. *Alice Doesn't.* Bloomington: Indiana University Press, 1984.

de Man, Paul. *Blindness and Insight: Essays in the Rhetoric of Contemporary Criticism,* 2d ed. *Theory and History of Literature,* vol. 7. Minneapolis: University of Minnesota Press, 1983.

———. *The Rhetoric of Romanticism.* New York: Columbia University Press, 1984.

———. *The Resistance to Theory. Theory and History of Literature,* vol. 33. Minneapolis: University of Minnesota Press, 1986.

de Rougemont, Denis. *Love in the Western World.* Trans. M. Belgion. New York: Pantheon Books, 1956.

———. *Love Declared: Essays on the Myths of Love.* Boston: Beacon Press, 1963.

Derrida, Jacques. *The Truth in Painting.* Trans. Geoff Bennington and Ian McLeod. Chicago: University of Chicago Press, 1987.

Doane, Mary Ann. *The Desire to Desire: The Woman's Film of the 1940s.* Bloomington: Indiana University Press, 1987.

Dolders, Arno. "*Ut Pictura Poesis:* A Selective Annotated Bibliography." *Yearbook of Comparative and General Literature* 32 (1983):105–124.

Dostoevsky, Fyodor. "*Anna Karenina* kak fakt osobogo znacheniia," *Dnevnik pisatelia.* July-August 1877. Polnoe sobranie sochinenie in 23 vols. Petrograd: Prosveshchenie: 234–239.

Dundas, Judith. "Style and the Mind's Eye." *The Journal of Aesthetics and Art Criticism* 37 (1979):325–335.

Dworkin, Andrea. *Intercourse.* New York: Macmillan, 1987.

Edwards, Lee. *Psyche as Hero: Female Heroism and Fictional Form.* Middletown, Conn.: Wesleyan University Press, 1984.

Elshtain, Jean Bethke. "Feminism, Family, and Community." *Dissent* 29 (1) (Fall 1982):441–449.

———. *Public Man, Private Woman.* Princeton: Princeton University Press, 1981.

Emerson, Caryl. "Problems with Bakhtin's Poetics." *Slavic and East European Journal* 32 (1988):503–525.

———. "The Tolstoy Connection in Bakhtin." *PMLA* (January 1985):68–80.

Erlich, Victor. *Russian Formalism. History. Doctrine.* New Haven: Yale University Press, 1955.

Ermarth, Elizabeth Deeds. *Realism and Consensus in the English Novel.* Princeton: Princeton University Press, 1983.

Fanger, Donald. *Dostoevsky and Romantic Realism: A Study of Dostoevsky in Relation to Balzac, Dickens, and Gogol.* Chicago: University of Chicago Press, 1965.

Fetterley, Judith. "The Temptation to Be a Beautiful Object: Double Standard and Double Bind in *The House of Mirth.*" *Studies in American Fiction* 5 (1977): 199–212.

———. *The Resisting Reader: A Feminist Approach to American Fiction.* Bloomington: Indiana University Press, 1978.

Flanders, Jane. "The Fallen Woman in Fiction." In Diane L. Fowlkes and Charlotte S. McClure, eds. *Feminist Visions: Toward a Transformation of the Liberal Arts Curriculum.* University: University of Alabama Press, 1984, 97–109.

Freeborn, Richard. *The Rise of the Russian Novel.* Cambridge: Cambridge University Press, 1973.

Freidenberg, Olga. "Three Plots or the Semantics of One: Shakespeare's *The Taming of the Shrew.*" In *Formalism: History, Comparison, Genre. Russian Poetics in Translation* 5 (1978):30–51.

Freud, Sigmund. "On the Relation of the Poet to Day-Dreaming." In *On Creativity and the Unconscious.* New York: Harper, 1958.

———. "A Child Is Being Beaten." In Philip Rieff, ed. *Sexuality and the Psychology of Love.* New York: Collier Books, 1963.

———. *Complete Psychological Works,* 24 vols. Revised and ed. James Strachey. London: Hogarth Press, 1953–1974.

Friedan, Betty. *The Second Stage.* New York: Summit, 1981.

Frieden, Ken. *Genius and Monologue.* Ithaca, N.Y.: Cornell University Press, 1985.

Gates, Barbara T. *Victorian Suicide: Mad Crimes and Sad Histories.* Princeton: Princeton University Press, 1988.

Gelley, Alexander. "The Represented World: Toward a Phenomenological Theory of Description in the Novel." *The Journal of Aesthetics and Art Criticism* 37 (1979):415–422.

Genette, Gerard. "Vraisemblance et motivation." *Figures II.* Paris: Editions du
   Seuil, 1969.

Gilbert, Sandra M., and Susan Gubar. *The Madwoman in the Attic: The Woman
   Writer and the Nineteenth-Century Literary Imagination.* New Haven: Yale
   University Press, 1979.

Graham, John. *"Ut Pictura Poesis:* A Bibliography." *Bulletin of Bibliography* 29
   (1972):13–15.

Hall, Jack, ed. *The Trollope Critics.* New York: Macmillan, 1981.

Heilbrun, Carolyn, and Margaret R. Higonnet, eds. *The Representation of
   Women in Fiction.* Baltimore: Johns Hopkins University Press, 1981.

Heldt, Barbara. *Terrible Perfection: Women in Russian Literature.* Bloomington:
   Indiana University Press, 1987.

Higonnet, Margaret R. "Speaking Silences: Women's Suicide," in *The Female
   Body in Western Culture: Contemporary Perspectives.* Susan Rubin Suleiman, ed. Cambridge: Harvard University Press, 1985, 1986:68–83.

Hinz, Evelyn J. "Hierogamy versus Wedlock: Types of Marriage Plots." *PMLA* 91
   (1976):900–913.

Irigaray, Luce. *Speculum of the Other Woman.* Trans. Gillian C. Gill. Ithaca,
   N.Y.: Cornell University Press, 1985.

Jakobson, Roman. "What Is Realism in Art?" Trans. Karol Magassy. In Ladislav
   Matejka and Krystyna Pomorska, eds. *Readings in·Russian Poetics: Formalist and Structuralist Views.* Ann Arbor: Michigan Slavic Publications, 1978,
   pp. 38–46.

James, Henry. Preface. *The Awkward Age.* New York: Penguin Classics, 1966.

Jung, Carl G., ed. *Man and His Symbols.* New York: Dell, 1968.

Kant, Immanuel. *Critique of Judgement.* Book II. Trans. J. H. Bernard. New
   York: Hafner, 1931.

Kovalevsky, M. *Modern Customs and Ancient Laws of Russia.* London: 1891.

Kramer, Dale, ed. *Critical Approaches to the Fiction of Thomas Hardy.* London:
   Macmillan, 1979.

Krieger, Murray. "Ekphrasis and the Still Movement of Poetry, or Laokoon Revisited." In Frederick McDowell, ed. *The Poet as Critic.* Evanston, Ill.:
   Northwestern University Press, 1967, pp. 3–26.

Lessing, Gotthold Ephraim. *Laocoön: An Essay upon the Limits of Painting and
   Poetry.* Trans. Ellen Frothingham. Boston: Little, Brown Co., 1910.

Levin, Harry. "What Is Realism?" *Comparative Literature* 3 (Summer 1951):
   193–199.

Lévi-Strauss, Claude. *The Raw and the Cooked: Introduction to a Science of
   Mythology I.* New York: Farrar, Strauss & Giroux, 1979.

Loraux, Nicole. *Tragic Ways of Killing a Woman.* Cambridge: Harvard University Press, 1987.

Lotman, Iurii. *Structure of the Artistic Text.* Trans. Ronald Vroon. Ann Arbor: Michigan Slavic Contributions, no. 7, 1977.

———. "The Origin of Plot in the Light of Typology." *Poetics Today* 1 (1979): 161–184.

———. "On the Spatiality of Plots in the Nineteenth-Century Russian Novel" [O siuzhetnom prostranstve russkogo romana XIX stoletiia]. *Trudy po znakovym sistemam* 20 (1987):102–114.

Lukacs, Georg. *Studies in European Realism.* New York: Grosset & Dunlap, 1964.

Mandelker, Amy. *New Research in Phonetic Symbolism: The Poetic Context.* Unpublished doctoral dissertation. Brown University, 1982.

———. "Russian Formalism and the Objective Analysis of Sound in Poetry." *Slavic and East European Journal* 27, 3 (1983):327–337.

Mandelker, Amy, and Roberta Reeder, eds. *The Supernatural in Russian and Baltic Literature: Essays in Honor of Victor Terras.* Columbus, Ohio: Slavica, 1988.

Markiewicz, Henry. "*Ut Pictura Poesis*. . . A History of the Topos and the Problem." *New Literary History* 18 (1987):535–558.

Martinsen, Deborah. *Dostoevsky and the Temptation of Rhetoric.* Unpublished doctoral dissertation. Columbia University, 1990.

Miller, J. Hillis. *The Form of Victorian Fiction.* Notre Dame: University of Notre Dame Press, 1968.

———. *The Ethics of Reading: Kant, de Man, Eliot, Trollope, James, and Benjamin.* New York: Columbia University Press, 1986.

Miller, Nancy. *The Heroine's Text: Readings in the French and English Novel.* New York: Columbia University Press, 1986.

Mills, Patricia Jagentowicz. *Woman, Nature, and Psyche.* New Haven: Yale University Press, 1987.

Mirsky, D. S. *A History of Russian Literature from its Beginnings to 1900.* New York: Vintage, 1958.

Mitrofanova, V. V. *Zagadki* ("Riddles"). Leningrad: ANSSSR, 1968.

Moers, Ellen. *Literary Women: The Great Writers.* New York: Doubleday, 1976.

Morson, Gary Saul. "Prosaics: An Approach to the Humanities." *The American Scholar* 57 (Autumn 1988):515–528.

Nepomnyashchy, Catherine Theimer. *The Poetics of Motivation: Time, Narrative, and History in the Works of Solzenicyn, Sinjavskij, and Pasternak.* Unpublished doctoral dissertation. Columbia University, 1987.

Neumann, Erich. *Amor and Psyche—The Psychic Development of the Feminine: A Commentary on the Tale by Apuleius.* Princeton: Princeton University Press, 1956.

Paigels, Elaine. *Adam, Eve, and the Serpent.* New York: Random House, 1988.

Paperno, Irina. *Chernyshevsky and the Age of Realism: A Study in the Semiotics of Behavior.* Stanford, Calif.: Stanford University Press, 1988.

Park, Roy. *"Ut Pictura Poesis:* The 19th Century Aftermath." *The Journal of Aesthetics and Art Criticism* 28 (1969):155–164.

Pliny the Elder. *Natural History.* H. Rackham, ed. Cambridge: Loeb Library, vol. 9, 1961.

Polhemus, Robert. "Being in Love in *Phineas Finn/Phineas Redux*: Desire, Devotion, Consolation." *Nineteenth Century Fiction* 37, 3 (1982):383–395.

Propp, Vladimir. *Morphology of the Folktale.* Trans. Laurence Scott. Austin: University of Texas Press, 1968.

Ransell, David. *The Family in Imperial Russia.* Urbana: University of Illinois Press.

Riffaterre, Michael. "On the Diegetic Functions of the Descriptive." *Style* 20, 3 (1986):281–294.

Ruddick, Sara. "Maternal Thinking." In Barrie Thorne and Marilyn Yalom, eds. *Rethinking the Family.* London: Longman, 1982.

————. *Maternal Thinking: Towards a Politics of Peace.* Boston: Beacon Press, 1989.

Sartre, Jean-Paul. *Les Mots.* Paris: Gallimard, 1968.

Schopenhauer, Artur. *The Art of Literature.* Trans. T. Bailey Saunders. Ann Arbor: University of Michigan Press, 1960.

Showalter, Elaine. *The Female Malady.* New York: Pantheon Books, 1985.

Simmons, Ernest J. "English Literature in Russia." *Harvard Studies and Notes in Philology and Literature* 13 (1931):251–307.

Smith, Mack, Jr. *Figures in the Carpet: The Ekphrastic Tradition in the Realistic Novel.* Unpublished doctoral dissertation. Rice University, 1981.

Sontag, Susan. "The Third World of Women." *Partisan Review* 40 (1973):188.

Steiner, Wendy. "The Causes of Effect: Edith Wharton and the Economics of Ekphrasis." *Poetics Today* 10:2 (1989):279–297.

Streidter, Jurij, ed. *Texte der russischen Formalisten,* 2 vols. Munich: W. Fink Verlag, 1972.

Tanner, Tony. *Adultery in the Novel: Contract and Transgression.* Baltimore: Johns Hopkins University Press, 1979.

Templeton, Joan. "The *Doll House* Backlash: Criticism, Feminism, and Ibsen." *PMLA* 104 (1989):28–40.

Terras, Victor. *Belinskij and Russian Literary Criticism: The Heritage of Organic Aesthetics.* Madison: University of Wisconsin Press, 1974.

Tomashevsky, Boris. *Teoriia literatury.* Moscow: Gosudarstvennoe izdatel'stvo, 1928.

————. "Literature and Biography." Trans. Herbert Eagle. In Vassilis Lambropoulos and David Neal Miller, eds. *Twentieth Century Literary Theory: An Introductory Anthology.* Albany: SUNY Press, 1987, pp. 116–123.

Toporov, V. N. *The Semiotics of Mythological Conceptions about Mushrooms.* Trans. Stephen Rudy. *Semiotica* special issue 53–54 (1985).

Torgovnick, Maria. *Closure in the Novel.* Princeton: Princeton University Press, 1981.

Trilling, Diana. "The Liberated Heroine." *Partisan Review* 45 (1978):501–522.

Uspensky, Boris. *A Poetics of Composition: The Structure of the Artistic Text and Typology of Compositional Form.* Trans. Valentina Zavarin and Susan Wittig. Berkeley: University of California Press, 1973.

Wachtel, Andrew. *The Battle for Childhood: Creation of a Russian Myth.* Stanford, Calif.: Stanford University Press, 1990.

Wasson, R. G., and V. P. Wasson. *Mushrooms, Russia, and History.* New York, Pantheon Books, 1957.

Watt, George. *The Fallen Woman in the 19th Century English Novel.* Totowa, N. J.: Barnes and Noble, 1984.

Wellek, René. "The Nineteenth-Century Russian Novel in English and American Criticism." In John Garrard, ed. *The Russian Novel from Pushkin to Pasternak.* New Haven: Yale University Press, 1983.

Wimsatt, W. K., and Monroe C. Beardsley. "The Intentional Fallacy." In Vassilis Lambropoulos and David Neal Miller, eds. *Twentieth Century Literary Theory: An Introductory Anthology.* Albany: SUNY Press, 1987, pp. 103–115.

Wittgenstein, Ludwig. *Tractatus Logico-Philosophicus.* Trans. D. G. Pears and B. F. McGuinness. London: Routledge & Kegan Paul, 1961.

Tolstoy

Adelman, Gary. *"Anna Karenina": The Bitterness of Ecstasy.* Twayne's Masterwork Series. Boston: J. K. Hall, 1990.

Aldanov, M. *Zagadka Tolstogo.* Berlin: I. P. Ladyznikov, 1923.

Alexandrov, Vladimir E. "Relative Time in *Anna Karenina.*" *Russian Review* 41 (1982):159–168.

Al'tman, M. S. "'Zheleznaia doroga' v tvorchestve L. N. Tolstogo." *Slavia* (Prague) Rocnik 34 sesit 2 (1965).

Anna Karénine. Cahiers Léon Tolstoi 1. Paris: Institut d'Etudes Slaves, 1984.

Armstrong, Judith. *The Unsaid Anna Karenina.* New York: St. Martin's Press, 1988.

Babaev, E. G. *Roman i vremia: Anna Karenina L. N. Tolstogo.* Tula: Priokskoe knizhnoe izdatel'stvo, 1975.

———. "Tri kursiva v *Anne Kareninoi. Russkaia rech'*: *Nauchno-populiarnyi zhurnal* 5 (1987):47–49.

Bayley, John. *Tolstoy and the Novel.* New York: Viking Books, 1966.

Benson, Ruth Crego. *Women in Tolstoy: The Ideal and the Erotic.* Urbana: University of Illinois Press, 1973.

Bidney, Martin. "Water, Movement, Roundness: The Epiphanic Pattern in Tolstoy's *War and Peace.*" *Texas Studies in Literature and Language: A Journal of the Humanities* 23 (1981):232–247.

Blackmur, R. P. "*Anna Karenina:* The Dialectic of Incarnation." *Kenyon Review* 12 (1950):433–456.

Bloom, Harold, ed. and introd. *Leo Tolstoy's "Anna Karenina".* New York: Chelsea House, 1987.

Blumberg, Edwina J. "Tolstoy and the English Novel: A Note on *Middlemarch* and *Anna Karenina.*" *Slavic Review* 30 (1971):561–569.

Call, Pau. "Anna Karenina's Crime and Punishment: The Impact of Historical Theory upon the Russian Novel." *Mosaic* 1 (1967):94–102.

Carroll, Traci. "Sports Writing and Tolstoy's Critique of Male Authority in *Anna Karenina.*" *Tolstoy Studies Journal* 3 (1990):21–32.

Chertkov, V. G. *O polovom voprose: Mysli L. N. Tolstogo.* Christchurch: Izd. Svobodnogo slova, 1901.

Christian, R. F. "The Passage of Time in *Anna Karenina.*" *Slavic and East European Review* 45, 104 (1967):207–210.

———. *Tolstoy: A Critical Introduction.* Cambridge: Cambridge University Press, 1969.

———. "The Problem of Tendentiousness in *Anna Karenina.*" *Canadian Slavonic Papers* 21 (1979):276–288.

Cockrell, Roger. "The Bayreuth Connection: Tolstoy as Wagnerophobe." *Journal of Russian Studies* 44 (1982):34–42.

Coetzee, J. M. "Confession and Double Thoughts: Tolstoy, Rousseau, Dostoevsky." *Comparative Literature* 37 (1985):193–232.

Coulton, John. "Anna Karenina's Tragedy of the Bedroom." *English Studies in Africa: A Journal of the Humanities* 28 (1985):109–117.

Edel, Leon. "Dialectic of the Mind: Tolstoy." In *The Modern Psychological Novel.* Gloucester: Smith, 1972, pp. 147–153.

Edgerton, William B. "Tolstoy, Immortality and Twentieth Century Physics." *Canadian Slavonic Papers* 21 (1979):289–300.

Egan, David R., and Melinda Egan. *Leo Tolstoy: An Annotated Bibliography of English Language Sources to 1978.* Metuchen, N.J.: Scarecrow Press, 1979.

Eikhenbaum, Boris. *The Young Tolstoy.* Trans. Gary Kern. Ann Arbor: Ardis Press, 1972.

———. *Tolstoy in the Seventies.* Trans. Albert Kaspin. Ann Arbor: Ardis Press, 1982.

Evans, Mary. *Reflecting on Anna Karenina.* London: Routledge, 1989.

Fedosiuk, M. I. "Portret v Anne Kareninoi." *Russkaia rech': Nauchno-populiarnyi zhurnal* 6 (1986):52–57.

Futtrell, M. H. *Dickens and Three Russian Novelists: Gogol, Dostoevsky, and Tolstoy.* London: 1955.

Gibian, George. *Tolstoy and Shakespeare.* The Hague: Mouton, 1975.

Gifford, Henry. "Anna, Lawrence and 'The Law.'" *Critical Quarterly I* (1959): 203–6. Reprinted in Henry Gifford, ed. *Leo Tolstoy: A Critical Anthology.* Harmondsworth, Middlesex: Penguin, 1971, pp. 299–303.

————. *Tolstoy.* Oxford: Oxford University Press, 1982.

————, ed. *Leo Tolstoy: A Critical Anthology.* Harmondsworth, Middlesex: Penguin, 1971.

Greenwood, E. B. "The Unity of *Anna Karenina.*" *Landfall* XV (1961):124–34.

————. *Tolstoy: The Comprehensive Vision.* New York: St. Martin's Press, 1975.

Grossman, Joan Delaney. "Tolstoy's Portrait of Anna: Keystone in the Arch." *Criticism* 18 (1976):1–14.

Gudzii, N. K. "Istoriia pisaniia i pechataniia *Anny Kareninoi.*" *PSS* 29:577–643.

Gustafson, Richard. *Leo Tolstoy: Resident and Stranger.* Princeton: Princeton University Press, 1986.

Hajnadi, Zoltan. "O 'vseobshchnosti' tragedii: *Anna Karenina.*" *Acta Litteraria Academiae Scientiarum Hungaricae* 24 (1982):191–201.

Hardy, Barbara. *The Appropriate Form: An Essay on the Novel.* London: Athlone, 1964.

Hogan, Rebecca S. *The Wisdom of Many, the Wit of One: The Narrative Function of the Proverb in Tolstoy's "Anna Karenina" and Trollope's "Orley Farm."* Unpublished doctoral dissertation. University of Colorado, 1985.

Holderness, G. "Tolstoi and Art." *Durham University Journal* 73 (1981): 135–146.

Holquist, James M. "Did Tolstoj Write Novels?" *American Contributions to the 8th International Congress of Slavists* 2 (1978):272–279.

Holquist, Michael. "The Supernatural as Social Force in *Anna Karenina.*" In Amy Mandelker and Roberta Reeder, eds. *The Supernatural in Russian and Baltic Literature: Essays in Honor of Victor Terras.* Columbus, Ohio: Slavica, 1988, pp. 176–190.

Jackson, Robert L. "Chance and Design in *Anna Karenina.*" In Peter Demetz, et al., eds. *The Disciplines of Criticism: Essays in Literary Theory, Interpretation, and History.* New Haven: Yale University Press, 1968.

————. "On the Ambivalent Beginning of *Anna Karenina.*" In E. de Haard, T. Langerak, and W. G. Weststeijn, eds. *The Semantic Analysis of Literary Texts.* Amsterdam: Elsevier, 1990, pp. 345–352.

Jahn, Gary R. "The Image of the Railroad in *Anna Karenina.*" *Slavic and East European Journal* 25 (1981):8–12.

————. "A Note on the Organization of Part I of *Anna Karenina.*" *Canadian American Slavic Studies* 16 (1982):82–86.

————. "The Unity of *Anna Karenina.*" *Russian Review* 41 (1982):144–158.

————. "Tolstoj and Kant." In George Gutsche and Lauren Leighton, eds. *New Perspectives on 19th Century Russian Prose.* Columbus, Ohio: Slavica, 1982, pp. 60–70.

Jones, W. Gareth. "George Eliot's *Adam Bede* and Tolstoy's Conception of *Anna Karenina*." *Modern Language Review* 61 (1966):473–481.

Jones, Peter. *Philosophy and the Novel: Philosophical Aspects of "Middlemarch," "Anna Karenina," "The Brothers Karamazov," and "À la recherche du temps perdu" and of the Methods of Criticism.* Oxford: Clarendon Press, 1975.

Karimov, E. "Printzpy khudozhestvennogo izobrazheniia sredy i cheloveka v romane L. Tolstogo, *Anna Karenina*." *Voprosy literaturovedeniia i iazykoznaniia* kn. 4. Tashkent: ANSSR, 1962.

Knapp, Shoshona. "Tolstoj's Reading of George Eliot: Visions and Revisions." *Slavic and East European Journal* 27 (1983):318–326.

Knowles, A. V., ed. *Tolstoy: The Critical Heritage.* London: Routledge & Kegan Paul, 1978.

Leavis, F. R. *Anna Karenina and Other Essays.* London: Chatto & Windus, 1967.

LeBlanc, Ronald. "Levin Visits Anna: The Iconography of Harlotry." *Tolstoy Studies Journal* 3 (1990):1–20.

Lucas, Victor. *Tolstoy in London.* London: Evans Bros., 1979.

McLean, Hugh, ed. *In the Shade of the Giant: Essays on Tolstoy.* Berkeley: University of California Press, 1989.

Matlaw, Ralph, ed. *Tolstoy: A Collection of Critical Essays.* Englewood Cliffs, N.J.: Prentice Hall, 1967.

Morson, Gary Saul. "Tolstoy's Absolute Language." *Critical Inquiry* 7 (1981): 667–687.

———. *Hidden in Plain View: Narrative and Creative Potentials in "War and Peace."* Stanford, Calif.: Stanford University Press, 1987.

———. "Prosaics in *Anna Karenina*." *Tolstoy Studies Journal* 1 (1988):1–12.

———. "The Tolstoy Questions: Reflections on the Silbajoris Thesis." *Tolstoy Studies Journal* 4 (1991):115–141.

Muchnic, Helen. "The Steeplechase in *Anna Karenina*." In *Russian Writers: Notes and Essays.* New York: Random House, 1971.

Nabokov, Vladimir. "Anna Karenin." In *Lectures on Russian Literature.* New York: Harvest, 1981, pp. 137–243.

Obolenskii, L. "L. N. Tolstoi o zhenskom voprose, isskustve, i nauke." *Russkoe bogatstvo* 4 (1886):167–176.

Parker, David. "Social Being and Innocence in *Anna Karenina*." *The Critical Review* 27 (1985):110–123.

Pearson, Irene. "The Social and Moral Roles of Food in *Anna Karenina*." *Journal of Russian Studies* 48 (1984):10–19.

Pomar, Mark G. "Tolstoy's *Anna Karenina*." *Explicator* 41 (1983):32–33.

Pomorska, Krystyna. "Tolstoy: Contra Semiosis." *International Journal of Slavic Linguistics and Poetics* 25–26 (1982):383–390.

Posse, V. A. *Liubov' v tvorchestve L'va Tolstogo.* 1917.

Pursglove, Michael. "The Smiles of *Anna Karenina.*" *Slavic and East European Journal* 17 (1973):42–48.

Rogers, Philip. "Lessons for Fine Ladies; Tolstoj and George Eliot's *Felix Holt, the Radical.*" *Slavic and East European Journal* 29 (1985):379–392.

———. "Scrooge on the Neva: Dickens and Tolstoj's *Death of Ivan Ilić.*" *Comparative Literature* 40 (1988):193–218.

———. "A Tolstoyan Reading of *David Copperfield,*" *Comparative Literature* 42 (1990):1–28.

Rowe, William W. *Leo Tolstoy.* Boston: Twayne, 1986.

Rzhevsky, Nicholas. "Tolstoy's Ideological Order: Herzen and *War and Peace.*" In *Russian Literature and Ideology.* Urbana: University of Illinois Press, 1983.

Schultze, Sydney. *The Structure of "Anna Karenina."* Ann Arbor: Ardis Press, 1982.

Sen, Samudha. "State Dignitaries, Liberal Landlords and Peasants: The Political World of *Anna Karenina.*" In J. V. Paul, ed. *Studies in Russian Literature.* Hyderabad, India: Central Institute of English and Foreign Languages, 1984, pp. 36–46.

Shklovsky, Viktor. "Paralleli u Tolstogo." In *Khod konia.* Berlin, 1923.

———. *Lev Tolstoy.* Moscow: Progress, 1978.

Shukman, Ann. "Bakhtin and Tolstoy." *Studies in Twentieth Century Literature* 9 (1984):57–74.

Silbajoris, Rimvydas. *Tolstoy's Aesthetics and His Art.* Columbus, Ohio: Slavica, 1991.

Skabichevsky, A. "Graf L. N. Tolstoy o zhenskom voprose." *Sochineniia v dvukh tomakh,* vol. 2. Spb 1905, pp. 176–194.

Sloane, David A. "Pushkin's Legacy in *Anna Karenina.*" *Tolstoy Studies Journal* 4 (1991):1–23.

Smith, Mack. "Tolstoy and the Conventions of Representation." *Renascence: Essays on Value in Literature* 37 (1985):220–237.

Sorokin, Boris. *Tolstoy in Pre-revolutionary Russian Criticism.* Columbus: Ohio State University Press, 1979.

Stenbock-Fermor, Elisabeth. *The Architecture of "Anna Karenina": A History of Its Structure, Writing, and Message.* Lisse, Belgium: Peter de Ridder Press, 1975.

Stern, J. P. M. *"Effi Briest, Madame Bovary,* and *Anna Karenina.*" *Modern Language Review* 52 (1957):363–375.

Stewart, David H. *"Anna Karenina:* The Dialectic of Prophecy." *PMLA* 79 (1964):266–282.

Usmanov, L. D. "Roman L. N. Tolstogo *Anna Karenina* i nauchnye spory 60–70x godov XIX veka." *Russkaia literatura: istoriko-literaturnyi zhurnal* 3 (1985):104–117.

Wasiolek, Edward. *Tolstoy's Major Fiction.* Chicago: University of Chicago Press, 1978.

————, ed. *Critical Essays on Tolstoy.* Boston: G. K. Hall, 1986.

Wilson, A. N. *Tolstoy.* New York: W. W. Norton & Co., 1988.

Zytaruk, George. "D. H. Lawrence's *The Rainbow* and Leo Tolstoy's *Anna Karenina:* An Instance of Literary 'Clinamen.'" *Germanoslavica* 5 (1987): 197–209.

The Woman Question

Atkinson, Dorothy, Alexander Dallin, and Gail Lapidus, eds. *Women in Russia.* Stanford: Stanford University Press, 1977.

Blake, Kathleen. *Love and the Woman Question in Victorian Literature: The Art of Self-Postponement.* Totowa, N.J.: Barnes & Noble, 1983.

Clements, Barbara Engels et al., eds. *Russia's Women: Accommodation Resistance, Transformation.* Berkeley: University of California Press, 1991.

Costlow, Jane. "Love, Work and the Woman Question in mid-Nineteenth Century Women's Writing." Unpublished ms., 1992.

Davidoff, Leonore, and Catherine Hall. *Family Fortunes: Men and Women of the English Middle Class 1780–1850.* Chicago: University of Chicago Press, 1987.

de Maegd-Soëp, Carolina. *The Emancipation of Women in Russian Literature and Society.* Ghent: Slavica Gandensia Analecta 1, 1978.

Dunham, Vera S. "The Strong Woman Motif." In Cyril Black, ed. *The Transformation of Russian Society.* Cambridge: Harvard University Press, 1960.

Engel, Barbara. *From Feminism to Populism: A Study of Changing Consciousness among Women of the Intelligentsia 1855–1881.* Unpublished doctoral dissertation. Columbia University, 1974.

Helsinger, Elizabeth, Robin Lauterbach Sheets and William Veeder. *The Woman Question: Society and Literature in Britain and America 1837–1883, vol. 3: Literary Issues.* Chicago: University of Chicago Press, 1983.

Matich, Olga. "A Typology of Fallen Women in Nineteenth Century Russian Literature." *American Contributions to the 9th International Congress of Slavists,* vol. 2. Columbus, Ohio: Slavica, 1983, pp. 325–343.

McDermid, Jane. "The Influence of Western Ideas on the Development of the Woman Question in Nineteenth-Century Russian Thought." *Irish Slavonic Studies* 9 (1988):21–36.

Mill, John Stuart, and Harriet Taylor Mill. *Essays on Sex Equality.* Chicago: University of Chicago Press, 1970.

Neff, Wanda F. *Victorian Working Women: An Historical and Literary Study of Women in British Industries and Professions 1832–1850* (1929; reprint, New York: Humanities Press, 1966).

Obolenskii, Leonid. "Voprosy v noveishei belletristike." *Russkoe bogatstvo* 3 (1890):188–200.

Poovey, Mary. *Uneven Developments: The Ideological Work of Gender in Mid-Victorian England.* Chicago: University of Chicago Press, 1988.

Selivanova, N. N. *Russia's Women.* New York: E. P. Dutton, 1923.

Shashkov, Serafim S. *Istoria russkoi zhenshchiny.* Petersburg: Suvorin, 1879.

Stanton, Theodore, ed. *The Woman Question in Europe,* New York: G. P. Putnam's Sons, 1884.

Stillman, Beatrice. "Sofya Kovalevskaya: Growing up in the 60s." *Russian Literature Triquarterly* 9 (1974):276–301.

Stites, Richard. *The Women's Liberation Movement in Russia: Feminism, Nihilism, and Bolshevism, 1860–1930.* Princeton: Princeton University Press, 1978.

Tishkin, G. A. *Zhenskii vopros v Rossii: 50-60-e gody XIX v.* Leningrad: Izdatel'stvo Leningradskogo Universiteta, 1984.

Vicinus, Martha. *Independent Women: Work and Community for Single Women 1850–1920.* Chicago: University of Chicago Press, 1985.

———, ed. *Suffer and Be Still: Women in the Victorian Age.* Bloomington: Indiana University Press, 1972.

Vorontsova, Liubov Andreevna. *Sofia Kovalevskaiia 1850–1891.* Moscow: Molodaia Gvardiia, 1957.

INDEX

The Theory and Interpretation of Narrative Series

James Phelan and Peter J. Rabinowitz, Editors

The series publishes studies of narrative that offer interpretations of particular narratives and address significant theoretical issues underlying those interpretations. The series is interested in new interpretations of narratives to the extent that these interpretations are grounded in theoretical discussions that have implications for our understanding of narrative in general or for the interpretation of other narratives. The series does not privilege any one theoretical perspective but is open to studies from any strong theoretical position. It especially welcomes works that investigate the relations among different theoretical perspectives on narrative.

Psychological Politics of the American Dream: The Commodification of Subjectivity in Twentieth-Century American Literature
  LOIS TYSON